DISCARD

DATE DUE

BRODART, CO.   Cat. No. 23-221

Just Politics

A volume in the series

CORNELL STUDIES IN SECURITY AFFAIRS

edited by Robert J. Art, Robert Jervis, *and* Stephen M. Walt

A list of titles in this series is available at
www.cornellpress.cornell.edu.

Just Politics

HUMAN RIGHTS AND THE
FOREIGN POLICY OF GREAT POWERS

C. WILLIAM WALLDORF, JR.

Cornell University Press

ITHACA AND LONDON

First published 2008 by Cornell University Press

Printed in the United States of America

Library of Congress Cataloging-inPublication Data

Walldorf, C. William (Charles William), 1967–
    Just politics : human rights and the foreign policy of great powers / C. William Walldorf, Jr.
        p. cm. — (Cornell studies in security affairs)
    Includes bibliographical references and index.
    ISBN 978-0-8014-4633-7 (cloth : alk. paper)
    1. Human rights. 2. International relations. 3. Alliances. 4. United States—Foreign relations—1945–1989. 5. Great Britain—Foreign relations—1837–1901. II. Title. II. Series.

    JC571.W146 2008
    323—dc22

2008001248

Cornell University Press strives to use environmentally responsible suppliers and materials to the fullest extent possible in the publishing of its books. Such materials include vegetable-based, low-VOC inks and acid-free papers that are recycled, totally chlorine-free, or partly composed of nonwood fibers. For further information, visit our website at www.cornellpress.cornell.edu.

Cloth printing 10 9 8 7 6 5 4 3 2 1

To Jennifer, Will, Amy, and Anson

Contents

Acknowledgments

Writing a book does a lot to one's own humanity. In my case, I have been personally stretched and challenged through the comments and encouragement of many colleagues, family members, and friends along the way. Most of the contributions that led to this book, I owe to them. Any mistakes, I claim for my own.

I am especially indebted to those at the University of Virginia who encouraged me to look at commitment termination and humanitarian norms. Jeffrey Legro, John Owen, Allen Lynch, and James Hunter offered exceptional guidance and devoted many hours to the project. I owe a special thanks to Jeff for his rigorous pursuit of a better product in the early stages. While difficult to swallow at the time, his insights paved the way, in the end, to making this a better book. For that I am grateful.

I am also grateful to David Adesnik, Spencer Bakich, Steven Brooks, Kelly Erickson, Mark Haas, Holger Schmidt, Christianne Hardy Wohlforth, William Wohlforth, and Benjamin Valentino for comments on various parts of the research that went into the book. Some deserve special mention. Ben Valentino and Steve Brooks read and re-read several chapters. Ned Lebow, Steven Walt (as series editor), and an anonymous reviewer for Cornell University Press read the manuscript in its entirety. Their abundant comments and close attention to detail were especially helpful in sharpening and expanding the argument. As with many others who have come before me, I appreciate Roger Haydon's commitment to the book and his guiding hand through the review and production process at Cornell University Press. Karen Laun and Martin Schneider helped repair numerous mistakes and oversights with their masterful editing. For research support, I appreciate the help of Engin Erdem, Marianne Scott, and Nan Swift.

On the financial side of the equation, I thank several units at the University of Virginia, including the Center for Russian and East European Studies, the Graduate School of Arts and Sciences, the Center on Religion and Democracy, and the Institute for Advanced Studies in Culture. The latter two provided not only resources but the opportunity to enter a vibrant intellectual community that helped expand my perspective beyond political science on norms, ideas, and justice in international politics. The Institute for the Study of World Politics, Gordon College, and Dartmouth College contributed valuable support as well. I am especially grateful to the College of Liberal Arts and the Office for the Vice-President of Research at my home institution, Auburn University, for summer funding toward completion of the book's final revisions. I also am grateful for permission in chapters 1 and 3 to reprint portions of my article "When Humanitarianism Matters: Liberalism and the Termination of Strategic Commitments," *Security Studies* 14, no. 2 (April–June 2005), 232–73. Reproduced by permission of Taylor and Francis Group, LLC., www.taylorandfrancis.com.

Many others provided various forms of help and encouragement. I appreciate the commitment of my parents, Charlie and Flora Walldorf, to my education from an early age. Their support, along with that of my in-laws, Patty and Cartter Frierson, was invaluable in producing this book. Furthermore, I have been blessed with inspiring places to write, most notably the library at the Center for Christian Study in Charlottesville, Virginia, and the Frierson Farm in the mountains of north Georgia. On the latter, there is nothing like the smell of hot summer grass, great mountain views, and the occasional sound of a train whistle in the distance. Finally, I cannot imagine completing this book without my wife, Jennifer, and our three children, Will, Amy, and Anson. I told them more times than I would like to remember, "Daddy needs to work." Their patience and support has been amazing. They knew that I could finish, even when I had my doubts. Mistakes aside, this book is as much theirs as it is mine. It is only appropriate that I dedicate it to them.

Just Politics

Introduction
Human Rights and Foreign Policy

The conventional wisdom in international relations is that human rights matter little, if at all, in the foreign policy of great powers, especially when that policy involves strategic endeavors like the war on terror. U.S. behavior since 9/11 seems to reflect this belief. In addition to its own abuses at Abu Ghraib and Guantanamo Bay, Washington appears to be overtly endorsing the inhumanity of partner regimes in countries ranging from Kazakhstan and Pakistan to Saudi Arabia and Egypt. These relationships are underwritten by a series of military and economic assistance commitments by which the United States has provided billions of dollars in aid. Under the strategic guise of fighting terror, the leading liberal great power in the international system appears to be acting anything but liberal. World affairs, in essence, have returned to politics as usual after a brief respite following the Cold War. Human rights are a natural casualty. Whether or not this is a positive outcome is a subject of longstanding debate. Some say that democratic states, in particular, should press inhumane regimes, even allies, to liberalize and respect human rights. Others want to jettison human rights from foreign policy altogether, since they detract from important security concerns. The debate is not limited to policymakers, either. It stands at the heart of academic deliberations about what matters more in driving international politics—material factors and the national interest or ideas and identity.

This book takes a definitive stand in these debates. More specifically, I show that while there may be some truth to the conventional wisdom on human rights, by and large it is wrong. Rather than play a marginal role, humanitarian norms are often at the heart of the foreign policy of great powers, especially in liberal democratic states. In fact, humanitarian considerations led the two greatest democratic powers in history—nineteenth-century Great Britain and the postwar United States—to terminate core security commitments to a host of important strategic partners. In the case of Britain, informal empire commitments, through which London pledged to protect the hegemony of allies in regions of great geostrategic importance, were critical to British power in the nineteenth century.[1] Yet Britain ended pledges like these to the Ottoman Empire and Portugal in the 1870s and 1880s. As for the United States, Washington ended numerous military and economic assistance pledges like those at the center of the war on terror amidst the insecurity of Cold War competition with the Soviet Union. U.S. commitments to partners such as Turkey, South Africa, Chile, Argentina, and many others were terminated.

Many international relations scholars, especially realists, would expect this behavior to occur only when partners become less strategically valuable. Yet in the above cases—and many others like them—the United States and Britain unilaterally ended commitments not because partners became enemies or lost their value due to geostrategic changes. Key decisionmakers in Washington and London believed that their actions did or would damage perceived strategic objectives. Yet they acted on humanitarian impulses all the same. The British cabinet, for instance, panicked as its humanitarian-inspired restraint in the Ottoman case allowed Russian troops to come within nine miles of Constantinople, threatening access to India, its imperial gem.[2] Henry Kissinger privately worried about dominoes falling across Latin America in the event that Chile or Peru became a communist state, arguing that such occurrences could affect the vitality of the NATO alliance.[3] Various U.S. leaders, including President Ronald Reagan, feared that sanctions against South Africa would end America's access to several vital strategic minerals and compromise sea lanes for Middle East oil.[4] Finally, the termination of security assistance to Cuba (1958) and Nicaragua (1978) for humanitarian reasons arguably contributed to the rise of the Castro and Sandinista regimes, respectively, creating costly security problems for Washington in the last three decades of the Cold War.[5] In hindsight, some of these threat perceptions may appear exaggerated. But at the time, policymakers were quite serious about them and nevertheless took what they saw as strategically self-destructive steps for humanitarian reasons.

How do we explain this type of punitive action against strategic partners? Why and when do humanitarian norms lead democracies to terminate or preserve strategic commitments? These are the main empirical questions addressed in this book.

I define a strategic democratic commitment as a promised course of action, communicated via treaties, executive agreements with legislative approval, or executive orders, for the purpose of supporting a partner in a perceived strategic endeavor.[6] I focus on British and U.S. security commitments that fit this definition. While these two democracies share a common Anglo-Saxon heritage that might make them more prone to embrace human rights, they constitute an important starting point. Any argument seeking to establish the efficacy of humanitarian norms in strategic relationships must begin with the two greatest democratic powers in history. Furthermore, Britain and the United States are the historical exemplars of presidential and parliamentary democracy, respectively. They offer, therefore, a necessary baseline for understanding how humanitarianism matters in different types of democracy.

In this book, I look inside the democratic state, at the institutional and ideational processes that bring humanitarian values to the center of the democratic foreign policy process. In so doing, I draw on some of the logic of the conventional wisdom, namely that the presence of strategic concerns makes consideration of humanitarian action more difficult. But since these strategic concerns are inherently ideational and their relevance to policy is dependent upon domestic institutions, this book is more than a mere supplement to realism. Rather, it offers a different paradigm, one rooted in sociological and liberal approaches, for understanding commitments in international politics. Domestic-level factors, namely humanitarian norms, ideas about the strategic relevance of partners, and institutions are the turnkey issues in explaining humanitarian politics in liberal states. They also inform, summarily, the policy suggestions that I offer for the war on terror.

My argument involves three broad factors: democratic legislatures, the pressure of activist groups or nongovernmental organizations (NGOs), and the perception of commitment partners on the part of legislatures. More specifically, I expect that legislatures will terminate strategic commitments when a partner demonstrates a pattern of illiberal behavior and activists apply enough pressure to counterbalance the perceived value that policymakers attach to that partner. Commitments are most likely to be sustained, in turn, when activists fail to engage the policy process or apply the wrong type of pressure and when partners take liberalizing reforms to correct past illiberal behavior. Under these circumstances, legislatures view partners with greater deference and generally refrain from taking action. Domestic contestation about foreign policy, then, is more than an inconsequential annoyance—more than just politics, as the conventional wisdom would have it. Instead, it comprises the core means by which ideas about justice affect the political process in great powers, especially democracies.

It might seem unusual to base an argument about humanitarianism around legislatures. In democracies we traditionally associate human rights with executives, like President Jimmy Carter. Yet liberalism in fact assigns legislatures a special interest in humanitarian issues, as major humanitarian movements in history from antislavery and anti-apartheid to efforts to ban landmines in the 1990s attest. In the absence of legislative pressure, humanitarian actions by the executive branch tend to be more tempered by geostrategic considerations and, hence, less severe. In the 1970s, this proved the case in U.S. policy. The Carter administration elevated the rhetoric of human rights, yet the U.S. Congress drove the human rights movement both before and after President Carter's term in office. It also took decisive steps against states on humanitarian grounds despite the resistance of the Carter administration for strategic reasons.[7] Legislatures most consistently serve as the locus of humanitarianism in democratic states.

The argument involves more than legislative norms, however. Legislatures often express concern for certain humanitarian values decades before they act on them. They also are inconsistent in when they take humanitarian action. Stated differently, for every humanitarian "success" like Argentina or South Africa, there are instances like the Philippines under Marcos or Iran under the Shah where a democratic power like the United States did not act. In short, sometimes norms appear to "fail." A norms-based argument needs to account for both action and inaction in order to demonstrate its efficacy. Why do humanitarian norms matter when they do?

The answer turns again on ideational and institutional dynamics within liberal states. Humane legislative foreign policy does not emerge easily. Liberal policymakers, especially in great powers, face competing ideational pressures, both strategic and humane, that often generate competing interests in foreign policy. Consequently, though legislatures care about human rights, they feel the weight of the perceived strategic value of certain partners, which often militates against humanitarian considerations. Furthermore, legislatures traditionally take a back seat to executives in making foreign policy, especially in the formation of commitments. When threats like 9/11 arise, legislatures tend to show excessive deference to executive leadership. Strategic-minded executives thus often gain a free hand to establish partnerships with regimes of all types, including inhumane governments such as those in Uzbekistan or Kazakhstan.

It takes a great deal of institutional fervor to generate the legislative initiative to overturn strategic commitments. I believe that the behavior of partners and the level of activist pressure are critical to producing this fervor and, with it, commitment termination. Activists must first apply the appropriate level of pressure for legislatures to terminate pledges to inhumane partners. For partners perceived as strategically vital by policy-makers, activists generally need higher forms of pressure, namely public opinion support, in order to get legislatures to end commitments. If partners are perceived merely as important, lower forms of activist pressure, namely information produced in reports by groups such as Amnesty International (AI), are usually sufficient. Congress did not terminate aid to inhumane regimes in Iran and the Philippines as it did to other vital Cold War partners (Turkey and South Africa) because activists never rallied public opinion support. In the next chapter, I explore the conditions under which activists succeed and fail at generating these higher levels of pressure through public mobilization.

The argument is not exclusively about activist pressure, though. The behavior of partners factors in as well. Activists will find success against partners that demonstrate a pattern of illiberal behavior. Thus, when partners initiate liberal reforms to correct past human rights abuses or when there is confusion over who is responsible for illiberalism, legislatures are likely to sustain commitments regardless of activist demands. At the height of political pressure from a nationwide grassroots movement against apartheid in South Africa, the U.S. Congress chose not to press further sanctions against South Africa for a time because of liberal steps by the South African government to end some of the most heinous features of apartheid. Partner liberalization must be genuine and progressive to have this kind of affect. Sometimes, piecemeal liberalization by clever allies can stave off legislative action temporarily. But the façade almost always collapses, leading back to excessive inhumanity and, consequently, punitive action by legislatures. After initially staving off U.S. congressional sanctions with modest reforms, the Somoza government faced a complete severance of U.S. military aid just a few months later as a result of a sudden outburst of brutal repression against civilians by the Nicaraguan military. In short, humanitarian-inspired commitment termination by democratic states is most likely when activists apply pressure against knowingly inhumane governments that show no sign of reform.

Norms generally need institutions in order to matter, and institutions operate as important conveyors of liberal values, a crucial fact. One finds, thus, a logic of both humanitarian *action* and *inaction* in relations between liberal states and strategic partners. Apparent inconsistencies by the former to defend human rights do not automatically translate into cases of "failed norms," as the conventional wisdom concludes. Disturbing as it may be from a value-based grid alone, a democracy can be close friends with certain nondemocratic (and even somewhat inhumane) regimes without abandoning, or even conflicting with, its core liberal humanitarian beliefs. This becomes clearer when we look at the politics of humanitarian norms in liberal states.

The findings in this book have several implications, especially for major strategic endeavors, like the war on terror. If history is any guide, the stability of relationships between the United States and its allies in the war on terror will not be determined by strategic considerations alone. Washington was able to sustain pledges to Cold War partners in Nicaragua, South Africa, and Argentina for years despite less-than-perfect human rights records in each. The findings in this book indicate that the strategic value of these states to the United States did not dictate Washington's behavior. Instead, each progressed, though not perfectly, toward liberal change. When change suddenly halted, the United States ended commitments, in many instances jeopardizing its own broader strategic objectives. In the war on terror, the course of human rights among U.S. partners will likely matter as well. While grassroots activity remains relatively quiet, activist monitoring of U.S. partners has increased and Congress has taken several steps indicating that human rights need to be a more prominent feature in relations with our allies in the war on terror.[8] Historically, developments like these have often been the prelude to strategically damaging action. The best approach for Washington is to promote liberalization aggressively among its allies in the war on terror now, especially with those that are nondemocratic. Furthermore, the U.S. president needs to take the lead here. A proactive executive branch will help defray legislative activism and preserve a coherent policy that avoids disruptions in aid to important allies.

Some might find this approach unnecessary with allies like Saudi Arabia, Egypt, and Israel. Given their extreme importance to the United States, it is very difficult to imagine Washington terminating assistance for humanitarian reasons. In any given era, it seems, there is always a handful of states (for instance, Germany and Great Britain during the Cold War) that are perceived as ultra-vital and, hence, largely immune from sanctions. However, few countries typically fall into this category. Whether these Middle East allies of the United States today fall into it is debatable. If some or all of them do, it may not necessarily be for strategic reasons, though. Related to the discussion of mobilization in the next chapter, longstanding pro-Israeli sentiments dating to the formation of the Jewish state are strong among many segments of American society. Hence, Israel is surely the most improbable state to face sanctions, since the emergence of a requisite public opinion movement against this highly valued ally is very unlikely. Commitments to Egypt and, especially, Saudi Arabia might be another story, however. There is deep sentiment among many quarters of the U.S. public that Islam, especially in its radical forms, facilitates inhumanity, as the method of the 9/11 terrorist attacks, for example, attests. Some blame the Saudi government, in particular, for indifference toward, and perhaps even encouragement of, these ideas within its country. This could be the basis at some point for a shift in public opinion against either or both allies in the United States. These types of changes should not be viewed as wishful thinking for those that care about human rights. It is worth recognizing that in the 1960s and 1970s few would have expected the United States to sanction either Turkey or South Africa—both appeared too strategically vital and there was little public or constituent impetus to act. But, as this book explores, change in public sentiment came dramatically, and U.S. policy changed with it. For that reason it seems wise to press humanitarian issues with allies in the war on terror all the more, despite their perceived importance at the present time.

[1]

Humanitarianism and Commitment Termination

Democratic states sometimes terminate commitments to strategic partners. Why does this occur? In my effort to answer this question, I specifically draw on three approaches to international politics: realism, institutionalism, and humanitarian norms—this being a hybrid liberal-constructivist framework. Each approach presents unique explanations of commitment termination. The first two—realism and institutionalism—reflect the conventional wisdom discussed in the prior chapter. I also discuss the methodology of the project and the logic of using case studies from the specific core British and U.S. security commitments at hand.

HUMANITARIAN NORMS

A humanitarian norms explanation of commitment termination combines elements of both constructivist and liberal thought. As such, it brings liberal norms into the picture and explores the ways that institutions serve as conveyors of those norms. In the context of strategic commitments, I anticipate that legislatures will force executives to terminate pledges when partners act illiberally and activist groups apply pressure for policy change. In the absence of patterned illiberalism by partners or certain levels of activist pressure, commitments are likely to be preserved.

A couple of qualifications are important. First, this book focuses on political, as opposed to economic and social, rights. The reason for this is that most of the humanitarian movements addressing the foreign policy of great powers have revolved around issues like life, liberty, and human dignity.[1] Second, the argument rests on a single assumption. Namely, once legislatures adopt anti-commitment interests, the executive will terminate pledges. In reality, policymaking is not always as straightforward as this assumption implies. Executives sometimes defy legislative objectives, even those encoded in law. The Reagan administration's decision to provide covert aid to the Contra rebels in Nicaragua despite congressional restrictions is one memorable example. Politics matters as to when executives respect legislative preferences. For space reasons, I do not explore the political cost-benefit calculations of these executive decisions. It should be noted, though, that in most instances, when legislatures act, they tend to get their way eventually. Once Reagan's actions became public, for example, aid to the Contras abruptly ended, an outcome that would not have transpired without legislative pressure.

Liberal Thought and Humanitarianism

Understanding legislative humanitarian action begins with an exploration of the basic identities of democratic states. Liberalism is the central legitimating worldview, or core identity, of modern democratic states. I define liberalism as a system of thought rooted in the autonomy and equality of the individual. Liberal scholars explore how these ideas serve as the foundation for humanitarian concern and action internationally. On this score, liberal societies reify the "equal worth and dignity of each and every person [regardless of] social utility" and respect the basic political right to "equal concern and respect."[2] Choice of the life one leads becomes a critical factor. "Equal and autonomous rights-bearing individuals are entitled to make fundamental choices about what constitutes the good life (for them), with whom they associate, and how," notes Jack Donnelly.[3] Liberty to define the good life is not license, however, to pursue one's wishes regardless of others. The autonomy of one can not be used to hinder the autonomy and equality of another. Noncoercion and tolerance therefore emerge as valuable to any liberal conception of society. Individuals stand free to define the good as they please as long as it does not encroach upon the capacity of another individual to do the same.

The state plays an important role as a servant toward this end. Government receives "its power from the governed with whom . . . [it] signed a contract."[4] The purpose of the state becomes consistent with what society values, namely, autonomy and equality. John Locke captured the place and responsibility of the liberal state: "[State] power, in the utmost bounds of it, is limited to the public good of society. It is a power that has no other end but preservation, and, therefore, can never have a right to destroy, enslave or designedly to impoverish its subjects."[5] For Locke and other liberals, the state role includes the active element, as well, of limiting excesses by one individual within society against another.[6] Under these conditions, liberals expect the greatest potential for human flourishing. No doubt some contemporary liberals take issue with this strictly contractarian bent, claiming that it misses the responsibility of the state to promote economic and social equality as well.[7] As it is farther removed from the task at hand, I do not wish to wade into that argument here. Instead, it is adequate to note that liberals of all stripes understand and expect a state imbued with liberal ideas to defend and advocate for individual autonomy and equality: "The function of government is the protection of natural rights."[8]

The liberal identity does not stop with a recasting of the domestic relationship between a state and its citizenry. An international dimension exists as well. Liberalism holds equality and freedom as universal rights. Liberal ideas create a lens through which liberal states view and judge the plight of humans beyond their own borders. "The principles of common morality plainly imply a more positive concern for the welfare of people outside one's own community," contends one liberal scholar, "For the general positive obligations to others included within common morality are not limited to people with whom we are bound in community by contract."[9] Not surprisingly, liberal democratic states have been at the center of many of the major humanitarian movements across history, from the codification of human rights in international law to the abolition of slavery in the United States and the movement against South African apartheid. The centrality of the individual produces a natural affinity for global humanitarianism in liberal states, especially relative to illiberal regimes.[10]

This statement is not without controversy. Important contextual issues related to what actors are considered human across time and the balance between strategic and humanitarian interests in liberal states need to be addressed here. The definitions of those believed to be "human" and therefore worthy of defense internationally has varied substantially between liberal states across history. In this book, for instance, nineteenth-century Britain vigorously defended Ottoman Christians while ignoring other oppressed minorities in the Ottoman Empire. This picture contrasts sharply with leading democracies since the middle of the twentieth century. While witnessing historically contingent movements revolving around specific states or groups (for instance, the anti-apartheid movement in the 1980s), U.S. foreign policy has reflected a trend common for most liberal states today in its defense of universal rights applicable to all, regardless of race, religion, or geographical location. How is *human* defined by liberal states, and how do these definitions change over time?

Constructivists are helpful on this point. The definition of *human* is historically contingent, deriving from social interactions and extant ideas. Who is human, thus, emerges from variations within liberal identities across history. "We tend to help those we perceive as similar to ourselves," notes Martha Finnemore.[11] For Britain in the nineteenth century, the definition of human was rather narrow, having mostly to do with Christianity and civilizational biases about the superiority of European culture and society. As Finnemore observes, the people of Africa "appeared utterly strange and therefore not 'human'" to Europeans.[12] Likewise, when it came to the Ottoman Empire, British humanitarian action was aroused exclusively when Christians suffered at the hands of the Turks, who were viewed in Britain as less civilized than their Christian subjects.[13] Christians fit the prevailing definition of human while other suffering non-Christian groups were ignored. Identity explains the more expansive definition of the human common across international politics since the late nineteenth century as well. Liberal beliefs about "natural" rights expanded dramatically across the nineteenth and twentieth centuries, as was reflected in a series of egalitarian movements, including the abolition movement. Human-ness, thus, eventually became a category not limited to Christians and Europeans but included all individuals as a matter of birthright.[14] Many see the United States, with its unique revolutionary history rooted from its very inception in individual rights, as an important actor in this changing definition of who is human.[15]

There are a variety of pathways and factors that help us understand how normative definitions of humanity, including those assessed in this book, emerge and change over time. Moral agents or entrepreneurs are often a critical starting point. "Norms do not appear out of thin air," note Martha Finnemore and Kathryn Sikkink. "They are actively built by agents."[16] From William Wilberforce on ending slavery to the International Red Cross on banning landmines, identifiable agents have been at the center of new and changing humanitarian values. Agents are the starting point; they envision and initiate the movement toward change. Their methods are many, focusing generally around persuasion, the framing of new ideas, and personalization techniques intended to generate empathy from unsympathetic audiences.[17]

Reflecting a prevalent theme in this book, agents do not operate in a vacuum, however. Success often depends on factors beyond their control. Most importantly, extant norms and ideas within society present both opportunities and hindrances to activist appeals. If persuasion and the framing of new norms are to be successful, appeals must resonate, or fit well, with existing values. Many authors find this part of the process critical in explaining the expansion of human rights to black Africans in the related movements of abolition and decolonization. By creating cognitive dissonance, activist appeals succeeded because they drew sharp contrasts between these western practices and the core values of liberalism, namely equality, self-determination, and democracy.[18] Likewise, activists sometimes need to wait until extant social norms change before their efforts resonate. Anti-apartheid activists in the United States repeatedly failed to draw attention to racism in South Africa until the mid-1970s. The civil rights movement in the United States provided a critical normative change that later served as the basis for the anti-apartheid movement.[19]

Related to extant norms, another structural feature to which constructivists draw attention as a condition for normative change is external events or shocks. This is especially important to my argument. Generally, a series of shocking events creates societal trauma over existing policy or state practices.[20] This trauma, in turn, confirms or reinforces activist appeals, creating space for activists to change norms. Several highly publicized incidences of brutality in overseas colonies created popular disapprobation toward the practice of colonialism as a whole in Britain, France, and Portugal during the nineteenth century.[21] Likewise, highly publicized brutality against unarmed civilians by U.S. and South Vietnamese troops during the Vietnam War created a foundation for the human rights movement of the 1970s in the United States. And, decolonization in southern Africa in the mid-1970s drew greater attention to South African apartheid, fueling anticipation that change was possible.[22] The long-term trauma from a series of shocking events is often important to norm change.

One final set of factors often facilitates the dispersion of new humanitarian ideas. While great powers are unlikely to have new norms forced upon them by other states, elements of what might be called international peer pressure can affect decisions to adopt new values. When a large number of states adopt a norm, it is possible that they will coalesce into a tipping point that leads to a norm cascade, where others in the system race to adopt it.[23] While initially instrumental, states that adopt norms this way often become habituated to them over time. In addition to common cultural and religious factors, Britain became interested in the plight of Ottoman Christians early in the nineteenth century out of an effort, in part, to ensure that Russia and France did not use the issue for strategic gain.[24] Combined with other factors already noted, the strategic rationale for defending Ottoman Christians soon took on a life of its own in Britain. This type of habituation can also occur when leaders justify strategic goals in ideological language. The beliefs can come back later to matter in ways that they did not intend. Looking at the cases discussed in this book, there is some evidence of this in the ways that the norm of the "freedom fighter" became prominent in U.S. foreign policy in the 1980s. In sum, identities, agents, and structures help us understand both the narrow definitions of human-ness in the past and how those definitions have expanded over time.

A second issue involves the tension between humanitarian and security impulses. This topic is vital for my argument. Most liberals agree that liberal states possess unique concerns for humanitarianism internationally. But they also recognize that international politics involves tackling perceived strategic challenges. A robust debate exists over which should take precedent, the humane or the strategic.[25] Along with cosmopolitan concerns for fellow humans, classical liberals did discuss the effect of the strategic challenges inherent to foreign policy on the extensiveness of moral behavior internationally. Jean-Jacques Rousseau stood by the universality of natural law, used the categories of "just" and "unjust" wars, and wrote of the "natural repugnance to see any sensitive being perish or suffer, principally our fellow man."[26] At the same time, Rousseau recognized the countervailing pressures to morality in the international domain: "the bodies politic, thus remaining in the state of nature . . . soon experienced the inconveniences that had forced individuals to leave it. Hence arose national wars, battles, murders and reprisals which make nature tremble and shock reason."[27] Immanuel Kant's writings demonstrate the same tension. It is a "duty" of the moral politician to hold the rights of man sacred and advance peace among nations toward a future order of perpetual peace. Yet, in the process of getting there, heads of state must "ensure . . . [the] existence of the commonwealth" against external enemies.[28]

Contemporary liberals discuss the same tensions. Some take a more cosmopolitan focus, arguing that humanitarian considerations should predominate over all others in the foreign policies of liberal states. "A concern for human freedom cannot stop with the satisfaction of one's own society or clan," argues Judith Shklar. "One must put cruelty first and understand the fear of fear and recognize them anywhere."[29] On the other side of the debate, Keith Shimko points to theoretical similarities between realist and liberal thinking, opening the door to security-first logic. "American students of international relations can be realists without shedding their liberal predispositions," he argues.[30]

Today, the security-rights tension echoes throughout the debates over the U.S. war on terror. The issue is whether it is appropriate for the United States and its allies to suspend certain rights and even use interrogation methods indistinguishable from torture. Michael Ignatieff has been a leader on the security-first side of the debate. While advocating certain checks on power, he claims that the greater good comes before attention to individual rights. Extreme interrogation methods would, in this sense, "be a lesser evil than allowing thousands of people to die."[31] Some critics of this argument take an absolute stand that rights should, under no conditions, be surrendered.[32] Others try to find a middle ground. Fernando Teson, for instance, argues for a stringent set of conditions to ensure that security measures do not unnecessarily infringe on rights. He claims that the acid test is to ensure that illiberal measures are "justified by reference to the need to protect liberty," rather than appeals to order or stability, or consequentialist approaches that can end in tyrannical government.[33]

As will become apparent, I take a definitive position in defense of human rights in the war on terror. But, for my purposes at this point, the philosophical debate between cosmopolitan and security-first liberals is most valuable for the empirical reality to which it points. Namely, there is an almost universal tension facing policymakers in liberal states: the natural proclivity toward humanitarianism versus equally pressing strategic challenges. How and when does the former take center stage in the foreign policy process? In short, when do humanitarian norms matter?

The Significance of Non-Executive Institutions

Institutional arrangements in liberal democratic states serve as a starting point in answering these questions. In both classical and contemporary liberalism, a distinct, though not absolute, bifurcation of interests exists between executive and non-executive institutions. Democratic executives generally think and act in terms of the broad national strategic and material needs of the state. Non-executive institutions, on the other hand, stand as the primary advocates for liberal foreign policy objectives. There are, of course, exceptions to this rule—sometimes executives promote liberal ends and sometimes non-executive institutions quite forcefully advocate strategic goals. But by and large, the distinction holds considerable merit and is useful theoretically. In explaining peace among democracies, non-executive institutions like the media, interest groups, and regular elections are found to restrain executives focused on material gain, prestige, and power from going to war with other democratic states.[34] "Liberal ideology prohibits war against liberal democracies, but sometimes calls for war against illiberal states," writes John Owen, a democratic peace scholar. "Democratic institutions allow these drives to affect foreign policy and international relations."[35] Mutual domestic

[14]

institutional restraint of democratic executives provides, among other things, time for the settlement of disputes, which explains the high rate of peace among democracies.

In the day-to-day realm of democratic foreign policy, legislatures and, as I discuss in greater length below, certain interest groups stand as the primary institutional advocates in liberal states for humanitarian objectives internationally. The relative propinquity of executives and legislatures to the alternative sources of strategic and humanitarian pressures explains the different tendencies of these two state-level institutions of policymaking authority. Executives stand closer to the exigencies of the international system. In effect, they face the state of nature in international politics most directly. As representatives of the nation and managers of the day-to-day foreign policy of democratic states, the uncertainty of the international arena forces executives to think primarily in terms of the strategic material well-being of the nation as a whole.

Legislatures are not only more removed from the international context institutionally, they also stand closer to the repository of liberal values within liberal democratic states in the form of the general populace. Again, this stems from the way that liberal ideas constitute the state. Consistent with concepts of the social contract or cosmopolitan society, the people comprise the foundation of liberal ideas and a liberal political order.[36] As the people's institution at the level of the state, legislatures possess a natural sensitivity toward liberal humanitarian concerns.[37] Kant similarly notes that right government, where the governed have a voice, can only be found in a representative system.[38]

Liberal political theorists are not alone in observing these differences between legislative and executive interests in the realm of foreign policy. Numerous scholars point to legislatures derailing strategic initiatives with policy demands based on liberal values and popular opinion.[39] History demonstrates, furthermore, that legislatures stand as the primary and most unwavering advocates of humanitarianism in liberal states. In the nineteenth century, the British Parliament pursued two humanitarian crusades that deeply influenced international politics: antislavery and the protection of Christians within the Ottoman Empire. In U.S. foreign policy, Congress drove the human rights campaign of the 1970s and the anti-apartheid movement against South Africa in the 1980s. The U.S. Congress and the British Parliament played the central role, as well, in creating policies to curb international drug trafficking and prostitution in the early twentieth century.[40] Legislatures in Canada, Belgium, the United States, and the United Kingdom led efforts to ban the use of landmines in times of war in the 1990s.[41] Finally, an extensive quantitative study finds that the

U.S. Congress stood as the most consistent and primary advocate for "pro-liberalization," including humanitarian, objectives in U.S. military interventions during the twentieth century.[42]

These institutional generalizations should not be taken to mean that executives ignore human rights and legislatures care little for strategic issues. No doubt, legislatures also recognize perceived strategic challenges. In this study, spirited debates and close legislative votes on action against commitment partners reflect this. As explored below, these challenges also contribute to certain institutional hurdles to legislative action on foreign policy issues. Liberal executives, likewise, are liberals. Consequently, they cannot entirely ignore inhumanity beyond their borders. As in the case of U.S. President Jimmy Carter, some liberal heads of state pay a great deal of attention to human rights and expend considerable amounts of energy promoting humanitarian causes. All the same, executives are not naturally inclined to take humanitarian action that could jeopardize strategic objectives. As we will see in chapter 3, Carter was no exception, his great attention to human rights notwithstanding.

The Legislative Foreign Policy Problem

Stating that legislatures care about humanitarian values and terminate strategic commitments on that basis only gets us so far. We still do not know why and how these values matter when they do. Sometimes legislatures apply norms to some commitment cases and ignore them altogether in parallel instances. Still further, legislatures often voice support for certain humanitarian proclivities for decades on end before taking actual policy steps informed by those values.

The groundwork for understanding case-by-case humanitarian action by liberal states begins with the inherent difficulty of legislative foreign policy leadership within democracies generally. In democratic systems of all types, executives traditionally possess a lead role in making decisions and shaping policy. In the liberal tradition itself, this is almost an unspoken assumption.[43] Legislatures tend to delegate leadership to executives for the sake of national interest clarity, such that a nation "speaks with one voice." Coordinating hundreds of voting representatives within a legislature on a large array of complex foreign policy issues is very cumbersome. Executive leadership, on the other hand, ensures cohesive, quick responsiveness to international events. This executive authority is endowed both legally and traditionally. In divided power presidential systems, constitutions often grant executives foreign policy leadership. In parliamentary systems, party and coalitional dynamics serve the same end.[44] In the domain of commitment politics, executive leadership is especially pronounced at the commitment-making phase in response to newly perceived strategic challenges and opportunities. Given this fact and the greater strategic focus of executives, it should be little surprise that democracies sometimes make cooperative pledges to nondemocracies. This can lead to contradictions as well. In the 1970s, as the United States cut ties to inhumane regimes in Latin America, for instance, relations with equally illiberal regimes like China warmed. The institutional division of labor within democracies helps account for this.

Some might wonder if the political dynamics in parliamentary systems make the foreign policy problem so intense that legislative leadership is virtually impossible. Unlike presidential systems, parliamentary rebellion against executives could lead to extreme outcomes like votes of no confidence, the collapse of the government, and new elections. All of these a majority in parliament prefers to avoid, making independent legislative action highly improbable. This seems especially true of systems like those of the British Commonwealth, where cabinets come from a single majority party in parliament.[45] In short, legislative foreign policy appears likely only in presidential systems.

While accepting the fact that legislative policy rebellion might be less frequent in parliamentary systems, I rely on a growing literature that recognizes similarities between presidential and parliamentary systems. Some analysts point out that parliaments often employ indirect methods to force preferences on executives without actually generating "no confidence" votes.[46] Others add that fragmentation and independent parliamentary action in multi-party coalitional governments can be expected due to ideological differences.[47] Even in the British Commonwealth, party discipline is not always as steadfast as many scholars expect. "The British Cabinet's concern today is not for its majority over the opposition, because that is almost automatic, but for its majority inside its own party," a former member of the British Parliament observes, "The only doubt the prime minister has is about his own supporters."[48] Kenneth Waltz similarly argues that "the requisite art for a Prime Minister is to manage the party in such a way as to avoid the defiance of the many or the rebellion of the few." Dissension of even a small number of MPs carries significant weight in cabinet circles. "The Prime Minister can only ask for what his party will give," Waltz suggests. "The English system concentrates power in the hands of the Prime Minister but provides effective, though informal, checks against its impetuous use."[49] Overall, their common liberal core provides a foundation to compare presidential and parliamentary systems.

[17]

While differences between presidential and parliamentary systems may not matter much to the intensity of the legislative foreign policy problem, the policy context of strategic commitments does. Great powers value some partners more than others. In this sense, they tend to view strategic partners as either "vital" or "important."[50] The perceptions of policymakers about how a partner fits into the great power's grand strategy for ensuring military strength and survival determines these value.[51] "Vital," thus, refers to states that leaders deem as valuable due to their perceived ability to provide forward defense positions in facing strategic challenges (often, these are allies with established militaries or basing facilities for the great power, like U.S. relations with the Philippines or South Korea during the Cold War); countries with natural resources that are perceived essential to strategic survival (South African minerals considered important to the United States during the Cold War); or countries that lie in geostrategic locations viewed as important, often near the great power's homeland or along sea lanes/transit routes to perceived forward defense or vital resource states (for example, the Ottoman Empire along British transit routes to India). States are merely "important" when they lie near states that are perceived as being vital but are perceived by leaders to face few challenges from adversaries of the great power. These states are close enough to vital interests that if, in time, such perceived challenges should emerge, important states could themselves become vital. The influx of weapons that Cuba supplied to Sandinista-led Nicaragua, for instance, moved Central America from the category of *important* to *vital* for the United States during the 1980s due to its geographic proximity to the U.S. mainland and the threat to sea lanes viewed as strategically vital in the Caribbean.[52]

Policy context affects the legislative foreign policy problem. I anticipate that when policymakers perceive a partner to be vital, policymaking authority shifts more pronouncedly to the executive branch. Legislative intrusion then becomes far less likely, although not altogether impossible as legislatures tend to follow the executive's lead all the more due to the high priority issues at stake. Executives summarily possess a relatively free hand to determine and change policy. When policy context is perceived as important, legislative intrusion increases somewhat over vital cases, but deference to executive leadership still remains pronounced due to the belief that issues of security are still at stake.[53] In short, legislative policy intrusion is especially difficult in foreign policy. That difficulty is compounded all the more when important strategic partners are the issue and still further with partners perceived as vital.

Agents of Change: Nonstate Actors and Humanitarian Norms

This study focuses on security commitments that are deeply affected by the legislative aversion to meddling in foreign policy. The interaction between two variables—illiberal developments and the pressure of moral activist groups—helps explain when liberal norms are most likely to drive legislatures to overcome this aversion and press executives to end security commitments. I focus on illiberal developments in the discussion below on causal pathways. Moral activists require additional attention at this juncture.

Liberals and constructivists both posit the responsibility—indeed, the necessity—of nonstate actors to move liberal values and norms onto the policy agenda of states.[54] Humanitarianism is no different. There are two questions to be addressed here. The first is why nonstate actors choose to apply pressure in some instances rather than others. The second is about activist mobilization. As we shall see, activists mobilize different levels of pressure, and they are most likely to influence policy when they generate some form of public opinion support. The question is, how do they mobilize?

If one overlooks *why* nonstate actors choose to act when they do, one might argue that the alternatives for commitment termination offered by realism and domestic institutionalism answer this question, thus accounting for an important part of my argument. This, however, is not the case. Relative to what realists and institutionalists expect, I contend that none of the following generally factor into group decisions on whether to apply pressure to terminate pledges: geostrategic shifts; renegotiation of commitments; or the violation of commitment agreements by partners (see below for a discussion of realism and institutionalism).

Work on social movements and organizational theory is most helpful in addressing this issue. Three factors in general repeatedly affect group choices for action: threats to group creeds, available resources, and perceived windows of opportunity within the policy process. In the end, the former and latter prove most important. Threats to group creeds represent the first and primary grid in a group's decisionmaking process. Creeds define the boundaries of issues in which interest groups care. "Purpose provides a principal criterion in determining what things are to be done," notes Herbert Simon[55] Group interests vary in breadth. Humanitarian activists might define their creedal concerns narrowly, around the protection of certain ethnic or religious groups in specific states, or more broadly, around an extensive set of rights on a global scale.

Whatever their nature and extent, creeds establish a baseline for group monitoring and help determine cases in which action might be necessary. Humanitarian activists ask a range of questions in analyzing government behavior. Are prisoners treated fairly? Is torture a regular practice? Is summary execution common? Are the accused granted due process? Any negative answers to these questions hone the attention of a group on this or that case and initiate a deeper assessment of whether or not to take action.

For some groups with narrow creeds and extensive resources, the mere violation of creeds will determine when they act. Many ethnic lobbies in the United States, like the Israeli lobby, fall into this category. They act at nearly every instance where ethnic kin are threatened. This is a luxury, however, usually not enjoyed by broader human rights organizations with wide agendas. For these groups creedal violations alone do not generate action. Many of them also must "worry about costs and benefits" or whether they have "resources to accommodate goals."[56] Groups, such as AI, often operate on shoestring budgets. Gathering information on a specific country or organizing and promoting public opinion campaigns or protests involves extensive costs.

How do groups choose campaigns when bound by limited resources but face multiple cases of interest? Creeds, along with openings in the policy process, take center stage. In short, groups will choose to publicize the worst cases of creedal violation from among those that show the most promise of gaining the attention of policymakers. On the latter, groups form perceptions of openings in the policy process by assessing the past interests of policymakers, through ongoing discussions with policymakers, and current statements by policymakers on recent developments in specific countries.[57] The large number of human rights abuses in Argentina coupled with public statements of concern by numerous members of Congress caused human rights NGOs to focus extreme attention on that country in the mid-1970s. At the same time, groups like Amnesty International (AI) delayed action on Nicaragua until later in the decade due to constraints on resources and the limited attention that the Somoza regime had received to that point among policymakers.[58] In this explanation of activist behavior, some might question whether activist pressure contributes to outcomes at all. If policymakers have already focused on a particular case, do activists really matter? As I discuss both theoretically and empirically in the pages to follow, activist pressure is a necessary condition in the process of commitment termination. In fact, no cases of humanitarian-inspired action against core security commitments like those in this study occurred without activist engagement.

[20]

Table 1.1 Conditions for mobilization by stage

Lowest pressure (stage one)	(stage two)	(stage three)	*Highest pressure* (stage four)
Single NGO reports	Multiple NGO reports	Constituency group	Public opinion/ social movement
	Condition(s): Gatekeeper NGO	*Condition(s):* NGO initiative; target group anxiety; cognitive liberation; complicity events	*Condition(s):* Constituency group demonstration; media attention; connection to broader social values

A second issue of importance is how nonstate actors mobilize pressure once they decide to act. Different levels of pressure can contribute to different outcomes in terms of commitment termination or preservation. For the sake of this study, I consider activist pressure a continuous variable ranging from low to high (table 1.1). For humanitarian activists, a single report by an NGO detailing illiberal developments in a certain country represents the lowest form of pressure (stage one). Pressure increases as other NGOs produce additional reports (stage two) and as activists rally support from an identifiable public constituency, like an ethnic or minority group (stage three). Finally, activist pressure reaches its highest level when domestic protests and demonstrations occur (stage four). The question of interest at this point is why do other groups and individuals join the effort in stages two through four?

As a blanket requirement, activists must be viewed as credible, both by policymakers and target constituents, to create constituencies and coalitions. While credibility is generally contingent on history, it often means that activists must be seen as prophetic, speaking from outside the political system on the basis of moral values rather than representing narrow interests or being political insiders. Given these parameters, it should be little surprise that the most successful humanitarian activists have historically been churches, civic organizations, and NGOs with some natural distance from the policy process, like AI.

Drawing from social movement and social psychology literatures, I argue that a mix of factors including the strategic choices of activists, events, broader norms within society, and certain group dynamics are critical to the emergence and timing of higher levels of mobilization. A stage-by-stage discussion is helpful here. As noted already, a single human rights group like AI will publicize, investigate, and produce reports on a certain case(s) depending upon the decision making process discussed above.

Stage two mobilization, involving other activists producing reports, occurs when these actions generate demonstration effects that draw other activists to follow. While networks among groups and framing by the lead group probably make some difference, numerous scholars have pointed out that this demonstration effect depends largely upon the reputation of the lead group. Clifford Bob notes, for instance, that in many issue areas there are "gatekeeper" NGOs with high credibility. When gatekeepers take action, others tend to follow. According to Bob, AI and Human Rights Watch have been the major gatekeepers in recent decades on human rights issues. Not surprisingly, they have been at the forefront of initiatives involving multiple NGOs that have focused around information-gathering and dissemination.[59] In sum, stage two mobilization depends largely on a gatekeeper NGO initiating action, which later draws other groups into the process.

More factors come into play at higher levels of mobilization, including stage three constituency group mobilization. The first necessary condition in order to connect with or build a constituency of supporters is a decision by a leading activist group to initiate action. This is not as obvious as it seems. Especially in the domain of human rights, there are many groups like Amnesty International that are either not equipped for or interested in building constituencies.[60] Groups that choose to create a constituency network are usually focused on direct lobbying of government. They generally initiate constituency-building when they believe that government officials are particularly unresponsive to the group's demands via standard lobbying methods.[61] Closed doors, in short, force groups to choose alternative methods. During the early years of the Reagan administration, the African-American lobbying group TransAfrica found the policy process in Washington, D.C., unresponsive to its anti-apartheid concerns. So TransAfrica began to build a nationwide network of supporters at the state and local levels in the United States that later became the foundation for the Free South Africa Movement (FSAM), which undertook a major drive for sanctions against South Africa.

In mobilizing stage three pressure, activists must sequentially build a constituency and then call its new supporters to action.[62] These processes involve several different factors. Activist framing is important to both, with groups building networks based on information about partner inhumanity that it and other organizations produce. Ultimately, though, structural and social-psychological variables are usually the most significant factors in successfully garnering public support. Similar to the discussion above on changing norms, successful activist appeals do not exist in a vacuum but must instead tap the "life world" of potential target constituents.[63]

An activist group begins building a constituency by identifying a target population of like-minded groups that it believes might be sympathetic to its cause. Success at creating a common vision or consensus for action depends, first, on the levels of anxiety and distraction within targeted populations. In other words, if the anxiety of the target population about issues perceived as being close to the activist appeal is high and if that population is not distracted by other major political endeavors, then the possibility for consensus mobilization is high as well. Anxiety is a constant theme across social movement scholarship.[64] Most often, this anxiety is a product of groups becoming discontented or alienated by events that threaten their core values and interests. This state of strain creates a sense of loss and assessments that "something is wrong" with the current social environment, generating great uncertainty and ambiguity.[65] TransAfrica successfully created a broad network of anti-apartheid supporters in political districts across the United States with 10 percent or more African-American voters. Its success was facilitated by discontent among local groups over the lack of attention to issues of interest to African Americans during the early Reagan years as well as a search for new political avenues by these groups to express that discontentment.

There is an additional factor that matters to creating a constituency base. Anxiety drives individuals to search for a framework of action, but individual strain will not translate into a mindset for action unless important group dynamics are in place. As Doug McAdam argues, individuals must give up all inhibitions about acting and come to believe in both a common group goal and the potential that their action can produce that goal. This process of "cognitive liberation" emerges most consistently through communication among group members.[66] The process of "milling" with other anxious individuals about the message from activists produces collective definitions of the situation at hand, helps create a grid for interpreting old and new events, and facilitates the creation of a common injustice framework within the group.[67] This is all made possible via the communication context offered by the interaction of members through established or emerging groups. Hence, churches, trade unions, and even nonpolitical civic organizations can serve as the context for cognitive liberation. Cases of humanitarian mobilization are not unique here. A network of local organizations and churches in Britain served as the foundation of the social movement in support of Christian subjects in the Ottoman Empire during the 1870s. Likewise, the Greek Orthodox Church and other Greek-American civic organizations were the bedrock of a grassroots movement against the second Turkish invasion of Cyprus in the mid-1970s. In short, if face-to-face contact is high within an anxious and focused target population, activist efforts are more likely to mobilize consensus among a network of new supporters with a shared vision.

Once established, constituencies must be moved to act. Events play a vital role here, especially when those events give constituents the impression that their own government is either an accomplice or uninterested bystander to injustice. These complicity events evoke both guilt and anger. They become "a symbol of cumulated grievances," as Neil Smelser has written.[68] Activist leaders play the part of pointing out complicity and calling constituents to action.[69] In each of the constituency-based movements in this study, the apparent callousness of the British or U.S. government to developments overseas sparked action. What followed in every instance was a full flourishing of stage three mobilization with constituency groups lobbying governments directly through letter-writing, public meetings, and even small-scale protests and demonstrations.

Stage four mobilization in which protests broaden beyond a smaller constituency to the public at large is more historically contingent but seems to occur most consistently when several factors are present. These include stage three demonstration by a constituency group, media attention, and a perceived fit to broader social values. Much as stage one relates to stage two, a demonstration effect by an identifiable constituency group is often the first step toward mobilizing broader public support. Constituency action creates a public display of the group's grievances. Publicity of these actions and the perceived fit of the grievances to broader social values give public legitimacy to the group's claims. Publicity involves first and foremost media attention, which "rapidly increases the number of individuals who are aware of the problem and strengthens the mobilization underway."[70] According to sociologists William Gamson and Andre Modigliani, the media is part of the way that broad "issue cultures are produced."[71] Widespread press reports of the early protests by the FSAM helped expand the anti-apartheid movement to campuses and cities across the United States. By contrast, the Greek-American movement against Turkey's invasion of Cyprus in the mid-1970s gained very little media attention and consequently remained at the level of stage three mobilization.

Finally, the emergence of broad social protests depends on public perceptions that the activist appeals and grievances relate to core values of society writ large. Perceptions along these lines play a role in media decisions to publicize activist appeals from the start. If journalists and editors see a fit, then publicity is more likely.[72] Even so, other social groups and individuals must make their own decisions about the fit between movement appeals and social norms before engaging in protest. A constituency movement "must justify its values by the sacred values of the society," note Ralph Turner and Lewis Killian, "The Constitution, certain religious symbols, historical personages such as Washington and Lincoln, all constitute such sacred values in American society."[73] The movements in this book testify to this reality. The FSAM touched the nerve of racial equality that had been a part of U.S. culture and politics since the 1960s. The British movement for Ottoman Christians resonated in similar ways with broad social concerns about civilization and the plight of co-religionists.

A point about movement decline deserves mention. Higher levels of mobilization often prove difficult to sustain. Almost by definition, supporters in the broader public are less attached to a movement than core constituents. Stage three movements are often made up of previously apolitical participants.[74] In the absence of quick results, fatigue and movement collapse constantly threaten movements. Furthermore, activists rally support around simple messages of who is to blame and how to fix the humanitarian crisis. Consequently, failure to gain success can lead to doubts about tactics and disillusionment, which cause constituents to fall away.[75] For example, the failure of U.S. sanctions to compel Turkey to negotiate over Cyprus contributed a great deal to the exhaustion and decline of the Greek lobby in the 1970s.

The Humanitarian Norms Hypothesis

Table 1.2 demonstrates predicted outcomes for strategic commitments given various combinations of activist group pressure and illiberal developments in partner states. The left-hand column lists the possibilities of activist group action, while the other two columns represent the nature of partner behavior. I consider "liberalizing" and "dispersed responsibility for illiberalism" as one category, given the similarity of their impact on the

Table 1.2. Humanitarian norms: Predictions for commitment termination or preservation

	Partner behaviors	
Activist group action	Illiberal	Liberalizing[1]
Pressure with public opinion support	1 Termination most likely	4 Preservation
Pressure with information	2 Termination more likely	5 Preservation
No pressure	3 Preservation	6 Preservation

[1] This column also applies to situations where responsibility for illiberalism is dispersed or difficult to assign.

legislative policy process. There are six possible causal pathways. Each cell notes the likelihood of commitment termination or preservation. Let us look more closely at these pathways.

The Pressure/Illiberal Pathways

As seen in cells 1 and 2, the likelihood of strategic commitment termination increases when a pattern of inhumane behavior occurs in a partner state and activist groups simultaneously pressure the legislature for policy change. A pattern of illiberal behavior consists of repeated and sustained human rights abuses within the borders of a partner state.[76] These combined factors do two things specifically. They make the disparity between partner illiberalism and extant humanitarian values impossible for legislatures to ignore and mitigate the already noted institutional hurdles to legislative foreign policy leadership.

Legislatures face disadvantages relative to executives in obtaining information on overseas developments. Due to their natural leadership role on foreign policy issues, executives control and possess unencumbered access to the intelligence network and the diplomatic corps—a privilege not directly available to legislatures. Consequently, legislatures and their committees charged with overseeing foreign policy rely largely on secondary accounts, especially those in the media, in order to follow international events.[77] Information on abuses or potential abuses from these sources often provokes humanitarian concerns within legislatures. Speeches, hearings, and the passage of resolutions represent the primary means by which legislatures express their concerns. In nearly all instances, the charge here is initiated by identifiable legislators. Inspired primarily by the patterned illiberalism of partner states, these legislative advocates are critical as publicists of media reporting about specific inhumane partners. They are especially important in generating wider attention, particularly in the early stages of debate, among legislators distracted by large, multi-issue agendas.

As cell 3 indicates, legislatively driven policy change remains unlikely in the absence of activist group pressure, though.[78] A leading reason for this lies in the nature of information. Media reporting is often speculative and incomplete, especially on events in illiberal countries that generally do not value press freedoms. Media uncertainty about the extensiveness of and blame for abuses in turn creates legislative uncertainty. Given legislative deference to executive leadership on foreign policy, preliminary and unsubstantiated knowledge of abuses generally fails to produce the collective legislative will that is necessary to overturn strategic commitments.

The engagement of humanitarian activist groups, in particular, shakes legislatures from these states of deference to executive leadership and produces steps to terminate strategic pledges. Activists that engage with mobilized public support (that is, stage three or four in table 1.1) are most likely to find success in generating commitment termination. With legislators facing competing ideational pressures—the humane versus the strategic—a public statement helps tip legislators toward the former. I anticipate, in fact, that if humanitarian considerations are going to matter in cases involving vital partners, then public opinion pressure is all but a prerequisite. Consistent with the discussion on policy context, legislatures hesitate the most in applying human rights sanctions against partners perceived as vital. A strong statement for humanitarianism from the public is the best means to push the legislature to defend human rights in these instances. Given legislative sensitivity to reelection, electoral politics often serves as an important part of the discourse when public opinion pressure is at issue.[79] Few would dispute that the United States, for instance, entered negotiations to end the Vietnam War and later ended pledges to defend South Vietnam because of a broad grassroots protest movement that brought about congressional pressure for change.[80]

Absent public opinion support, humanitarian activists often utilize lower-end information pressure in order to encourage legislatures to end commitments on humanitarian grounds (cell 2). Similar to what some call "accountability politics," groups like AI use information to shame or prick the moral conscience of legislatures.[81] In this sense, reports that provide detailed examples of illiberal partner behavior from on-site investigations or in-country activist networks serve to erase informational uncertainty by *validating* the provoked sentiments of legislatures. This effectively creates a "See, I told you so" dynamic among legislators as an impetus to take decisive action.[82] NGO information establishes a clear pattern of abuses and often assigns blame for those abuses (usually to the partner government).[83] It also levels the institutional playing field between legislatures and executives. It effectively eradicates—or at least gives a legislature the impression of eradicating—the informational deficiency that legislatures possess relative to executives. This further increases legislative boldness to interject humanitarian norms into the foreign policy fray. Like evidence in a judicial proceeding, group information serves to *invalidate* executive arguments for retaining the status quo, even when strategically important.

U.S. aid to Cuba in 1958 offers a good example of information pressure. The United States terminated military assistance to the Batista government in Cuba prior to the rise of Fidel Castro. Congress was the driving force behind the move. The reason lay with the combination of Batista's violation of U.S. congressional concerns about the repressive practices of military regimes in Latin America and information pressure on Congress from various activist groups.[84]

The Pressure/Liberalizing Pathways

If our analysis ended with cells 1, 2, and 3, activist pressure would, in effect, tell the entire story. However, as cells 4 and 5 demonstrate, this is not the case. Here we find the second condition—policy windows of opportunity—that affect when activists matter. In the liberal worldview, the behavior of state authorities represents the most critical basis for judging the level of a regime's humanity. Consequently, it turns out that commitment termination depends just as much on the course of events within the partner state as it does on activist behavior. Partner actions, hence, can open and close windows of opportunity for activist groups.[85]

Above, we saw how illiberal behavior lays the foundation for activists to press the state toward commitment termination via either public opinion or information pressure. Cells 4 and 5 illustrate that activist pressure will fail to generate this outcome if one of two scenarios occurs. One scenario is that a partner that once acted inhumanely takes actual liberalizing steps. These might include ending states of emergency, enforcing measures to end torture or abuse, or initiating transitions to democracy. As a partner begins to correct its poor behavior, the impact on legislative decision making is understandable: why impose measures that could hurt a friend and important strategic ally if the friend is honestly trying to reform its wayward course? When illiberal partners pursue liberal reforms, legislatures often respond by adopting a "wait and see" approach. As long as the process of reform proceeds, commitments remain intact.

Similarly, legislatures will turn aside activist pressure if it cannot be established that the partner government is truly the most to blame for the inhumanity within its borders—in effect, if the responsibility for illiberalism is dispersed among other actors in society. Another party within the partner's borders, like an anti-government insurgency movement, might be a worse, or even the sole, violator of legislative expectations. Again, if an important partner government is not really responsible for what is going on or is responding to the acts of a more heinous illiberal actor, why punish it? Under these "lesser of two evils" scenarios, legislative deadlock often emerges and stymies progress toward commitment termination regardless of the force of interest group pressure. That leftist guerrilla movements in Argentina stood as the leading violators of human rights during the early 1970s led the U.S. Congress to preserve military aid pledges to the Argentine regime until 1977. In doing so, Congress turned aside pressure from human rights NGOs that claimed Argentine government abuses from 1973 forward. The ambiguity of the situation initially caused Congress to retrench to the policy status quo and support the commitment.

The No Pressure/Liberalizing Pathway

Cell 6 demonstrates a final scenario. Consistent with the importance of partner behavior and activist pressure, I expect the preservation of commitments if partners liberalize and groups fail to bring pressure against pledges to the partner. In the 1970s and 1980s, when many of Venezuela's neighbors saw the U.S. Congress terminate foreign assistance due to human rights violations, aid from Washington to Caracas increased. Venezuela had a good human rights record, and NGO complaints against it were, as a result, all but nonexistent.

Overall, the humanitarian norms argument offers the following hypothesis:

> Democracies are (a) most likely to terminate security commitments when a partner demonstrates a pattern of illiberal behavior and activist groups apply public opinion pressure on the legislature for policy change; (b) more likely to terminate commitments when a partner acts illiberally and activists apply information pressure; and (c) most likely to preserve commitments when activists do not apply pressure, partners take liberalizing steps, or responsibility for illiberalism is dispersed across various nonstate actors in the partner state.

REALISM

Broken commitments are no surprise to realists. Due to the structure of the international system, states fear interdependence and hence enter cooperative commitments only when strategically necessary. When these pledges become less valuable due to geopolitical changes, states prove more likely to desert them. A great deal of pressure inherent to the international system thus militates against stable long-term commitments and cooperation between states.

Given this skepticism about commitment vitality, realism should have something to say about the core security commitments of two of the greatest powers over the last two centuries, Great Britain and the United States. Some realists might take offense here, since this study focuses on great powers relations with developing world states. Realism applies most to relations between great powers, they might argue. Other realists might counter that the third world occasionally matters and deserves attention.[86] Without taking a position in this broader debate, I argue that realism should speak directly to the particular cases in this book. In each instance, key U.S. and British policymakers perceived security losses after commitments were terminated or believed prior to termination that severe losses would follow if Washington or London ended pledges. In the prior chapter, I noted the security losses that leaders perceived in Nicaragua and Cuba following the end of military assistance to the Somoza and Batista regimes. Similarly, U.S. President Gerald Ford cited a litany of strategic losses that followed the U.S. arms embargo of Turkey: Turkish military effectiveness declined; Ankara closed nearly two dozen U.S. military bases, harming among other things U.S. intelligence-gathering inside the USSR; and the Turks allowed Soviet ships of war to pass through the Dardanelles into the Mediterranean for the first time since the beginning of the Cold War.[87] In a similar vein, Argentina responded to U.S. military aid termination by ending naval cooperation with the United States in the South Atlantic at a point when Soviet naval activity in that region was significantly increasing. Argentina also became the leading sanctions buster in the U.S. effort to embargo grain sales to the USSR following the Soviet invasion of Afghanistan.[88]

Beyond strategic losses after the fact, British and U.S. officials believed prior to termination that the partners assessed in this study carried great strategic benefits and that the commitments at hand were vital to protecting those benefits. Prime Minister Benjamin Disraeli and his cabinet panicked over Russian gains in the Balkans during the 1870s, because Disraeli felt that the Crimean War commitments to the integrity of the Ottoman Empire were critical "to maintain the interests of England and the British Empire."[89] National Security Advisor Henry Kissinger confessed to deep concerns about the costs of a communist government in Chile. He designated Chile a "maximum danger area," noting that in addition to the impact on Latin America, communist success in Chile "would have implications for the future of communist parties in Western Europe, whose policies would inevitably undermine the Western Alliance."[90] South Africa was likewise viewed as vital for strategic minerals and sea lanes and "of critical importance" as a surrogate for the United States in combating the Soviet-Cuban presence in Angola.[91] Along these same strategic lines, Assistant Secretary of State Chester Crocker and others in the Reagan administration viewed Mozambique as a partner that "could provide the context for cooperation in undercutting the Soviet position and eliminating Soviet military influence and presence" in the southern

Africa region.[92] In short, many countries in the developing world carry strategic value in the perceptual grid of great powers. Given that much of day-to-day international politics involves relations, like those assessed in this book, between great and mid-level powers, realism should matter all the more.

As the most prevalent form of security cooperation expected by realists, alliances offer the best starting point for developing general realist propositions about commitment termination. According to realists, anarchy generates extreme uncertainty about the intentions of other actors in the international system. As a result, states fear for and jealously guard their security. They do so by closely monitoring the capabilities of other states within the system, attempting to balance the power of the strongest and, thus, most threatening international actor(s). As power shifts in varying directions, states summarily take steps to counterbalance new centers of power. Here, we find the deepest realist motivation for state behavior as well as the central element to a realist proposition of commitment termination: change in the systemic distribution of power.[93]

Since states in an anarchic world distrust other actors, they prefer to balance these shifts in power with unilateral initiatives, such as arms increases. Yet, because states often do not possess the means alone to balance an overwhelming power, actors tend to commit to cooperative forms of balancing through alliances.[94] States do not enter the dependence of alliances lightly. This raises a second important element to a realist theory of commitment termination. For realists, the decision of states to enter, sustain, and end alliance commitments involves a careful calculation of costs and benefits: "States form or join alliances, we may suppose, if the benefits of doing so are greater than the costs. The benefits are counted chiefly in terms of the increased security resulting from the partner's commitment, and the costs largely in terms of the autonomy sacrificed in the commitment to the partner."[95] Costs also stand at the center of decisions to end alliances. Shifts in power often yield shifts in commitment costs as well. Cost-benefit recalculations follow, which always bring the potential for commitment termination.

Realist Hypothesis on Commitment Termination

Realism points to two specific types of geopolitical shifts that are likely to increase commitment costs above benefits, leading a state to terminate strategic pledges. The first type of geopolitical change involves a decreased threat. States make cooperative security commitments in order to counter specific threats, whether actual or potential. At times, geopolitical changes create entirely new threats or lessen the severity of old threats, requiring a state, in response, to shift its own resources accordingly. Commitments established prior to the new threat may be deemed unnecessary or too costly in the face of the new challenge.[96] Sound historical evidence indicates, for instance, that in the 1890s, Great Britain abandoned longstanding commitments to protect Italy and Austria against Russian imperial designs in the Balkans because London felt more threatened by the emergence of German power in Europe than it did by the lingering threat of Russia. A change in Britain's threat calculation due to a shift in systemic power led to commitment termination.

The second type of geopolitical change involves increased partner dependence. Commitment partners often find themselves in situations that increase their dependence on the state. This, in turn, increases the costs of the commitment for the state. In the realm of alliances, realists discuss two such situations. First, a commitment partner may decline in relative power. George Liska, a realist, notes, "A marked decline in the capability of a crucial ally is even more likely to set off [the] dissolution" of the alliance relationship.[97] Second, a commitment partner might engage in provocative behavior (a military endeavor being the most extreme) that requires an increase in the state's assistance. A new cost-benefit calculation may follow, as Paul Huth explains: "The willingness of the defender to incur the costs of using military force to protect its protégé depends on the economic and military value of the protégé."[98] This new calculation might affect the state's desire to sustain the broader commitment in and of itself. Some might argue, for instance, that the United States ended support for French hegemony in Indochina in 1954 due to France's weakened position militarily against the Viet Cong and the potential entrance of China into the war. A negotiated settlement between North and South Vietnam seemed less costly to Washington than continued assistance in the French project to retain control over Indochina.

A single realist hypothesis emerges from these two propositions:

> States terminate strategic commitments when geopolitical changes make the costs of sustaining pledges greater than the benefits.

DOMESTIC INSTITUTIONALISM

Institutionalism offers an alternative liberal explanation to the humanitarian norms argument. In the concluding chapter, I discuss ways that the two approaches can build upon each other toward a more comprehensive explanation of democratic commitments. At this juncture, I turn attention to institutionalism alone. According to recent work in this genre, the making of commitments by democracies often involves broad social and legislative coalition-building that uniquely binds democratic states to their pledges. This, in turn, enhances the probability of credible commitments and cooperation. Given these domestic processes, institutionalists expect that terminating commitments will follow renegotiation of the original commitment with a commitment partner or a commitment partner's own unilateral abandonment of pledges to the democratic state. Domestic institutionalism should be well positioned to explain core British and U.S. security commitments in the nineteenth and twentieth centuries, respectively. The British Parliament and U.S. Congress ratified each of the pledges in this study at their inception in addition to re-ratifying them at several points prior to commitment termination.

Domestic institutionalist expectations of commitment termination begin with the logic of credible commitment signaling. The starting point is the standard collective action problem that states face in an anarchic international system. States often recognize the benefits of cooperating with others, but anarchy makes collective action difficult. In the absence of commitment enforcement mechanisms in international politics, the costs of potential defection by a commitment partner outweigh the benefits of cooperation. States, therefore, often choose the safer road by shirking mutually beneficial cooperation.[99]

To overcome this dilemma, states must signal credible commitments to potential partners. Institutionalists claim that unique features of the commitment-making process in democratic states allow for democracies to send these signals more easily than nondemocracies. Specifically, when a democratic executive makes an international pledge to action, a web of domestic coalitions emerges within the democratic polity to endorse the commitment. The partner sees this domestic political endorsement as creating stronger political disincentives for the executive to defect from the commitment later. This assurance increases the probability that the partner will enter into cooperation with the democratic state.[100]

For my purposes, it is important to see how institutionalist logic extends beyond the negotiating context. Institutionalism rests on the expectation that once engaged, institutions increase the probability that democratic pledges will remain resilient over time. Like their nondemocratic counterparts, democratic heads of state face various incentives to defect from existing commitments. Executives may worry about the unknown costs of a commitment or face pressure from important domestic political constituencies to change policy. Or new executives with new foreign policy ideas might come to power.[101] Institutionalists expect that whereas such pressures often cause nondemocracies to terminate pledges, democracies are more likely to remain steadfastly committed to their pledges. Lisa Martin explains the underlying logic in reference to treaty commitments in the U.S. policy process:

> Gaining ratification of a treaty is a course that is not lightly reversed in the future, even by new executives. Systems like the United States, with multiple veto points, are well-known for inducing status quo bias. . . . Once put in place, policies are difficult to change. This is certainly the case with treaties. Once Senators have gone on record by ratifying a treaty, they will be more reluctant to allow a president to abrogate it than if they had not gone through with the formal ratification process. Part of the logic of commitment lies simply in the complexity of the legislative process.[102]

As Robert Keohane, among others, notes, legislative engagement in particular embeds international pledges within the state as domestic law, creating an array of political, and sometimes legal, restraints against executive efforts to adopt policies that violate international commitments.[103] Martin points to the importance of legislatures as well, noting that they often operate as an international regime at the domestic level by blocking the efforts of executives to renege on prior commitments.[104]

The broader public can also play the role of domestic endorser. In analyzing pledges to use force in threat situations, several scholars argue that the mere public pronouncement of a threat by a democratic executive rouses the honor of the nation. The executive is likely to face severe "audience costs" (usually in a later election) if he or she decides to disgrace the nation by backing down from the pledge.[105]

Domestic Institutionalist Hypothesis on Commitment Termination

For domestic institutionalists, the termination of strategic commitments is most likely to follow interaction with a partner that reduces the domestic political costs to the executive to taking such a step. In effect, domestic commitment endorsers within the democratic state must either be neutralized or appeased in order to give the executive political space to terminate pledges. Theoretically, two interactive conditions between a democracy and its commitment partner are most likely to bring this about.

First, if the commitment partner abandons its end of an agreement to the democratic state, the latter can terminate the pledge as well. Like all other states, democracies attempt to enter relationships with credible partners. But the potential for defection always exists.[106] When this occurs, domestic constituencies that endorsed the pledge often lose interest in continued adherence to the commitment arrangement. In short, if a partner state breaks its promise, the treaty or pledge is null and void.

Second, if the executive can cooperatively restructure the commitment relationship with its partner in a manner that appeases domestic constituencies, commitment termination becomes more likely. Scholars that focus on international institutions discuss this logic extensively. Since international regimes force states to "eschew independent decision making," states must, in effect, commit in order to de-commit.[107] For domestic institutionalists, this process involves a two-level game. An executive must reenter the bargaining context with a partner and seek satisfactory side payments for the domestic endorsers of the old commitment.[108] Pledges end only when an executive reaches an agreement acceptable to both the commitment partner and commitment endorsers at home.[109] Facing the global economic recession of the 1970s, leading industrial states did not abandon their commitments under the General Agreement on Tariffs and Trade (GATT) in order to protect domestic constituents. Instead, they negotiated new provisions, such as voluntary export restrictions, to meet domestic need. "In a period of economic difficulty, governments seek to protect their constituents from the costs of adjustments to change," Keohane notes of the institutional realities of this period, "A feature of the modern world economy is that they have done so as much through illiberal measures of international cooperation . . . as through unilateral action leading to escalating discord."[110]

These two propositions lead to a single domestic institutionalist hypothesis:

> A democratic state is most likely to terminate a commitment when interaction with a commitment partner appeases or negates domestic political endorsers of the commitment.

THE METHOD OF THIS BOOK

This project anticipates that humanitarian norms account, at times, for decisions by the United States and Britain to terminate and preserve core security commitments. The methods for measuring the variables in my argument both demonstrate their presence independent of outcomes and determine their impact on the policy process. I measure legislative *humanitarian values* through the most telling expression of collective legislative concerns: adopted legislation. This book focuses on general human rights norms as well as norms related to the protection of specific groups of people at different times. Bills, amendments, and resolutions prior to decisions for commitment termination or preservation paint a picture of these legislative values.

I measure *partner behavior* by tracing the historical record of partner actions using data from secondary and media sources. In each of the cases in this book, a number of respected scholars provide information on the political developments, including the numbers and types of human rights abuses, in the countries of interest. Across the decision points in each case, I use these figures to demonstrate whether there is a pattern of illiberal behavior in light of extant legislative norms. Process-tracing from media sources allows me to demonstrate the picture of events in partner states that U.S. or British policymakers saw at each decision point, helping to determine to what extent partner behavior was publicly evident. In the same fashion, I use secondary and media sources to note any liberalizing steps to correct past or ongoing abuses of humanitarian norms.

After illustrating patterns in partner behavior, I demonstrate the impact, if any, of this behavior on legislatures by tracing connections between changes in partner behavior and actions by legislatures. Do legislatures take steps (for instance, committee hearings, parliamentary inquiries, or legislation to express concern short of commitment termination) at the time of partner violation of legislative norms? In doing so, do members of the legislature tie these steps to specific acts and developments within a partner state? Likewise, do members justify inaction on the basis of liberal reforms or ambiguity over who is to blame for illiberal events inside a partner state?

I apply a similar two-step approach in order to measure *activist group action* and its effects. First, I use secondary and media sources as well as activist group literature, like newsletters and annual reports, to show where, when, and how groups sought to influence policy. For information activists like AI, gathering and disseminating firsthand information on developments within a country represents the essence of group activity and the foundation for effective political pressure. For these groups, engagement comes via published reports of findings from investigatory missions to a particular country and information provided by in-country affiliates. I determine the presence of information group engagement when NGOs release reports on the subject. Given their credibility, a single NGO report can prove sufficient to move a legislature toward action.[111]

Public opinion activists, by contrast, use broad popular support in order to exert political pressure for policy change. Protests, rallies, and demonstrations represent the primary methods that groups use to communicate public opinion pressure. On this basis, I determine that public opinion pressure is present if groups organize and lead a series of public demonstrations as captured by secondary and media sources as well as group publications. For the sake of this study, I define *series* as more than one demonstration in more than one geographic location—a clear indication of broader appeal—within the democratic state. I measure *non-engagement* as the absence of an NGO report or protests at a particular decision point.

Second, I trace connections between the presence and absence of activist groups within the course of legislative policy. Does termination follow the application of pressure by interest groups? Do members of the legislature justify their approach with reference to specific groups, information provided by these groups, protests, or public opinion? Likewise, with legislative inaction, do we find an absence of group pressure or members of the legislature justifying commitment preservation by a lack of activist engagement?

One final point on measurement is necessary. As noted, individual statements by legislators are an important tool in assessing the impact of partner behavior and activist pressure. This presents an aggregation problem: how can one use the opinions of individual legislators to determine the motivations of the legislature as a whole? I overcome this problem with the use of two techniques in each case. First, I look for dominant trends in the statements of individual legislators on why they support certain steps regarding a partner. In identifying trends, one gains greater confidence that these statements resonated across the legislature as a whole—or at least among a majority within it—and served as the main determinant of collective legislative action. This approach is not without its flaws, of course. While painting a good cross-sectional picture of the sentiments of the most vocal legislators, it relies on outcome to determine whether belief collectivization occurred or not.

In order to address this problem, I crosscheck these findings with a parallel technique. I assess statements by specific legislators and executive branch officials about the factors that drove the legislature as a whole. Statements by legislative leaders and, especially, opponents of proposed measures often discuss the "mood," "sentiments," and "overarching concerns" that predominate on a given decision. Since these statements describe the posture of the legislature as a whole, rather than merely detailing the positions of individual legislators, they serve as particularly good indicators of the factors that contributed to legislative action. Where available, assessments from secondary sources prove helpful as well.

I test the predictions of my argument in cases of British and U.S. relations with strategic partners. The specific commitment types for nineteenth-century Britain involve pledges to protect the territorial hegemony of important allies, a phenomenon that John Gallagher and Ronald Robinson called "informal empire."[112] With respect to the United States, I analyze military assistance and strategic trade/aid commitments in the postwar period, especially in the 1970s and 1980s, to various Latin American and African states.

Leaders in London and Washington believed that many informal empire and foreign assistance obligations were critical to sustaining the international power and prestige of their countries. As demonstrated by Gallagher and Robinson, British imperialism in the nineteenth century consisted, in part, of a unique set of cooperative relations with ruling authorities in regions where those authorities possessed strong social and political organization. Free riding on these authority structures yielded imperial advantages for Britain without the cost of formal absorption and direct rule. London used this method to gain control over regions where it had economic or geopolitical interests. On the latter, Gallagher and Robinson note, "Imperialism may be only indirectly connected with economic integration in that it sometimes extends beyond areas of economic development, but acts for their strategic protection."[113] This project looks at cases that generally fall into this geopolitical category. Most notably, Britain sustained close alliance relations with the Ottoman Empire and Portugal until the late nineteenth century due in large part to their hold on certain colonies in the Balkans and Africa that London believed were geostrategically vital.[114]

With competition outside of Europe and North America perceived by U.S. policymakers as crucial to countering Soviet influence, the developing world witnessed the most intense fighting of the Cold War. For the United States, development, trade promotion, and military assistance stood as the leading tools for shoring up regimes both internally and externally. In this regard, scholars point to the close correlation between the region-by-region expansion of U.S. competition with the USSR and the parallel increase in foreign aid by Washington to those regions. An overwhelmingly clear trend exists, as well, of the United States providing both military *and* economic assistance as part and parcel of aid packages to assist non-communist friends.[115] Many agree that the foreign aid program represented "the basis of America's foreign policy" in the Cold War.[116] In this vein, I assess cases involving major allocations of assistance over an extended period of time during the Cold War.

I chose these types of pledges in large measure because they offer every opportunity for each of the three alternative explanations of commitment termination to matter. Relative to humanitarian norms, these cases involved active legislative processes throughout. As to realism, security-related considerations explain why these commitments emerged in the first place. Furthermore, perceived geopolitical changes made each case all the more strategically vital to the commitment-making state at the point of termination. Realist expectations of a "rally around the flag" effect at all levels of the state thus seem far more likely than bottom-up policy rebellion by norm-driven legislatures. Finally, each pledge was institutionalized at the domestic level. With the 1856 Treaty of Paris, Parliament formally ratified the British commitment to protect the integrity of the Ottoman Empire. Congress gave the authority for presidents to negotiate military and trade/aid pledges in addition to approving each at the point that funding began.[117] Since these U.S. and British pledges also required constant engagement with commitment partners, an interactive process consistent with the institutionalist explanation also seems far more likely than a sudden, unilateral overturning of the status quo by the U.S. Congress or the British Parliament.

The specific cases that I have selected for comparative study are listed in table 1.3. I focus on Great Britain and the United States because they represent two of the greatest powers in the history of international politics. Furthermore, they epitomize presidential and parliamentary democracy. Though they generally have fewer commitments to use as leverage, weaker liberal states often act much the same as their great power counterparts. I discuss examples along these lines in the concluding chapter.

The primary objective of this book is to deepen our theoretical understanding of humanitarian norms in democratic states. In line with other efforts to understand the causal pathways that lead to certain regularities in democratic foreign policy, I utilize case-studies to assess the argument.[118] In allowing me to supplement existing large-N work and present new directions for future research, case studies provide a better test of the dynamics at the center of human rights politics.[119] In the end, this book offers a more sophisticated understanding of humanitarian norms and, thus, better tools for assessing the three alternative explanations in larger statistical tests on the formation and termination of democratic commitments.

Even with the limitation of case studies, the book is empirically rich. In the case studies, I use a decision point approach. This allows me to assess multiple periods of commitment preservation prior to termination. The decision point approach, in the end, increases the number of observations in the main case studies to sixteen.[120] I also include a chapter of plausibility probes covering six additional cases from U.S. foreign policy. In the

Table 1.3. The process of de-commitment over time: A basis for study

Typology of commitment (time t)	Typology of recommitment (time t+1)	Typology of de-commitment (time t+2)
1. British pledge to protect *Ottoman* hegemony in the Balkans at the Treaty of Paris (1856)	1. British recommitment at Black Sea Conference (1871) and in Berlin Memorandum (May 1876)	1. British nonsupport of *Ottoman* hegemony in the Balkans at Constantinople Conference and neutrality in the Russo-Turkish War (1877–78)
2. U.S. foreign economic aid commitment to *Mozambique* (1984)	2. Recommitment annually with foreign aid legislation through 1992	2. No de-commitment
3. U.S. pledge of export promotion assistance to and unfettered trade with *South Africa* (1948)	3. Several recommitments to open trade relations, the last coming in 1984	3. U.S. imposes widespread economic sanctions, restricting most imports from and American business with *South Africa* (1985–86)
4. U.S. pledge to long-term military assistance to *Argentina* in a mutual security agreement (1964)	4. U.S. recommitment annually with foreign assistance legislation through 1976	4. U.S. termination of all military assistance to *Argentina* (1977)
5. U.S. pledge to long-term military assistance to *Chile* in a mutual security agreement (1952)	5. U.S. recommitment annually with foreign assistance legislation through 1973	5. U.S. termination of all military assistance to *Chile* (1974, 1976)
6. U.S. pledge to long-term military and economic development assistance to *Peru* in a mutual security agreement (1952)	6. U.S. recommitment annually with foreign assistance legislation to *Peru* into the 1980s	6. No de-commitment
7. U.S. pledge to long-term military and economic development assistance to *Nicaragua* in a mutual security agreement (1954)	7. U.S. recommitment annually with foreign assistance legislation to *Nicaragua* through 1977	7. U.S. termination of all military assistance to *Nicaragua* (1978)

chapter on U.S.-Latin American relations, I include data on the broad trends with all states in Latin America during the 1970s and early 1980s. In short, this book draws its conclusions from a dense empirical foundation of interesting and important historical cases.

The selected case studies meet general criteria of case selection. First, they offer extreme values on the dependent variable. Second, they are well matched for cross-case comparison, which allows for control against factors such as personality and context. I avoid the bias of sampling on the dependent variable in two ways.[121] The decision point approach allows me to examine multiple points of recommitment that occurred after the initial commitment and prior to commitment termination (table 1.4, recommitment column). For example, in the Balkan case, Britain's 1856 pledge to protect Ottoman hegemony was reconfirmed in the 1871 Black Sea Accord before British termination in 1877. The 1870 recommitment offers a case of commitment preservation, the inclusion of which in the study allows me to test the validity of any particular explanation of events at the point of commitment termination. Beyond decision points, I also include the Peru, Mozambique, and Nicaragua cases as a baseline of U.S. commitment consistency in the same time periods that the United States terminated commitments to Chile, Argentina, and South Africa. Third, in reference to the above discussion, I control for issue area by focusing exclusively on cases of strategic commitments.

[2]

Suffering Christians in British-Ottoman Relations

Throughout most of the nineteenth century, Russia stood as a leading strategic challenger to Great Britain's foreign policy goals. For Britain, this competition revolved around India, the center of its global empire. In this context, the Balkans and the broader issue of the integrity of the Ottoman Empire took on special meaning for London. The vast territory controlled by the Ottoman Empire was perceived as a crucial strategic buffer against Russian efforts to expand southward and hinder London's access to India. The Ottoman-controlled Balkans represented the geostrategic core in this respect for Britain. St. Petersburg had considerable leverage in the Balkans. Across the 1700s, it used common ethnic ties with the kindred Slavic nations to extend its influence toward the Black Sea and the Turkish Straits, directly challenging—indeed, in many ways usurping—Ottoman authority. For London, Russian encroachment brought St. Petersburg perilously close to the Ottoman capital of Constantinople and ultimately, the British believed, to India's border.[1]

In the Crimean War, Britain took its most decisive step in the nineteenth century to reverse the tide of Russian expansion into the Balkans. Joined by France and Austria, Britain led the way in repelling Russian attempts to gain even greater control over Ottoman territory. The ensuing Treaty of Paris (1856) terminated the Russian right to protect Slavic Christians in the Balkans and bound all signatories to respect and protect the integrity and independence of the Ottoman Empire. Britain joined France and Austria in signing three additional conventions in 1856 that made them guarantors of the Treaty of Paris. Article 2, herein, stated, "Any infraction of the stipulations of the said Treaty will be considered by the Powers signing the present treaty as *casus belli*."[2] Britain was obligated diplomatically and militarily to protect Ottoman integrity.

In the years that followed, the importance of the Mediterranean in its own right to British commerce soared. The planning and construction of the Suez Canal in the 1860s created a new, and far shorter, route of access to India. At the same time, London's ties to the Ottoman government grew closer, as British financiers extended substantial loans to the Porte (meaning the Ottomans) and invested in many development projects in Turkey. All the while, Britain stood by the Treaty of Paris. It reaffirmed its commitment to the treaty at the 1871 Black Sea Conference and refused as late as May 1876 to endorse international proposals for Balkan autonomy and independence.

November and December 1876 brought a dramatic change of course in British policy, however. At the Constantinople Conference of the European powers, Britain was the lead sponsor of an aggressive plan to strip the Balkan region from Ottoman control. Furthermore, in the spring of 1877, London adopted a treaty-violating posture of neutrality after Russia launched a military attack on Turkey with the sole purpose of ending Turkish dominion over the Balkans.

How do we explain British termination of a critical strategic commitment to Turkish integrity and independence? Furthermore, why did Britain sustain its commitment at several points, including the Berlin Memorandum in May 1876, only to radically change course in December of that same year?

Humanitarian norms help answer these questions. In 1876–77, the British Parliament brought unequivocal (though indirect) pressure to bear on the government in favor of Balkan independence. Parliament took this course following a massacre of Christians in Bulgaria that generated nationwide protests in Britain. Low levels of activist pressure or liberalizing steps by the Porte explain why Britain stood by the 1856 pledge in earlier periods.

Parliament, Humanitarianism, and the "Barbarous" Turks

For the twenty years that followed the Crimean War, Parliament shared the concerns of Britain's various cabinets over Russian ambitions. Paralleling these strategic interests, Parliament also displayed broader humanitarian concerns about the course of British foreign policy. In the case of the Ottoman Empire, these focused on the plight of Christian subjects of the Ottoman government.

The roots of British humanitarianism during the nineteenth century emerged, in large measure, from religious movements in the mid-Victorian period. R. T. Shannon, in particular, attributes two large Christian revivals and the Oxford Movement of the nineteenth century with raising moral sentiments throughout Britain. The second of the revivals occurred in 1859, just three years after the Treaty of Paris. In the political realm, these developments and others within society produced certain "ameliorative movements," which eventually reached Parliament.[3] The British legislature became the debating club for the heightened moralistic impulses of British society at large. In foreign policy during this period, the antislavery movement stands as the unrivaled example of the humanitarian tendencies of Parliament during the nineteenth century.[4] "In the last resort it was Parliament which abolished the slave trade and slavery," notes James Walvin. "It was the precise chronology of parliamentary debates, ministerial wrangles and government decisions which was crucial in the exact progress—or delay—in securing abolition and emancipation."[5]

As with antislavery, moral disdain for the Turkish administration and the Muslim foundation of the Ottoman state took hold in the British legislature. The Treaty of Paris brought Britain into a closer alliance with Turkey and, hence, greater complicity in the often repressive methods of administrative control over its Christian population. Parliament, thus, paid particularly close attention to the plight of co-religionist Christian subjects of the Porte.[6] On this basis, Parliament occasionally pressed the British government to encourage Turkish administrative reform to benefit Ottoman Christians.

The earliest parliamentary expression for Ottoman Christians came with the Greek war for independence. Following Turkey's ruthless suppression of the Greek rebellion, the British Parliament expressed deep sympathy for Greek independence.[7] In a July 1822 debate, condemnation of the Porte was rampant. Various speakers talked of the "barbarous ferocity" of the Turks, "Turkish inhumanity" and "tyranny" as well as the "wasteful and disgusting empire of the Turks."[8] Some Members of Parliament (MPs) sought liberation of the Balkans. To this effect, antislavery advocate William Wilberforce labeled the Turks "a nation of barbarians, the ancient and inveterate enemies of Christianity and freedom in Asia."[9] In the end, official policy came to reflect the demands of these and other MPs. In concert with Europe, Britain adopted steps that facilitated eventual Greek independence in 1830.[10]

The Treaty of Paris reflected concerns for the Christians as well. Britain negotiated a clause into the treaty regarding European hopes for good government by the Porte over its Christian subjects. While this provision did not constitute a quid pro quo for British or European support for

Ottoman integrity and independence, it received a warm welcome during parliamentary debate over the treaties. Above all else, Parliament showed considerable unease with unfettered Ottoman control over its Christian subjects.[11]

Parliamentary reactions to events in the 1860s demonstrated these concerns still further. In 1860, tensions between the Maronite and Druse populations of Lebanon erupted into open civil war. On 9 July, local Ottoman officials prosecuted a widespread massacre of Christian Maronites in which thousands were killed. A strong reaction from the British Parliament helped move the government to join other European powers for a joint response.[12] Lord Stratford de Redcliffe noted that the news was a "shock to all the best feelings of humanity." He called for Parliament to stand up on the basis of England's principles of "civilization and humanity."[13] The Marques of Clarincarde drew parallels to the Greek civil war and said that Turkey should not be allowed to "hold in a state of barbarism some of the finest districts in the world."[14] John Bright claimed that "the Turks returned to their tyranny, and the Christians again passed under the yoke of oppression."[15] The British government eventually endorsed the dispatch of European (mainly French) troops to restore order in Lebanon and a conference of the powers for a new administrative structure in Lebanon.[16]

A similar pattern of developments marked a dispute over Ottoman garrisons stationed in the independent state of Serbia, a Christian nation. In 1862, Ottoman forces from one of the garrisons clashed with Serb nationals and, as a result, shelled the Serb capital of Belgrade. Hundreds of innocent civilians died.[17] Again, the British Parliament erupted. In the House of Commons, Sir William Gregory announced his support for Ottoman integrity before complaining of "Turkish barbarism and misrule." He called for a "more Christian policy" of using "the moral weight of England" to "obtain for the Christian provinces of the Porte self-government as far as possible."[18] Grant Duff complained that the Turkish garrisons served no purpose except as "outposts against Christendom."[19] Another MP described the Christian population as, "in a word, outlaws" in Turkey who are merely "seeking to catch the light of Western Europe and to enter upon a new path of civilization and progress."[20] The Chancellor of the Exchequer noted the dominant posture in Parliament: "It is impossible not to notice that the discussion of this evening has been marked by a warm interest in the fate of the Christian subjects of Turkey."[21] In the end, Britain joined other powers in creating a timetable, with Turkish consent, for the removal of the garrisons. In 1867, the Porte completed the process on schedule.[22]

Lebanon and Syria demonstrate British parliamentary concerns over Ottoman inhumanity. Developments in both during the first decade or so after Crimea also demonstrate a willingness on the part of the Ottoman government to meet, at some level, broader desires within Britain and Europe for better government in rulings its Christian subjects. Turkey agreed to European peacekeepers and implemented new administrative measures over Lebanon. It also withdrew its garrisons from Serbia under international pressure. All of this helped the plight of Christians in those regions. But over time Turkish willingness to accommodate European concerns about Ottoman Christians faded. As this occurred and activist group pressure against Ottoman inhumanity increased in the late 1870s, parliamentary—and with it, British—policy moved away from the pledges in the Treaty of Paris.

Before we assess that change in policy, a brief look at parliamentary methods of exerting independent pressure on policymaking in the British system deserves attention. As we saw in the last chapter, open policy rebellion, in which the legislature passes legislation contrary to cabinet interests, is rare in parliamentary systems, especially in two-party systems like the British system, where the Cabinet is chosen exclusively from members of the majority party in Parliament. The majority will almost always vote with the government. The main reason for this lies with the fear among MPs that an open break with the government will lead to a vote of no confidence and an unpredictable general election. Hence, the picture of legislative policy influence in this chapter will look quite different from the U.S. cases to follow, where Congress struck out on its own in every case by passing bills contrary to executive wishes.

The British Parliament exerts pressure more indirectly than this. Prime ministers worry most about their own party. "The only doubt the Prime Minister has is about his own supporters," argues former British prime minister Richard Crossman. "They are the people who can challenge him and, in the last resort, overthrow him."[23] Debate in the House of Commons matters in this context. Prime ministers worry about the trouble that the opposition party can raise through questioning and parliamentary inquiries that could draw some members of the majority closer to the opposition cause. The nature and flow of dissension on the floor of the House of Commons matters, therefore, even if open majority rebellion is low. Prime ministers must be expert managers of their party, keenly aware of and preempting member grievances before they gain enough momentum to produce open party rebellion and votes of no confidence.[24] As we shall see, the British Cabinet moved to accommodate parliamentary concerns about Ottoman Christians only after members of its own party, the Tories, began to discuss in public their support for the cause.

In Britain, the structure of cabinet decisions also offers a unique opportunity for broader grievances in Parliament to affect policy. Unlike the U.S. system, where final policy decisions rest with the president alone, government decisions in Britain are a group product, a decision of the Cabinet as a whole. "The last thing Cabinets ever think of doing in America is to try to decide anything," writes Crossman. "It is not their function, whereas in the British system the Cabinet is the place of decision."[25] The prime minister's role in any cabinet debate is to "formulate" at some point a broad policy that reflects cabinet sentiment. But the prime minister in no sense makes the decision alone. In fact, decisions may at times go directly against his or her will. Since all cabinet members are MPs as well, this group-based decision process offers numerous potential inroads for broader parliamentary opinion to affect debates.[26] This was no less evident with the Disraeli government in the 1870s. As a conservative Tory, Benjamin Disraeli was an ardent supporter of Turkey due to its vital strategic location for the British Empire. Many members of his cabinet were concerned, though, about the public and parliamentary outrage stirred up in part by the Liberal William Gladstone over the plight of Ottoman Christians. Much to the consternation of Disraeli, his cabinet's policy eventually came to the defense of these Christians, even though doing so appeared to jeopardize broader strategic goals for Britain.

The Black Sea Conference (1871)

The Treaty of Paris included two measures intended to weaken Russian naval capacity for interfering in Turkish affairs. The first involved the neutralization of the Black Sea, meaning that ships of war could no longer use it. The second was the placing of the Turkish Straits under the unhindered control of the Porte with an additional provision that closed the Straits to foreign ships of war during peacetime.[27]

In November 1870, Russia announced that it no longer accepted the first of these provisions, the neutralization of the Black Sea. The British government called a conference of the Powers (France, Germany, Austria-Hungary, Russia, and the Ottoman Empire) in response. As Barbara Jelavich notes, it came at a time when Britain, more than ever, found passage through the Mediterranean important among the ever-growing imperial entanglements and interests in the East.[28] The Black Sea Conference proved a strategic success for Britain. While accepting the Russian request for de-neutralization of the Black Sea, the conference recommitted the Powers, at the demand of Britain, to the remaining clauses of the Treaty of Paris. It also strengthened the main strategic thrust of the treaty by increasing the hand of the Porte in its control over the Straits. "The Black Sea was no longer neutralized, but the rest of the Treaty of Paris remained intact," noted Jelavich. "The Straits settlement was changed in a manner which could benefit the Ottoman Government."[29]

The posture of the British government at the Black Sea Conference centered exclusively on protecting Ottoman integrity and independence. Nothing deterred the government of Prime Minister William Gladstone from this strategic end. On the topic of Ottoman Christians, Parliament, in particular, hardly raised the issue in its support of the government. The main reasons for parliamentary restraint on the Christian issue appeared to be the lack of noticeably illiberal steps by the Porte against its Christian subjects at the time. In fact, Turkish reforms in Lebanon and Serbia (see above) in addition to greater administrative autonomy for Crete in 1867 aided the Turkish cause in Parliament, an image that British newspapers reinforced. At the time of the conference, *The Times* (London) reported on Turkish cooperation with Greece in pursuit of a band of criminals that had crossed into Ottoman territory as well as concessions made by the Porte to Catholics living in Armenia.[30] At the time, Russian newspapers complained of mistreatment of Christians by the Porte. A correspondent for *The Times* directly refuted these claims, echoing a common theme in the media: suspicion over Russian intentions.[31]

In its appeal for parliamentary approval of the Black Sea accords, the British Cabinet used this state of affairs in Turkey to its advantage. In Parliament, Viscount Enfield recounted on behalf of the government the satisfactory plight of Christians in Turkey, stating, "The internal conditions of Christians in Turkey . . . [have] improved since the Crimean War."[32] In a later question about the plight of Turkey's Christian population, he elaborated, "All accounts in Turkey agree in confirmation of the progress . . . made towards toleration, and much has been done of late years towards raising the position of the Christian population in Turkey." Parliament appeared to concur. Enfield did not face a single challenge from MPs.[33]

Faced with Turkish liberalization and a lack of activist pressure, most MPs, in fact, defended the status quo of Ottoman integrity and independence during the Black Sea accord debates.[34] Prior to and during the conference, the only parliamentary inquiries called for the Cabinet to stand behind the Treaty of Paris. On 14 and 24 February, Conservatives complained that abandoning the Black Sea clauses of the Treaty of Paris would destroy the entire Crimean policy. The government responded on both occasions with statements of its firm resolve to protect the Crimean policy, noting that the Turkish navy was one of the strongest in the world, which made the Black Sea provisions unnecessary.[35] During the 30 March debate in the Commons, supporters praised the adherence and protection of Ottoman independence and integrity. The only criticism centered on whether the Cabinet should have done more to ensure the vitality of those commitments. Beyond that, nearly every parliamentarian who spoke sounded one of several themes: pro–Treaty of Paris, pro-Turkish, anti-Russian—or all of the above.[36]

The Berlin Memorandum (May 1876)

The next major challenge to Ottoman integrity came in May 1876. The outcome was much like the Black Sea Conference. In July 1875, Christians in Herzegovina rebelled against Turkey, with co-religionists in Bosnia soon to follow.[37] It was the first major clash of Christians and Muslims in the Ottoman Empire since the 1866 Cretan revolt. With support from Serbia, the insurgents overwhelmed the Turkish forces initially. Press reports detailed these developments, making no mention of inhumane behavior by the Turks.[38]

After a mildly worded note from the European powers failed to end the dispute, Russia began to press for more far-reaching reforms on the part of the Porte.[39] Along with Austria and Germany, it drafted a memorandum for reform that carried a veiled threat of European coercion if Turkey refused to comply. The British Cabinet of Benjamin Disraeli followed the policy of 1856. It saw the memo as a clear violation of Ottoman integrity. In order to back up its position, Disraeli sent the British fleet to Beşik Bay near the Turkish Straits and warned the European powers about infringing on Ottoman authority.[40]

Unlike the Black Sea Conference debate, the months leading up to the Berlin Memorandum brought out a noticeable coalition of interest groups and activists who demanded that Britain desert the 1856 commitments and support full independence for the Balkan provinces. The revolts in Bosnia and Herzegovina sparked this activity. In 1875, two organizations, the League of Suffering Rayahs of Bosnia and Herzegovina and the League in Aid of Christians of Turkey, were created. The former held a rally in September 1875. The latter followed with a highly publicized meeting, which included various dignitaries, in December 1875. Paralleling these organizations, a group of influential individuals began to demand changes to the Crimean policy. These included prominent Oxford historian E. A. Freeman, former prime minister and foreign minister Lord

Russell and leading humanitarian Dr. Humphrey Sandwith. Many British media sources also gave substantial sympathetic attention to the rebellions and the plight of Christians generally in the Ottoman Empire.[41]

Activist appeals fell on unsympathetic ears within Parliament. This was due, in part, to a lack of any form of informational or public opinion support. Activist pressure rested exclusively on claims of sympathy for the Christians, centering on generalizations about Turkish inhumanity with very little reference to specific cases. While supported by some MPs, the activists also lacked a public constituency.[42] Activist efforts were compounded as well by liberalization inside Turkey. Of greatest significance, a coup took place in Constantinople in late May. Much as in Crete, the new Turkish government promised extensive administrative reforms in Bosnia and Herzegovina. The proposed changes included the introduction of local and regional representative governments, like Crete, as well as reforms that made the taxation and justice systems more equitable for Christians.[43]

The British Parliament stood behind the government's policy. On 15 June, when asked to state the government's position on the 1856 commitments, the foreign minister, Lord Derby, read the treaty aloud. He then said, "These are the words of the Treaty; and as far as I know that Treaty has not been invalidated or modified by any subsequent Treaty or diplomatic document whatever."[44] No challenge followed. On 22 May, the government announced its refusal to sign the Berlin Memorandum. This, again, drew no challenge from Parliament.[45]

The Porte's endorsement of reforms stood at the heart of parliamentary restraint. Wary of the Christian issue, Disraeli appealed to Parliament for patience in waiting for the Porte to reform. He pressed this argument at several points without challenge from the House of Commons. On 9 June, for instance, he praised the Porte for its new reform initiatives. At the same time, he pointed out that the Christian provinces of the Ottoman Empire congratulated and supported the new sultan. The most ardent humanitarians in Parliament were swayed by the prospects of reform. The Marquess of Hartington from the opposition bench said on the issue that he did not "believe there exists in the country [that is, Britain] any distrust . . . of Her Majesty's Government" in the handling of the Berlin Memorandum, so he refused to press a debate with the Government.[46] After an appeal by Disraeli for MPs to wait on "the consequences of the steps recently taken by the Government at Constantinople," Lord Hartington called the reforms "interesting" and backed away from a debate.[47] "The Turkish Revolution suddenly transformed the situation and seemed after all to justify the British Cabinet," observed Hugh Seton-Watson. "Who could not argue that the new sultan and his reforming ministers must be given the necessary breathing-space in which to carry out their program?"[48] Liberalizing events thus helped allay parliamentary action. Within a matter of weeks, though, the Porte's behavior changed, and so did the British Parliament's attitude.

Termination of the Crimean Policy (May 1876–1877)

From the opening of the 1876 legislative session in February until late July, Parliament did not have a single debate on foreign policy. The legislature faced little incentive to interfere with executive prerogatives on the Ottoman question or any other foreign matter. Events in Bulgaria changed that entirely.

The Bulgarian massacres started in the week of 4 May 1876. Amidst nationalist uprisings, the Porte called upon armed radical Muslim groups called "irregulars" to suppress the rebellion. The irregulars did much more than that. After crushing the insurgents, they attacked unarmed men, women, and children across the region. In the process, they burned more than fifty towns to the ground. Death toll estimates for Christians ranged from twelve to sixty thousand.[49] News of the massacres reached Britain on 23 June when the *Daily News* published the first in a series of articles by Edwin Pears from Constantinople giving extensive details of the killings.[50] Pears's information came from American missionaries in Bulgaria. The reports carried vivid details: young girls sold into slavery by the irregulars; a town of six hundred houses burned to the ground; the destruction of three hundred and fifty houses in another village where nearly two thousand women, children, and elderly people died; and the burning of forty women to death in a barn.[51]

The reaction of Parliament was, as George Thompson notes, "to fly to the Ministers for information" and determine what the British government "intended to do in view of the facts."[52] In several debates through July, MPs made strong statements against Turkish inhumanity. In response to Pears's findings, John Jenkins stated, "The news that has been received in this country within the last few hours has created everywhere the greatest anxiety. . . . We feel that matters are so serious and have arrived at such a crisis, that we are entitled to ask the Government for some further, more real explanation." He was not alone. John Bright called on Britain to aid "the subjects of the Porte to free themselves from . . . dominion." Henry Fawcett referred to the "galling and unendurable thralldom" under which the Christians were suffering and demanded that the government make its policy clear. William Forster noted "the pain—I may say horror" of reports from Bulgaria. Anthony Mundella said the "facts are horrible," a "disgrace to humanity." Conservative MPs spoke up as well. One complained of the "evils of the Turkish Government." Another drew parallels to Greece and Lebanon, saying the Porte never recognized "civilization."[53]

Forced to rely on media reports alone, Parliament remained cautious through July, however, and followed the government's lead. In a major debate on 31 July, the Liberal leader in the Commons, the Marquess of Hartington, complained about the slow response of the government to the developments in Bulgaria but then concluded with his grudging support for government policy. The former Liberal prime minister, William Gladstone, also offered a broad critique of Turkey with only a veiled reference to Bulgaria. He too stood behind government policy, stating that Parliament "shall not presume to announce a definite judgment" on Bulgaria until the completion of the inquiries by the government. Publicly, Disraeli felt undeterred by the debates in June and July. He criticized MPs for their excitement, calling the information provided by Pears and others "coffee-house babble" and "imaginary atrocities." He concluded with a firm commitment to Ottoman integrity, stating that British policy did not emerge from any intrinsic love for the Turks but "was to maintain the interests of England and the British Empire."[54]

Behind the scenes, the government showed greater sensitivity to parliamentary concerns. After the July debates, Derby instructed Sir Henry Elliot, the British Ambassador to Turkey, to assess the extent of the atrocities and protest to the Porte about them.[55] After receiving a petition signed by forty MPs, Derby suggested that the government might consider pressing "local or administrative autonomy" in the Balkans.[56] All the same, suggestions of deserting the 1856 policy never emerged. By early August, in fact, the government considered the issue all but dead in Parliament.

Two major changes occurred in late July and early August, however, which propelled Parliament to demand a change in policy toward the Porte. First, activist groups initiated a movement in late July that led to nationwide protests against the Treaty of Paris commitments to Turkey. Second, and more immediately, two separate reports by respected figures offered firsthand accounts of the atrocities in early August. Steps toward commitment termination soon followed.

In late July, the League in Aid of Christians of Turkey along with other leading activists initiated a pressure campaign on Parliament that by the fall had blossomed into a full-scale public opinion upheaval. The movement's formation generally followed the theoretical course discussed in chapter 1. Namely, through the organization and use of smaller group settings, activists built a network of supporters that eventually set off a broad grassroots movement. On 27 July, the League helped organize a meeting in London. Events in Turkey validated the longstanding complaints of the League and gave it greater credibility as a leading authority on the issue. Forty-eight MPs and twelve other leading political figures attended the event. Lord Shaftsbury oversaw the meeting, and E. A. Freeman, serving as the keynote speaker, demanded that the government press the Porte to accept full autonomy for the Christian provinces of Turkey. The format and tone of the meeting became a model for others that started in cities across England in late August and September. The July gathering received substantial media attention: *Saturday Review* noted, accurately as it turned out, that this and other meetings of the same type "could determine the future policy of the country."[57]

The League received a boost from new information coming out of Turkey. In the middle of July, two separate missions left for Bulgaria from Constantinople. Walter Baring, the assistant secretary at the British Embassy in Constantinople, led one inquiry on behalf of the British government. Much like British Ambassador Elliot, Baring was known for his strong pro-Turkish sentiments. In light of this, missionaries from the United States requested that the U.S. Embassy send a mission of its own to Bulgaria. The secretary of legation and consul-general, Eugene Schuyler, was chosen for the task. J. A. MacGahan, a correspondent for the London *Daily News,* accompanied Schuyler.[58]

A letter from MacGahan published in the *Daily News* on 7 August bolstered the cause of the League and other activists. MacGahan gave vivid details of what he and Schuyler had discovered to that point. Focusing on the Bulgarian town of Batak, in particular, he described the brutal methods by which Turkish irregulars murdered the majority of the population, which included the burning of a church with many of the town's inhabitants inside.[59] British government officials read a letter in Parliament from Baring that confirmed much of the MacGahan article. Shannon captured the consequences: "The combination of MacGahan and Baring gave the British Parliament and public the most profound stir it had experienced since the opening of the Bulgarian question."[60] Above all else, the uncorroborated press articles from late June gave critics of Turkey instant credibility; the Disraeli Government, which had previously claimed that the atrocities had been exaggerated, found itself on the defensive.

In Parliament, MPs from both parties demanded a change in the course of British policy toward Turkey. Debates occurred in the final days of the parliamentary session. Each MP that spoke acknowledged the pressure of activists, referencing either the 27 July meeting of the League or MacGahan's reports. Mundella, for instance, claimed that the "testimony of M. Schuyler" proves the necessity of ending the British alliance with Turkey. Hartington pointed to the credibility of MacGahan's report and said that "unless some complete defense against these atrocities can be put forward, the Turkish Government will lose as it has lost, and is rapidly daily losing, all traces of the sympathy previously shown" by Britain. Evelyn Ashley called the MacGahan report a confirmation of Turkish barbarism and a sound reason to pursue "freedom on behalf of oppressed nationalities." These sentiments crossed party lines. William Forsyth, a Conservative, asked, "Could we, as a Christian nation and a free people, continue to give moral countenance and support to a nation whose Government had allowed these horrors . . . to be perpetrated, unchecked and un-reproved." Another Conservative, Sir H. Drummond Wolff, criticized Elliot for his overly pro-Turkish approach, a perspective he claimed was not shared with the country or Parliament.[61]

During the debates, the government called on Britain to remember its imperial interests. "All classes of the community, without distinction of class or Party, felt exactly the same sentiments of horror as described by Mr. Forster," said Robert Bourke, the under-secretary of state for foreign affairs. He warned, though, against allowing these feelings to override the "interests of the country." Disraeli admitted as well that "even the slightest estimates of the horrors that occurred in Bulgaria is quite sufficient to excite the indignation of the country and of Parliament," adding, "I am sure that as long as England is ruled by English Parties who understand the principles on which our Empire is founded, and who are resolved to maintain that Empire, our influence in that part of the world [Ottoman Empire] can never be looked upon with indifference."[62]

Behind closed doors, the government's posture was less defiant to the changing parliamentary tide. The Cabinet started to take steps away from the Treaty of Paris in response to parliamentary pressure. On 8 August, the day after the first debate sparked by MacGahan's article, Derby wrote to Elliot that the "accounts of the atrocities committed in Bulgaria continue to give rise to discussion, and are exciting much reprobation. . . . You cannot speak too strongly of the horror which the statements have aroused in the Government and the people of this country."[63] Disraeli made perhaps the most profound admission of Parliament's impact. Despite his strategic tone in Parliament, the Prime Minister wrote to Derby after the debates, "We have had a very damaging debate on Bulgarian atrocities and it is lucky for us, in this respect, that the session is dying."[64]

In light of domestic constraints, the government realized that diplomatic developments required action. In early July, Serbia and Montenegro moved to strengthen their strategic positions by declaring war against

Turkey on behalf of the Bosnians and Herzegovinians. Bolstered at the time by Parliament's support of the Berlin Memorandum decision, the Cabinet remained aloof, hoping that the Porte would easily defeat Serbia and Montenegro. By August, those hopes had come to fruition, as Turkey made significant gains in the war. However, with Russia beginning to agitate for war on behalf of Serbia and stiff domestic political restraints emerging in Britain against alliance with Turkey (as demonstrated by Parliament, in particular), Derby made an about-face in mid-August. With war on behalf of Turkey impossible, peace was Britain's only means for sustaining its interests: keeping Russia from gaining in the Balkans and achieving access to the Straits. Derby's efforts to this end eventually brought Britain to violate the 1856 treaty.[65]

The peace initiative emerged in a barrage of telegrams from Derby to Elliot in August and early September. Derby repeatedly cited the domestic developments that had forced Britain into its new posture. While perhaps overstating the level of public disdain at the time, his words proved prophetic, as public pressure soared during the fall and winter. On 22 August, he wrote to Elliot:

> Any sympathy which was previously felt here towards that country has been completely destroyed by the recent lamentable occurrences in Bulgaria. The accounts of outrages and excesses committed by the Turkish troops upon an unhappy, and for the most part unresisting population, has roused an universal feeling of indignation in all classes of English society, and to such a pitch has this risen that in the extreme case of Russia declaring war against Turkey, Her Majesty's Government would find it practically impossible to interfere in defense of the Ottoman Empire. Such an event, in which the sympathies of the nation would be brought into direct opposition to its Treaty engagements, would place England in a most unsatisfactory, and even humiliating position, yet it is impossible to say that if the present conflict continues the contingency may not arise. The speedy conclusion of a peace under any circumstances most desirable, becomes from these considerations a matter of urgent necessity.[66]

The next day, Derby, citing Bulgaria and British opinion, sent a message directly to the Porte demanding an end to the war with Serbia. Following a Serbian appeal for mediation on 24 August, the foreign minister again sent notes calling for Constantinople to negotiate peace. Finally, on 1 September, Derby instructed Elliot to move to the center of Turkish-Serbian negotiations and broker an armistice before Turkey's relations with Russia were irreparably harmed.[67]

Meanwhile, the end of the parliamentary session did not dampen public-parliamentary support for Balkan Christians, as Disraeli hoped. Instead, the call for action reached its height over the fall of 1876. A large public meeting expressing sympathy for Balkan Christians occurred on 22 August in Darlington. Three days later, Darlington held another meeting. From that point, meetings rapidly spread across the north of England, with fourteen cities holding large public gatherings before August was out. The South followed more slowly. By 6 September, all cities in the North and half of the major cities and towns across England had held protest meetings.[68] On 25 September, the *Daily News* estimated a total of 262 meetings across Britain starting in late August.[69] Leaders at the meetings repeatedly appealed to broad national values, support for suffering Christians, and the civilizational backwardness of the Porte. Each adopted a series of petitions that were later sent to the Foreign Office. The petitions were similar: each expressed indignation over the atrocities in Bulgaria and disdain for the pro-Turkish policy of the government and ended with an appeal for self-government or independence for the Balkan nations. By the end of 1876, the Foreign Office had received a total of 455 petitions that comprised six published volumes.[70]

As discussed in chapter 1, meetings of civic groups and small ad-hoc gatherings serve as the fuel for developing a collective set of grievances as the foundation of social movements. That appeared to be the case here. City and town mayors, trade unions, and political associations as well as other organizations called and sponsored the gatherings of the agitation across Britain during the fall of 1876. Most scholars grant special attention to the way that a small group of organizers—the Oxford Group—used the flow of reports from MacGahan and Schuyler in September to build nationwide support for the movement that led to these meetings. The Oxford Group included Farley, Freeman, and Cannon Liddon, among others.[71] Churches, especially nonconformist ones, proved crucial to the initiation and spread of the movement. They had special credibility among the public as voices on the issue of suffering Christians. As one of the few members of the Anglican hierarchy to press openly for Turkish reform in the Balkans, Liddon used the pulpit as a means to spread the message of responsibility to change the Crimean policy.[72] Many nonconformist clergy and lower-level priests in the Anglican Church across England did the same.[73]

With the surge of public activity, political leaders joined the movement as well. At the request of Liddon and others, Gladstone became the leading figure in early September.[74] He was joined by other Liberal backbenchers and, more importantly, Conservative MPs. Conservatives held an anti-Turk meeting in London on 18 September, for example. At a

31 August meeting, a Conservative MP introduced the anti-Turk resolution that the participants adopted, and another Conservative MP in attendance claimed that he would ensure that Disraeli knew that this particular meeting was bipartisan. At meetings in Bristol and Plymouth in the first week of September, two Conservative MPs presented letters to be read aloud. Conservative MPs were also in attendance at protests in Christchurch and Cardiff on 7 September.[75]

The Cabinet responded to the pressure. As parliamentary under-secretary, Bourke was "naturally most alive to the Parliamentary reaction." On 25 August he sent Derby, and later Disraeli, suggestions on steps in the Balkans that might allay the public concern. In doing so, Bourke noted, "I continue to receive daily letters from members of Parliament recording the indignation of their constituents about Bulgarian atrocities."[76] Bourke cited a 31 August meeting as evidence.[77] Cabinet members with seats in the House of Commons also expressed the need to change policy. For several, there was deep concern over the weakening of the government amidst charges of cabinet complicity in the Porte's inhumanity.[78] The war secretary, Gathorne Hardy, appealed to public opinion and Bulgarian atrocities as the basis for forcing peace on the Porte. In a note to the Lord Chancellor in the Cabinet, he conceded as well that he hoped Disraeli was "mindful" of public opinion. Stratford Northcote, chancellor of the exchequer, told Disraeli of the need for Britain to propose Balkan autonomy or independence. He feared that otherwise, "British opinion unchecked might possibly carry the country into immediate opposition to its own best interests."[79]

Disraeli reluctantly bowed to the pressure from below. With a nod to activist pressure, he complained to Derby in September of "this . . . crew of High Ritualists, dissenting ministers, and 'the great Liberal party.' " He later told Lord Salisbury, the India secretary, that dealing with the agitation was "the most difficult business I have ever had to touch." The prime minister added that he had serious misgivings about "our new point of departure" but captured its domestic political necessity when he labeled the turn "wise because inevitable."[80]

As we have already seen, the 1856 commitment to Ottoman integrity translated into two specific things for Britain: a vigorous defense of the Porte militarily against Russian encroachment and a refusal to reduce the Porte's sovereignty over its subject populations. The domestic political upheaval in Britain generated progressive backpedaling from these commitments by the Cabinet through 1878. At each turn, the Cabinet sought minimum damage to its strategic commitments while hoping to appease pressure at home. Hamstrung by the latter, it eventually had to stand by as Russian troops tore into the Balkans and nearly marched to the gates of Constantinople.

Britain started to alter its commitments in September. Facing pressure at home, the Cabinet moved aggressively against Turkey toward a Balkan solution. The Porte refused to submit to the call for an armistice in early September. On 21 September, Britain demanded that Turkey offer local autonomy for Bosnia and Herzegovina as well as implement measures to ensure no further injustices in Bulgaria as terms for peace with Serbia. After further delays by the Porte, Derby warned the Sultan on 5 October that a refusal to accept both an armistice with Serbia and a Conference of the Powers would lead to the withdrawal of Elliot and the end of all moral and material support from Britain. Facing this threat, Turkey reluctantly accepted the intervention of the Powers.[81]

Britain officially called the Powers to a conference at Constantinople in order to discuss the Balkan situation. Disraeli and Derby chose the India secretary, Lord Salisbury, as the British plenipotentiary to the conference over Elliot. Derby explained why in a letter to Salisbury: "Your tendencies are not supposed to be Turkish, and the choice would therefore satisfy the public . . . [and] you would be able to help the Parliamentary defense of your own acts."[82] The public and activist leaders received the announcement of Salisbury as an indication of change in government policy.[83]

Salisbury did not disappoint anti-Turkish activists and MPs. With Germany's declaration of neutrality, Russia and Britain dominated the discussions. During preliminary negotiations, Salisbury moved to establish a quick agreement with his Russian counterpart, Count Nicholas Ignatiev. The two settled on far-reaching autonomy for Bosnia, Herzegovina, and Bulgaria in addition to a restatement of the same status for Serbia and Montenegro. Agreement was made easier because Salisbury's initial proposal on this point outstretched that of Ignatiev. The two circumscribed Ottoman independence and integrity in the Balkans with a proposal to establish a European Commission at Constantinople in order to oversee the Porte's treatment of its remaining Christian subjects. Salisbury and Ignatiev also agreed on a plan for European appointment of governors over the Christian provinces of Turkey. The plan granted Europe, without the consent of the Porte, the sole authority to remove and appoint members of the commission and regional governors.[84]

Cabinet records show that the anticipated posture of Parliament drove the British position. Disraeli monitored the negotiations with great anxiety.[85] A Russian proposal for a European occupation force in Bosnia, Herzegovina, and Bulgaria drew particularly strong objections from the British Cabinet. Yet, at each turn, the Cabinet reluctantly agreed due to domestic politics. In mid-December, Salisbury justified his support for the occupation force to Derby:

> If the Porte accepts the decision of the conference and then an outbreak of massacres occurs, we shall be in an awkward position before Parliament, for Ignatiev will have left on the protocols of the conference his warning of danger. Then it will be impossible to resist or control the Russian occupation. England's power will be paralyzed by agitation at home and the Russians will cross the frontier and do as they like.

Disraeli seemed to agree with Salisbury, noting that a British force in the Balkans "would be cheerfully accepted in Parliament and be popular outside" with the public as well. Though a clear violation of Ottoman integrity and independence, the Cabinet eventually agreed to a Belgian occupation force.[86]

The conference officially opened on 11 December. As Millman notes, "The Turks made little effort to mask their disappointment and anger at what they considered British abandonment." Salisbury pressured the Porte to agree, but to no avail. The Porte refused to accede to the conference provisions on grounds of domestic political restraints.[87] Finally, on 20 January 1877, the conference ended in failure.

In disdain, each of the Powers withdrew their ambassadors from Constantinople. A Russian military attack now appeared inevitable. Through February and March, concerns about Russian intentions brought a more pro-Turkish position from the British Cabinet, amply demonstrated by a delay in signing a Russian protocol demanding reforms from the Porte, a refusal to sign a joint declaration of war against Turkey, and demands that Russia respect British interests with respect to Constantinople. The latter Russia refused, resulting in a tense deadlock in Russo-British relations in early 1877.[88]

The British Parliament returned to session in February 1877. There was deep socio-legislative concern that war on Turkey's behalf was imminent. When Derby reinforced these sentiments by indicating in mid-March that the highly unpopular Elliot would return to Constantinople, the House of Commons exploded in fury. For nearly everyone in Parliament, Elliot personified the Crimean War policy. Each MP that stood against Elliot in the debate made reference to broader public opinion. "He entirely differs from the opinion which we hold on this subject, which is held by the Government themselves, and which is certainly held by the country," said Forster, "therefore he ought to no longer represent this country at the Porte." Gladstone said that Elliot was not "in harmony with the general convictions of the country" as represented by the public agitation over Bulgaria. Indicative of the diffuse nature of anti-Turkish sentiments across Parliament, the two lone defenders of Elliot qualified their comments by indicating outrage at Bulgaria and sympathy with the agitation.[89]

The Cabinet responded. Each member except Disraeli and Derby supported the replacement of Elliot. Salisbury stepped into the fray and warned in a cabinet debate "that our [the Cabinet's] general retirement will be the consequence" in Parliament if the decision came in favor of Elliot's return to Turkey. Disraeli issued the final decision. In a public statement, he said that Elliot would not return "after the expression of feeling on the part of an almost unanimous Cabinet, and the report of the temper and prospects of the House of Commons given by its leader." On 31 March, the Government announced Elliot's replacement, Sir Henry Layard.[90]

Russia declared war on Turkey on 24 April 1877. Fearing that Britain would come to the Porte's defense, Gladstone proposed two resolutions, which Parliament debated in May. One condemned Turkey on the basis of Bulgaria, and the other stripped the Porte of any future assurance of British matériel or moral support. While the resolutions eventually ended in defeat, the Bulgaria-dominated debate forced the government to adopt a clear policy of neutrality, which sealed the fate of Ottoman control over the Balkans.

Gladstone opened the debate with a discussion of the Bulgarian atrocities and sentiment against Turkey in Britain. He gave special attention to both the autumn agitation and the more than one hundred meetings and demonstrations in the days leading up to the debate of his resolutions. Joseph Chamberlain followed Gladstone's lead, talking of the "tyranny of the Turks" and detailed the extent to which the agitation changed Government policy. Sir H. Drummond Wolff, a Conservative, proposed a counterresolution to negate any parliamentary moves intended to embarrass the government. In defense of his measure, Wolff expressed his sympathy for the agitation and then argued that Gladstone's resolutions were superfluous in light of the fact that the Government had already responded to public pressure by withdrawing support for Turkey.[91]

Asheton Cross, the home secretary, then commented on behalf of the government. Cross's speech stood as the most important of the debate. Adopting Wolff's tone, Cross began with deference to the agitation. "I can only say that I, for one, should have been ashamed of my countrymen if public expressions had not been given from one end of the land to the other of their utter detestations of the horrors which had been committed in Turkey," Cross stated. From there, he criticized Turkey as "utterly blind and foolish" and stated emphatically that the Cabinet stood unified behind "every word uttered by Lord Salisbury" at the Constantinople Conference. Cross then turned to current policy. He claimed that Britain would assume a posture of "absolute and strict neutrality" in the Russo-Turkish War. Of special importance was Cross's effective renunciation of British adherence to the *casus belli* provisions of the 1856 treaties: "We warned them [Turkey] . . . that they had nothing to expect from us. We warned them at the Conference and since then there has been no loss of time in the issue of our declaration of neutrality. In the war between Russia and Turkey we are absolutely impartial." Though deeply concerned about Russia's unwillingness to issue a public assurance that its troops would stop short of Constantinople, Cross noted in closing the conditions under which Britain would break its neutrality: a Russian attack on Constantinople, the Turkish Straits, or the Suez Canal. These areas represented Britain's minimal essential interests for sustaining its empire. Cross noted further that no geographical reasons existed for Russia to touch these regions if St. Petersburg's true intentions were to merely aid the Balkan Christians.[92]

The speech marked another emphatic break with the Crimean policy. Most noticeably, perhaps, British interests in the Ottoman Empire no longer included any mention of integrity or independence. Several MPs pointed this out with great relief. George Goschen, for instance, said, "There was something which used to be considered a British interest which has not been enumerated [by Cross and other Conservatives]: . . . the maintenance of the independence and integrity of the Ottoman Empire." Hartington echoed Goschen at the end of the debate: "The old formula . . . the integrity and independence of the Ottoman Empire, no doubt, has not been much heard in this debate." Forster brought in the agitation on this point, noting that supporters of the old policy "are in the minority in this House" because "honorable members generally, and almost all who pay attention to the matter out-of-doors have, I believe, given up hope" in Turkey to "regenerate herself."[93]

Cross's statement eased parliamentary concerns. In the four nights that followed the speech, MPs spoke their minds on the Russo-Turkish War and Britain's role in it. Eighty-one percent of them referenced the agitation or anti-Turkish public opinion as support for either the resolutions or neutrality. Fifty-four percent noted events in Bulgaria. Of the fifty-two total speakers, only five adopted an overtly pro-Crimean War, pro-Turkish posture. The majority of Conservatives who opposed Gladstone's resolutions did so because the government had already adopted a posture aligned with the agitation, making Gladstone's resolutions unnecessary. Even Liberal supporters of Gladstone's resolutions made positive references to Cross's statement. The speech "will do much to allay fear," Forster noted. The debate "compelled the Government to turn the peace side of its policy to the front," said Shaw Lefevre, also a Liberal. "The discussion had elicited from the Home Secretary a speech with which most of the Honorable Members of the [Opposition] agreed."[94]

The resolutions debate framed British policy for the remainder of the war. A month after the debate, Layard telegrammed Derby to indicate the extent to which the Porte felt abandoned by Britain. Derby's response captured the coils of public-parliamentary restraints. "I understand the disappointment produced as you say by our 'abandonment of the Turkish cause' but opinion here was practically unanimous," wrote Derby. "Dislike of war is just now the strongest feeling—and the outcry of last Autumn . . . derived most of its strength from the apprehension that we were about to be involved in another Crimea struggle."[95]

Gripped by the fear of major strategic losses, the British Cabinet stood by in a parliamentary-imposed state of paralysis during 1877 and 1878 as Russian troops advanced to within nine miles of Constantinople. After tense diplomatic wrangling, the Russian offensive finally ended and the Powers gathered at Berlin. The outcome, the Treaty of Berlin, marked the final nail in the coffin of the Crimean policy for Europe. Romania, Serbia, and Montenegro gained full independence. Bulgaria was divided into two provinces, with the northern province gaining political autonomy and the southern administrative autonomy. Overall, Turkey was badly defeated, having lost two-fifths of its empire. More importantly, with the European commitment to Ottoman integrity and independence in tatters, in the years leading up to World War I, Turkey witnessed one European state after another encroach into Ottoman territory.[96]

Great Britain played an undeniably significant role in this turn of events, more by its inaction than anything else. It abandoned longstanding pledges to defend Ottoman integrity both diplomatically and militarily. The humanitarian impulses of British society and Parliament stood as the central cause of London's dramatic policy change.

THE ALTERNATIVES: REALISM AND DOMESTIC INSTITUTIONALISM

Realism and domestic institutionalism offer alternative explanations for the British decision to terminate its Treaty of Paris commitments. However, neither accounts for these developments very well.

Realism

Realism expects that one of two geopolitical changes could generate British termination. The first was the emergence of a new threat that would make the 1856 pledges to the Ottoman Empire unnecessary. The second would involve a loss of power by the Ottoman Empire (especially in the event of losing a war), making the Porte a more costly and hence less valuable ally to London.

Europe witnessed significant geopolitical changes in the two decades after the Crimean War. The most important developments were France's defeat in the Franco-Prussian War and Germany's arrival as a major new actor in the European system. Despite these changes, however, neither of the realist propositions offers an explanation as strong as that of humanitarian norms.

With respect to the first proposition, a new threat, Germany's rise presents the most logical possibility. Anglo-German competition indeed increased dramatically in the nineteenth century and contributed to the spiral of competition that culminated in World War I. Timing presents a problem for this explanation, however. Anglo-German competition and suspicion began to increase in the late 1880s and did not reach its most extreme form until the 1890s. British termination of its Treaty of Paris commitments, on the other hand, came in 1877, well before Germany dominated British threat perceptions. The German posture in the period from 1876 to 1878 reinforced its status as a non-threat for Britain. Prior to both the Constantinople Conference and the Russo-Turkish War, Germany made itself a nonfactor when Bismarck publicly declared strict German neutrality. Bismarck committed to reconsider this position only if Austria entered the war and suffered major losses. Since this never transpired, Germany remained a peripheral factor in this period.[97]

Furthermore, if a new threat had arisen from Germany or any other power, British cabinet deliberations should demonstrate this. From start to finish, however, Russia stood as the foremost concern to Britain, as demonstrated at many points in the discussion above.[98] If anything, Britain's strategic panic over Russia at the time demanded a more vigorous defense of Ottoman integrity. At the very least, concerns over the Russian threat should have produced some tangible step, such as a show of force in order to prevent Russian moves beyond the Balkans toward Constantinople. Yet, no matter how much Disraeli desired to move, parliamentary restraints made action impossible.

It is possible that the geopolitical shifts did matter, but not by creating a new threat. By the mid-1870s, Britain faced a different set of European alignments. France and Austria, its two Crimean War partners, backed away from the 1856 pledges. The French defeat at the hands of Germany in the Franco-Prussian War left Paris struggling to regain its international status. Austria entered the Three Emperor's League, formed in 1873, bringing it into closer alignment with Berlin and its Crimean War foe, Russia.

These alignment changes, however, do not explain British action very well. First, Britain recommitted to the Crimean policy at the Black Sea Conference of 1871 and, more importantly, with the Berlin Memorandum in May 1876. Why did Britain suddenly change its policy in 1877, then? The realignments noted above were completed by 1873. With the members of the Three Emperor's League firmly behind the Berlin Memorandum, the realist prediction of British termination seems more likely to occur in May 1876 rather than in December, after Germany had withdrawn into neutrality. Something other than this realist proposition must explain the variation in British commitment policy during the 1870s.

Second, private conversations and memos at the cabinet level make little reference to the fact that these alignments precluded British defense of Turkey. Instead, the vast majority of private statements by cabinet members discuss the state of domestic political, especially parliamentary, opinion. Derby's previously cited statement on 22 August that the "sympathies of the nation" were driving the government into "opposition to its Treaty engagements" repeatedly explained British action through the Russo-Turkish War.[99]

Finally, the geostrategic changes of the early 1870s did not, in reality, leave Britain facing an insurmountable alignment of states ready to end Ottoman integrity and independence. Most notably, although Austria joined the Three Emperor's League and even signed a secret accord with Russia in early 1877 expressing Austrian neutrality, Vienna's natural interests were much closer to Britain than to Russia. For Austria, loose Ottoman hegemony in the Balkans offered the best solution to the Eastern Question. Hegemony kept the Balkan nations from inciting independence movements among Austria's multinational population. Knowing this, the Disraeli government looked upon Austria as a natural ally whose help, when enlisted, could easily overcome a Russian army, which was known to be far weaker than the one that had fought in the Crimean War.[100]

Reflecting their common interests, Britain and Austria talked on numerous occasions throughout the war about alliance. For Disraeli, in fact, alliance with Austria represented the most promising means to stymie Russia's advance, especially once Russian troops crossed the Balkan Mountains and headed toward Constantinople in violation of Russian commitments to Austria in early 1877.[101] Yet the state of British domestic politics presented an insurmountable snag in bringing an Austro-British alliance to pass. The parliamentary stand for neutrality influenced developments here in two ways. First, in the initial stages of the war, it kept the Cabinet from approving Disraeli's requests even to initiate serious overtures to Austria for the formation of an alliance. In May 1877, for instance, Disraeli pressed the Cabinet to consider alliance. Derby, however, resisted and won the support of his colleagues with the argument that this was a violation of neutrality, a step opposed by both public and parliamentary opinion.[102]

Second, when the Cabinet finally took the initiative to discuss alliance in late 1877, it found cooperation with Austria blocked by Austria's own distrust of London due to domestic politics in Britain. Austria's foreign minister, Count Andrassy, warned his ambassador in London that "British attitudes" dampened Britain's resolve.[103] Even as the situation in the war grew strategically desperate for Austria in 1878, Andrassy turned aside a British request for alliance. As Millman notes, "Andrassy expressed his disappointment that Parliament had not been asked for money, that Gallipoli had not been occupied, and that the fleet had not been sent to Constantinople." The Austrian Ambassador to Britain told the British Foreign Office at the time that Britain needed to "prove by some active and material step that she was in earnest" if London wanted alliance with Austria.[104] The demonstrable action that Austria sought proved impossible for a British Cabinet bound by public/parliamentary restrictions.

Relative to the second main realist proposition, did a decrease in Turkish power generate termination? Turkey indeed stood as a weak military power across the entire nineteenth century relative to other major actors in the European concert, which explains the initial Treaty of Paris commitments. Furthermore, Turkey's financial strength declined after 1856, and the Porte declared bankruptcy in 1875.

Financial issues did not appear to factor into British decision-making, however, especially when compared with the force of the Bulgarian agitation. Most importantly, financiers with stakes in Ottoman economic recovery represented the only identifiable lobby in London supporting the Treaty of Paris. For British lenders, Ottoman vitality as a whole proved essential to Ottoman financial recovery.[105]

Militarily, British leaders did not perceive a decrease in Ottoman military power after 1856. In fact, official opinion in Britain held a positive view of Ottoman military strength. The Gladstone government, for instance, felt comfortable in giving up the Black Sea clauses of the Treaty of Paris in part because the new Turkish navy was seen as one of the strongest in the world. Likewise, during the summer of 1876, Disraeli was confident that the Turkish army could defeat Serbia, Montenegro, and the other insurgent republics—expectations that the Porte indeed matched— by August 1876.[106]

Even during the war with Russia, the Ottoman forces showed considerable strength. Between August and November 1877, the Turks won several impressive battles against the Russian army, stalling the Russian advance to Constantinople. London took notice—in fact, several Conservatives urged the Cabinet to enter into an alliance with Turkey.[107] These signs of Turkish strength should be understood for what they were, however. The British Cabinet, at any rate, harbored no illusions about the Porte's strength. Prior to and during the war with Russia, members of the Cabinet universally believed that Turkish forces stood no chance of defeating Russia. "Turkey . . . is fighting a very costly war without money and without credit," wrote Salisbury prior to the Russian attack, "and is maintaining with success a desperate struggle for national existence without the aid of a single man of conspicuous ability." Numerous memos prior to the war reflect Disraeli's belief that without British military support, a war between Turkey and Russia would inevitably result in the outright partition of the Ottoman Empire.[108] From the very start of the Bulgarian crisis, British officials knew that Turkey stood no chance against the Russians. Without help, they would fight a losing battle—as in fact occurred.

Domestic Institutionalism

The British-Ottoman case should lend itself to domestic institutionalism. Parliament ratified the initial commitment to Ottoman integrity and independence in 1856 when it debated and approved British accession to the Treaty of Paris. As noted above, it also re-ratified integrity and independence with the Black Sea Conference in 1871 and the Berlin Memorandum decision in May 1876. Institutionalism expects one of two processes to explain British behavior. First, commitment termination could follow an agreement by Britain and Turkey to end London's 1856 pledges. It could also come if the Porte unilaterally violated any pledges that it had made in the Treaty of Paris.

These explanations do not offer much leverage in explaining British behavior, however. As noted above, termination did not transpire in cooperative negotiation with the Porte. In August, Britain unilaterally took the first anti-commitment steps when Derby instructed Elliot to inform the Porte that British domestic opinion made fulfillment of its obligations in the Treaty of Paris impossible, even in the event of a Russian attack. At the

Constantinople Conference, Salisbury agreed to terms with Russia that violated Ottoman integrity and independence. He then led a charge to force those terms on Turkey. When the Porte refused, amidst complaints of unilateral British abandonment, Salisbury firmly stated that in doing so, the Porte forfeited all matérial or moral support from the British government. The declaration of neutrality in response to the Russian attack followed the same unilateral course of action.

The second institutionalist argument proves equally deficient. The Treaty of Paris elicited far-reaching commitments from Europe, with the Ottoman Empire offering little in return. The only major expectation of the Porte involved Turkey sustaining its international power and preserving its stated responsibilities over the Turkish Straits. As we have seen, the Porte did both sufficiently from 1856 forward.

BRITAIN, PORTUGAL, AND THE CONGO

Turkey was not the only European power that faced British termination of informal empire pledges in the nineteenth century. Portugal's right to control the African Congo in the 1880s drew a similar fate. By the nineteenth century, Portugal maintained a substantial imperial presence in Africa, its main colonies being Angola and Mozambique. On the basis of a longstanding alliance and in the interest of expanding trade, Britain recognized Portuguese imperial control outside of these regions as well, including Portuguese control along Africa's western coast above Angola up to and beyond the Congo River. London committed to Portuguese dominion over the Congo in an 1817 treaty and recommitted to this arrangement in subsequent years despite various territorial disputes between the two powers.[109]

Despite British recognition, Portugal showed little interest in settling the region until the 1870s, when traders discovered a wealth of resources along the Congo River. By the early 1880s, British traders controlled nearly three-quarters of all trade in the region. At the same time, traders from other European countries, especially France, began to make inroads. In response, Britain initiated treaty negotiations with Portugal in 1877 that would provide British protection over the Portuguese Congo in return for uninhibited access to the region for British traders. The primary British requests consisted of free navigation on the Zambezi and Congo Rivers, a reduction in tariffs, favorable trading status for British goods, and a Portuguese commitment to suppress the slave trade. In February 1883, an agreement had been reached in principle.[110]

Cooperation all but ended there, however. In April, the British Foreign

Office suddenly stiffened its terms. The two countries signed an agreement in early 1884, but the British Cabinet never submitted the treaty to Parliament for consideration. In December 1884, London reversed course altogether, recognizing the sovereignty of King Leopold II of Belgium over the Congo.[111]

Strategic considerations played some role in the British decision to abandon the Portuguese option in late 1884. By that point, Leopold's lobbying had helped align the major European powers against the Anglo-Portuguese Treaty. Scholars agree that German support of Leopold, in particular, in the summer of 1884 played a major role in bringing a final decision from the British cabinet. By the same token, scholars also agree that if Britain had signed the accord when it was first approved in 1883, the rest of Europe would likely have accepted it. Roger Anstey contends that the return to the bargaining table "fatally delayed the conclusion of negotiations in the spring and summer of 1883 when there was an appreciably greater chance of obtaining international recognition of the treaty."[112] So the real issue is the delay in negotiations. Humanitarian norms best account for this.

The story begins with the antislavery movement and the humanitarian vision of free trade in nineteenth-century Britain. Britain's efforts to end slavery focused intensely on the coast of Africa. Pressed by Parliament, British heads of state, especially Lord Palmerston, who served as prime minister twice in the 1850s and 1860s, commissioned the navy to seize slave vessels and destroy slave-trading posts along the African coast. In these efforts, Britain sought also to replace the slave trade with legitimate means of commerce. As Anstey observed, "This was an age which believed that if licit trade could be established it would of itself play a part in ending the slave trade, and was deeply, if somewhat uncritically convinced of the moral value of commerce."[113]

For those who cared most about the slave trade, Portugal was among the least humane of European states. Palmerston noted that he preferred "to deal with the worst savages than with the best intentioned Portuguese."[114] Through the eighteenth century, Portuguese colonies and ships stood at the center of the slave-trading industry. Though Portugal outlawed the trading of slaves in the early nineteenth century, the trade continued from its colonies, especially in Africa. To a large degree, the reason for this was poor colonial administration. By the early 1800s, Portuguese power was in precipitous decline, leaving few resources to govern its African colonies effectively. The lawlessness of regions under Portuguese sovereignty allowed slavers to continue business. Protectionist trade policies encouraged it as well. Portugal retained a high tariff system in its colonies that precluded trade in other goods. The slave trade never lost its financial appeal.[115]

By 1883, when the British Foreign Office concluded the first round of negotiations on the Congo with Portugal, brutal practices in Portuguese Africa were still commonplace. British explorers and missionaries exposed continued examples of the slave trade from Mozambique and Angola. Reports of Portuguese officials flogging black Africans to death were common as well. The British government even confirmed specific cases of torture of blacks by Portuguese citizens in its African colonies.[116]

On the basis of Portuguese inhumanity, a broad consortium of commercial and humanitarian groups lobbied both the Foreign Office and Parliament against the Anglo-Portuguese Treaty beginning in 1882. The main groups consisted of the Anti-Slavery Society, the Baptist Missionary Society, and the Manchester Chamber of Commerce. Three individuals, John Kirk, James Hutton, and William Mackinnon, had ties to each of these groups and served as the main instigators of the agitation. In lobbying the British government, Hutton proved especially active from his post as the secretary and later president of the Manchester Chamber of Commerce, which sent a memorandum protesting the treaty to the Foreign Office in November 1882. The group complained of the lack of Portuguese "civilization and enlightenment" in addition to the treaty's blow to free trade. Over the next three months, memoranda poured in from the chambers of commerce of Liverpool, Glasgow, London, Dewsbury, Cardiff, Greencock, Bristol, Sunderland, Huddersfield, and Birmingham. Each echoed the initial Manchester memorandum, indicating Hutton's initiative.[117]

The Baptist Missionary Society and Anti-Slavery Society were active as well. In addition to putting pressure on the government, these groups gave "moral strength" to the movement, helping it avoid the impression that the activists cared about profit alone. The Baptist Missionary Society provided information on developments in Portuguese Africa that the London Chamber of Commerce, for instance, included in its memorandum. The Anti-Slavery Society sent memoranda to the Foreign Office and members of Parliament. It also made appeals against the treaty in its regular newsletter, *The Anti-Slavery Reporter*. The Foreign Office paid little heed to the movement against the Anglo-Portuguese Treaty, but Parliament was another story. Activists worked closely with MPs in organizing a parliamentary movement against the treaty. Hutton and Mackinnon met repeatedly with Conservative and Liberal MPs. Consequently, from December 1882 through

March 1883, various members raised questions about the treaty, its provisions, and the progress of negotiations.[118]

The height of parliamentary activity came on 3 April 1883. Jacob Bright introduced a motion that banned the creation of a treaty with Portugal that would "interfere with the freedom hitherto enjoyed by all civilizing and Commercial agencies at work" in the Congo region. In his case against Portugal, Bright pointed to Portugal's anti–free trade policies and discussed the memoranda by various chambers of commerce. He repeatedly spoke of Portuguese corruptness and "barbarity." In turning to slavery, he cited both the Anti-Slavery and Baptist Missionary Societies. "I cannot help believing that the Anti-Slavery Society has more knowledge of Portugal in relation to slavery than the Foreign Office," he said before delving into facts provided by the Society about the slave trade in Mozambique and Angola. In closing his discussion, Bright even compared Portuguese rule in Africa to that of Turkey in Eastern Europe, noting that both Lisbon and Constantinople "are corrupt and feed upon the Natives." Edward Whitley joined Bright. He regarded the treaty as a "retrograde step" that would thrust the peoples of the Congo region into "barbarism and obscurity."[119]

According to one cabinet member, the treaty "was virtually stopped by the House of Commons."[120] Given the dynamics of parliamentary government discussed earlier, one can see why this happened. William Gladstone, a Liberal, was prime minister at the time. Bright was leading a revolt from within the Liberal Party that Gladstone, for reasons of his government's political survival, could not ignore. Consequently, in the April 1883 debate, Gladstone took the unprecedented step of agreeing to a parliamentary review of the treaty before its final adoption by the Cabinet.[121] The Foreign Office subsequently reopened negotiations with Lisbon. Trying to meet the demands of Parliament, it presented an entirely new agreement with fifteen rather than seven articles. Nine of the articles included new conditions. The negotiations were tedious, taking nearly eight months to complete. The Foreign Office had little room to compromise since, as Anstey noted, "the Government knew in an unusually imminent sense that its actions were accountable to Parliament."[122]

In late February 1884, a new agreement emerged. Some MPs spoke of asking for further revisions rather than rejecting the treaty altogether. Hutton, Mackinnon, and Kirk wanted a full rejection and a British endorsement of Leopold's sovereignty over the Congo. The protests, subsequently, resumed. Protests from commercial groups and the Baptist Missionary and Anti-Slavery societies began again. Petitions against the treaty were more numerous than they had been in the winter and spring of 1883. MPs soon followed. Between March and June, a series of parliamentary questions were presented to the Cabinet demanding information and changes to the treaty. The Cabinet tried to rescue the accord. It appealed directly to the heart of the agitation when it sent a letter explaining the benefits of the agreement to the Manchester Chamber of Commerce in March. Behind the scenes, the Cabinet begged Hutton to appeal to Lord Granville in the House on behalf of the treaty.[123]

The initiative failed entirely, and the activists remained resolute. As Hutton noted, "It was too late, and I declined to entertain any more of their [the Cabinet's] trifling work." The Cabinet then changed course. It announced on 8 May that it would seek international endorsement of the treaty before turning to Parliament for approval. Fitzmaurice explained the reasoning behind closed doors: "It is I think beyond doubt . . . [that the government] may be beaten on the Congo question in the House of Commons . . . [and defeat] would be serious in the present conditions of affairs and very serious at Manchester from the party point of view."[124]

International events dealt the treaty its final blow. France almost immediately announced its opposition to the treaty. Bismarck did the same in early June. During the months of parliamentary delay in Britain, Leopold vigorously lobbied European capitals, promising both more humane administration of the Congo than Portugal and, even more enticing for France and Germany, nearly unfettered economic access to the Congo's wealth. France and Germany took Leopold at his word. Their opposition to the Anglo-Portuguese Treaty effectively sealed its doom. Britain conceded by supporting Leopold's bid for sovereignty over the Congo, which was granted at the Berlin West Africa Conference in 1885. Portuguese control quickly ended. Leopold, of course, turned out to be far worse than his promises suggested. Soon after gaining sovereignty, he closed the Congo almost entirely to foreign commerce and created a highly brutal regime over the local population. Hutton, Mackinnon, and others soon abandoned their support for the Belgian king. With the wilting of British trade in the Congo, the concerns of the Foreign Office came to pass.[125]

CONCLUSION

This chapter explored Britain's decisions to terminate certain informal empire commitments to European allies during the nineteenth century. The primary focus rested on the termination of London's pledge in the Treaty of Paris to Ottoman integrity and independence in the Balkans.

Table 2.1. Humanitarian norms by decision point: The British-Ottoman case

Parliamentary decision point	Illiberal behavior	Activist pressure	Commitment outcome
Black Sea Conference (1871)	No	No	Preserved
Berlin Memorandum (May 1876)	No (liberalizing)	Yes (information only)	Preserved
Constantinople Conference (December 1876)	Yes	Yes (public opinion)	Terminated
Russo-Turkish War (1877–78)	Yes	Yes (public opinion)	Terminated

Why did this action come, especially in light of Britain's endorsement of Ottoman integrity as late as May 1876?

Relative to realism and domestic institutionalism, humanitarian norms best explain both the timing and process of British desertion of its 1856 pledges. Table 2.1 compares the various decision points in the British-Ottoman case. In 1871, Britain reaffirmed its 1856 commitments at the Black Sea Conference in the absence of both activist group pressure and Turkish illiberalism. Amidst tranquil relations with its subject populations, the British government successfully defended the Porte as reforming. Liberalizing events dominated parliamentary decisions at the May 1876 recommitment. Despite growing activist group pressure against the Crimean policy, Parliament adopted a wait-and-see attitude following a coup in Constantinople that brought a government promising reforms for the Christian provinces.

London soon reversed course. Turkish inhumanity in Bulgaria and a public surge calling for Balkan independence yielded parliamentary pressure against the Treaty of Paris commitments. Parliament never passed legislation forcing a change in policy, but the letters and dispatches of British ministers indicate that legislative pressure all but dictated cabinet decisions to endorse Salisbury's proposals at the Constantinople Conference and the British declaration of neutrality in 1877.

The case of British relations with Portugal over the Congo is similar. Seeking to trump growing competition with other European powers for trade in the African Congo, the British Cabinet encouraged Portugal to fulfill treaty rights granted by London and assume responsibility over the region. Spurred by activist pressure over Portugal's inhumane rule in Africa, especially regarding slavery, Parliament fatally delayed the Anglo-Portuguese Treaty. The losses proved real for London, as King Leopold's control over the region ended British access altogether.

In sum, Britain found it difficult to remain allied with states that violated certain humanitarian norms regardless of their perceived strategic value. This proved particularly true when activist pressure and partner illiberalism existed simultaneously. As the next three chapters demonstrate, Great Britain has not been alone among liberal great powers in this regard.

[3]

Torture and Summary Execution in U.S.–Latin American Relations

Guided by the goal of avoiding "another Cuba," the foreign policy experts in the United States moved Latin America to the top of the list in Cold War planning after Fidel Castro's 1959 revolution. Security assistance (military grants, sales, and training) became the primary tool in Washington's arsenal for achieving this end.[1] This chapter grants primary attention to four of the largest aid recipients—Chile, Nicaragua, Peru, and Argentina—in the two decades following the Cuban Revolution. The first three of these states were among the earliest signatories of military assistance accords, or Mutual Defense Assistance Agreements (MDAAs), with the United States after World War II. Into the early 1970s, Chile ranked as the second-highest recipient of military assistance in Latin America behind Brazil—Peru was third. Argentina signed an identical agreement following the ascension of a pro-U.S. regime to power in 1964. It quickly became one of the largest annual recipients of U.S. credits, training, and sales in the region.[2]

These commitments were deeply institutionalized within the U.S. policy process. During the Cold War, security assistance through MDAAs represented an executive-legislative partnership. In the 1949 and 1951 Security Assistance Acts, Congress granted the president the authority to negotiate individual agreements with strategically important states. Once negotiated and approved by Congress, each agreement committed the United States to provide unspecified amounts of military assistance in each funding cycle (biannually by the mid-1960s) in exchange for partner coordination with U.S. strategic defense goals as stated in the MDAA. As each accord explicitly noted, termination required an exchange of diplomatic notes. The United States registered each agreement with the United Nations.[3] Given these parameters, William Mott refers to MDAAs as "legal commitments." Furthermore, he compares them in their "treaty-like" nature to U.S. commitments to the North Atlantic Treaty Organization (NATO).[4]

After years of uninterrupted deliveries of military assistance, U.S. policy to the four primary countries under study here went in very different directions. Specifically, the United States terminated all military assistance and sales to staunchly anticommunist regimes in Chile (1974 and 1976) and Argentina (1977). At the same time that Washington terminated aid to Argentina, the United States preserved assistances to the pro-U.S. Somoza regime in Nicaragua. In due course, that commitment too was severed. Peru, on the other hand, remained unaffected. The United States sustained aid to Lima throughout the 1970s and into the mid-1980s. Ironically, perhaps, a leftist military regime that at numerous points challenged U.S. strategic interests ruled Peru for most of this period.

Humanitarian norms help explain why these punitive steps came when they did, why they happened to some partners but not others. A movement for the international protection of a broad set of political rights (for instance, the rights to live and due process as well as prohibitions against torture, summary execution, and cruel punishment) became well entrenched in congressional foreign aid decisions by the early 1970s. Combinations of illiberal/liberalizing behavior by partners, and information pressure from nongovernmental organizations (NGOs) best account for congressional decisions to terminate and preserve assistance.

LIBERAL CONGRESSIONAL VALUES: DEMOCRACY AND HUMAN RIGHTS

By the early 1970s, the U.S. Congress increasingly demanded that recipients of foreign assistance respect liberal democratic values in the domestic governance of their populations. The movement to institutionalize human rights began with the Morse Amendment in 1958, which grew out of developments in Cuba. Starting in the late 1950s, the staunchly anticommunist Batista regime used brutal methods of torture, political assassination, and repression of the civilian population to counter the uprising of Fidel Castro. Foreshadowing later cases, media accounts of Batista's brutality generated concerns in Congress. Pressure from Cuban-American and other humanitarian groups led to congressional demands for aid termination, to which President Eisenhower acceded in 1958 when he ended all security assistance to Cuba.[5] Congress passed the Morse Amendment in order to limit assistance in future cases involving brutal regimes like that of Batista.[6]

The humanitarian trend in Congress intensified in the late 1960s and 1970s. The House Subcommittee on International Organizations and Movements, chaired by Representative Donald Fraser, served as the central proponent of this movement. In 1973, the subcommittee held fifteen hearings with forty-five witnesses on various aspects of humanitarianism and U.S. foreign policy. The goal of the hearings was unambiguous: "to enable the subcommittee to develop recommendations for raising the priority of human rights in U.S. foreign policy."[7] Complaining that humanitarian concerns are often "invisible on the vast foreign policy horizon of political, economic and military affairs," a 1974 subcommittee report laid out a specific set of guidelines for legislative action.[8]

The call for action found supporters on Capitol Hill. In September 1973, Senator Edward Kennedy criticized the State Department for promoting "a policy of silence toward human tragedy."[9] Senator George McGovern, among others, followed suit, saying, "I think nothing has damaged the support of the American people for aid programs more than our identification . . . with corrupt and brutal regimes overseas."[10] Congress took several concrete steps to bring humanitarianism to the fore in a set of legislative measures from 1973 to 1975. The first was the 1973 Foreign Assistance Act. A nonbinding "Sense of the Congress" resolution called for the administration to deny military and economic assistance to foreign governments that imprisoned their citizens for political reasons. The 1974 Foreign Assistance Act expressed much the same, as Congress attached yet another "Sense of the Congress" resolution stating that the president should suspend security assistance to governments deemed gross violators of human rights.

The most decisive congressional move came in 1976. The International Security Assistance and Arms Control Act instructed the president to avoid aid programs that associate the United States with repressive governments. In addition, it required a mandatory termination or restriction of security assistance to governments that repeatedly violated human rights, and it legally bound the State Department to file complete annual reports to Congress on the status of human rights in every country receiving U.S. security assistance. Those restrictions were eventually extended to economic development and trade assistance as well.[11] The debate on Capitol Hill over these measures revealed the depth of congressional concern about humanitarianism. Representative Dante Fascell noted that Congress intended to "raise the recognition and consideration of human rights to the high level where it belongs as an ethical and moral factor in the foreign policy of the United States." Representative Leo Ryan said that the message to people around the world was, "Look, we would like to help you, but you have got some meatheads in the capital who are trying to repress your rights." Representative Edward Koch closed the debate on the measure in the House: "I recognize that there are those who believe that we must never end assistance to any country . . . [on the basis of] the inhumanity of the Government. . . . I take a different point of view and believe that the elimination of such aid causes inhuman governments to lessen their inhumanity vis-à-vis their own people."[12]

Several points deserve further attention. First, Congress focused primarily upon political, rather than economic, rights. These pieces of legislation spoke, for instance, about torture or degrading treatment, extended detention without charges, and denials of life, liberty, and security of the person. Second, a clear burden of proof existed when deciding whether or not to end assistance. The 1973, 1974, and 1976 legislation shared the call for the termination of assistance to any government that "engages in a consistent pattern of gross violations of internationally recognized human rights."[13] In turn, Congress also proved sensitive to liberalization.[14] Congressman Tom Harkin, author of the 1976 legislation, pointed to specific steps, like the release of political prisoners or halting of indiscriminate arrests, that Congress considered positive signs of liberal change.[15] As evident below, steps of this nature often stymied pressure for ending pledges.

Third, within the federal government, these human rights concerns were largely unique to Congress. Presidents throughout the 1960s and 1970s proved sensitive to human rights only to the extent that Congress forced them to be so as a matter of politics. While the Carter administration was a slight exception, rhetoric often proved more severe than action. Carter lowered assistance to some countries but never terminated military or economic assistance on his own initiative. Whether direct or indirect, congressional pressure pushed the U.S. government to this extreme. Consequently, many scholars agree that Congress represented the true repository of democratic humanitarian values in the 1970s and 1980s.[16]

Finally, despite Congress's own sweeping gestures, it never terminated assistance to a state via the mechanisms detailed in the 1976 legislation. Instead, termination came by a seemingly haphazard process of attaching amendments to various pieces of legislation that targeted some violators while ignoring others.

HUMANITARIAN NORMS AND LATIN AMERICA: THE BROAD TRENDS

In security assistance relations during the 1970s, the argument developed in this book anticipates that Congress terminated pledges under two individually necessary and jointly sufficient conditions: when partners demonstrated a pattern of political rights violations, and activist groups used information or public opinion to press Congress to act. The argument anticipates the preservation of commitments in the absence of activist pressure, liberalizing steps by a partner government, or uncertainty over which party is most to blame for inhumanity.

By the mid-1970s, nondemocratic regimes with a high level of political rights abuses dominated the Latin American political landscape. Military governments ruled thirteen of the twenty-four Latin American members of the Organization for American States (OAS) at mid-decade, while civilian dictators governed two other OAS states.[17]

The 1970s also witnessed a sharp increase in both the number and country-specific activities of nongovernmental organizations with interests in human rights. Established nongovernmental organizations, like Amnesty International (AI) and the International Commission of Jurists (ICJ), turned more attention to affecting the policies of great powers like the United States.[18] They were joined by a host of new activist groups, the most influential being the United States Catholic Conference (USCC), the National Council of Churches (NCC), and the Catholic-based Washington Office on Latin America (WOLA). These groups did not seek to build constituency-based movements. Instead, their focus was (and, in most cases, continues to be) information. In this vein, they created a large network in Washington, D.C., called the Human Rights Working Group, which sought to coordinate research, information dissemination, and lobbying strategies.[19]

Much of this initiative focused on the U.S. Congress, where NGOs found a receptive audience. NGO evidence, in particular, laid the "factual groundwork upon which the Congress could act."[20] According to Philip Ray Jr. and Sherrod Taylor, NGOs provided "information that is difficult to acquire," which tended to raise "government's consciousness about human rights violations."[21] Another scholar argues, likewise, that "the human rights lobby filled an information vacuum" and "provided heretofore unavailable evidence."[22] This "evidence" was a particularly potent force in challenging the executive branch. Congressman Donald Fraser directly attested to this: "Nongovernmental witnesses . . . proved an invaluable resource in providing us with information with which to compare Department of State testimony."[23]

Table 3.1 details all Latin American cases (except those analyzed in case studies below) from the 1970s. It demonstrates U.S. policy against case-by-case changes in the two independent variables—that is, illiberal/liberalizing partner behavior and NGO pressure—within my argument.

Table 3.1. Sample of political situations, NGO pressure, and U.S. action in Latin America by country

Country	Partner behavior	NGO activity	U.S. policy
Bolivia	Repressive military regime promises elections in 1977; constitution created; elections in early 1980s with decline in human rights abuses	ILHR(P), ICJ(I, 1976), AI(TC, 1975–76)	Military assistance sustained
Brazil	Repressive military government early 1970s; liberal reforms mid-decade; return to high levels of repression in 1976	ILHR(P), ICJ(P, 1976), ICJ(I, 1976), USCC(R, 1974)	Congress terminated military aid (1977)
Colombia	Democratic government, no consistent human rights abuses	ICJ(M, 1974–75), AI(TC, 1975–76)	Praise for civilian government, aid increased
Costa Rica	Democratic government, no consistent human rights abuses	None	Praise for civilian government, aid increased
Dominican Republic	Repressive military regime promises elections in 1977; civilian government elected in 1978	AI(M TC, 1975–76)	Praise for democratic transition, aid sustained
Ecuador	Democratic government with interlude of relatively nonrepressive military dictatorship from 1973 to 1979; transition back to democracy beginning in 1978	None	U.S. government and AI praise return to democracy, military aid continues
El Salvador	Repressive dictatorship; fraudulent elections in 1977 followed by repression	AI(M, TC,1975–76)	Congress terminated military assistance (1977)
Guatemala	Repressive dictatorship and military regime	AI(M, 1975–76)	Carter administration lowered aid (1977) and Congress terminated it entirely (1977)
Guyana	Semi-democratic civilian government from 1968 to 1992	None	Aid sustained
Haiti	Repressive civilian dictator	ILHR(P), AI(TC, 1975–76)	Congressional hearings, some military aid suspended, though not terminated

Table 3.1. (Continued)

Country	Partner behavior	NGO activity	U.S. policy
Honduras	Repressive military regimes	AI(M, 1975–76)	Congress terminated military assistance (1977)
Jamaica	Civilian government through 1970s; martial law in 1976–77; human rights improve in late 1970s	AI(M)	Aid sustained
Mexico	Semi-democratic civilian government with reports of disappearances and torture through mid-1980s; human rights improvement and full democratization starting late 1980s	AW(M, 1984) AI(M, 1986)	Praise for transition to democracy, aid sustained
Panama	Civilian government with improving human rights situation throughout 1970s	None	Aid sustained
Paraguay	Repressive military government; fraudulent elections in 1978	ILHR(M)(1976), ICJ(P, I, 1976), AI(TC, 1975–76)	Congress terminated military aid (1977)
Suriname	Repressive military dictatorship to power in 1982	AI(M)	Congress terminated military assistance (1982)
Trinidad and Tobago	Liberal democratic government throughout 1970s and 1980s	None	Not a recipient of U.S. military or economic assistance (1970–1989)
Venezuela	Democratic government, no consistent human rights abuses	None	Praise for civilian government, aid increased
Uruguay	Oppressive military government from 1973 on	AI(M), ILHR(P), ICJ(P, 1976), ICJ(I)	Congress terminated military aid (1976)

NGO Key

Organizations:
ILHR: International League for
  Human Rights
ICJ: International Commission of Jurists
AI: Amnesty International
USCC: United States Catholic
  Conference
AW: Americas Watch

Organization Activities:
M: investigatory/observer mission,
  followed by report
P: protest of violating government
R: report based upon in-country
  networks
I: Publicized through regular
  publications (through 1977)
TC: torture campaign, based upon
  in-country network investigatory
  missions (AI only)

Individual cases fit into one of several different categories. In one category, we find, for instance, that Congress terminated military aid pledges to a host of inhumane regimes where NGOs applied significant pressure for action. U.S. policy toward El Salvador, Guatemala, Honduras, Paraguay, and Uruguay follow this pattern most neatly. Moreover, these cases tend to highlight the importance of the NGO side of the equation. In all, these states consistently violated human rights. Congress, however, acted only after NGOs targeted them specifically. In the case of Uruguay, for instance, the military took over the government in the summer of 1973 and quickly became one of the leading violators of human rights in Latin America. Congress, however, took action only in 1976 following large-scale NGO activity. An AI report on torture was the leading piece of evidence in Congress's termination of military aid.[24]

In numerous other cases, the United States sustained pledges when illiberal behavior and interest groups did not converge. Democratic regimes in Costa Rica and Venezuela, for example, produced low to nonexistent levels of human rights abuses and gained no major NGO attention. In other instances, liberalizing steps appeared to derail NGO pressure. The military governments of Bolivia and the Dominican Republic faced extreme activist pressure. Both made transitions to democracy soon after. The inactivity of Congress suggests that these reforms stymied NGO pressure on Congress to end security commitments.[25] The same pattern can be found in the Mexico case. Mexican human rights abuses received little attention in the 1970s due to NGO focus on more blatantly inhumane states. When NGOs turned to Mexico in the mid-1980s, liberal reforms by the Mexican government kept U.S. assistance intact.[26]

Brazil offers another case in this vein, though with a different outcome. Ruled by the military since 1964, the level of human rights abuses in Brazil fluctuated into the late 1970s. In 1974, Ernesto Geisel became the fourth consecutive military president of Brazil. He embarked on a liberalization campaign that resulted in a significant reduction in reports of torture. 1976, however, saw a major reversal with the suspension of the legislature and large increases in both torture and political arrests. NGOs made a concerted effort to bring attention to the situation. With U.S. congressional concerns on the rise, Brazil cancelled its foreign military aid request in 1977. Congress formally terminated the program in the same year.[27]

Finally, the case of Haiti seems to defy my argument. The United States knew the inhumanity of the ruling Duvalier family, and NGOs applied ongoing pressure in the 1970s and 1980s. Military assistance continued, however. Along with concerns that aid termination would be ineffective, the United States was consumed with combating the strategic push of the

Soviet Union into the Caribbean Basin.[28] There is some cover for my argument here. With Moscow's activity in Central America, aid to Haiti was maintained at a point when allies in the Caribbean Basin had become especially vital to U.S. security. As discussed in chapter 1, policy leadership moves decisively to the executive in this context. Especially when activist pressure is solely information-based, as it was in this case, humanitarian norms should matter less. If nothing else, the Haiti case demonstrates the falsifiability of the argument developed in this book.

A look at the U.S. commitment relationships with Chile, Argentina, Nicaragua, and Peru can help us determine the efficacy of the general findings in table 3.1.

THE UNITED STATES AND CHILE, 1973–76

The decline in U.S.-Chilean relations that resulted in Washington's termination of military assistance began with a military coup against the democratically elected government of Salvador Allende in September 1973.[29] Allende assumed the presidency in 1970. An avowed socialist, he institutionalized a series of draconian reforms, including the nationalization of all industries, and redirected Chilean foreign policy away from its traditionally close relationship with the United States. In doing so, he increased ties with the hemispheric pariah, Cuba, as well as initiated arms purchases from the Soviet Union and nations in the Warsaw Pact.

With General Augusto Pinochet at the helm, the fiercely anticommunist leaders of the 1973 coup that deposed Allende moved Chile back to its traditionally close strategic association with the United States.[30] The junta imposed a state of siege, a strict curfew and restrictions against travel that included suspension of the constitution. Reports indicated that Marxist insurgency groups, which were well armed and trained due to Cuban support, numbered between ten and fourteen thousand. Insurgents tapped deep resentment of the population in industrial areas affected by the economic chaos of the prior months.[31] Pinochet moved to restore economic order and root out all communist elements. The Nixon administration tacitly endorsed these initiatives, doubling military assistance for the remainder of 1973 and requesting a 50 percent increase the following year. The Ford administration continued to press Congress for similar levels of funding.[32]

Despite humanitarian concerns about Pinochet, Congress granted these requests in 1973. That posture soon faded, however. In 1974, Congress terminated military loans and credits, which amounted to more than 90 percent of Chilean security assistance. In 1976, the legislature ended the last vestiges of assistance when it terminated all cash and commercial sales of military equipment to Santiago.[33] The intersection of Chilean government behavior and activist pressure—with special emphasis on the latter—is critical to understanding the reasons for and timing of congressional action.

A Provoked Congress Delays Action: September–October 1973

Pinochet's campaign to restore order led to an almost immediate pattern of human rights abuses that continued throughout his regime. A 1991 study found that by December 1973, between 1,500 and 2,000 civilians had been tortured to death, executed without trial, or hunted down by vigilantes.[34] Human rights scholar Lars Schoultz sets the number of deaths slightly higher during this period. He concludes that by October 1973, two to three thousand people had died in Chile, most of them by summary execution.[35] As many as seven thousand individuals were detained for weeks without due process or trials at a Santiago sports stadium immediately following the coup. Many eventually ended up in prison camps. In the same period, the regime shipped fifty former senators, cabinet ministers, and academics who had supported Allende to a prison camp without trial, where they routinely suffered inhumane treatment; many of them were tortured.[36]

Despite tight restrictions against travel and press freedoms, western media sources in Chile presented snapshots of these developments. Between the coup on 11 September and the mid-October congressional action on the foreign aid bill, the index of the *New York Times* indicates the publication of thirty-nine articles about political arrests, torture, and summary executions in Chile.[37] Just three days after the coup, one article noted that at least one thousand had been arrested for political reasons.[38] As early as 17 September, a *New York Times* article reported the detention of more than three thousand people at the stadium in Santiago where an indeterminate number were apparently killed by summary execution.[39] Articles later in the month referenced groups of people laid out on the field of the stadium prior to being shot.[40] Several other articles detailed the suspension of normal legal proceedings and the creation of military courts to try over five thousand individuals with leftist political ties in addition to the suspension of all political party activity.[41]

The details that came out of Chile via the media aroused the human rights concerns of the U.S. Congress. "News reports . . . have provoked increasing alarm," said Senator James Abourezk in September. "It has been reported by a variety of news sources that killings have already exceeded 5000."[42] Another representative referenced news reports in discussing the seven thousand stadium prisoners. Some spoke of the "death of South America's most stable democracy" and "the tragedy" that the army "forced out a democratically elected government."[43]

Within weeks of the coup, various members of the House of Representatives introduced a total of seven different resolutions related to Chile. Congress attached a nonbinding resolution to the foreign assistance bill in 1973 asking President Nixon to consider suspending military assistance. Debate on the Senate floor reflected the humanitarian rationale for the measure. The resolution's author, Senator Edward Kennedy, said that the amendment expressed his "own deep sense of shock" at the continued violation of human rights occurring in Chile. Senator Humphrey called it "a vital and important step." Senator Stuart Symington cited an article from *Newsweek* detailing human rights abuses in Chile, declaring, "If this is true . . . this is one of the most reprehensible, illegal takeovers of government I have ever heard of." The measure proved so uncontroversial that it passed by a voice vote.[44]

Why did Congress not terminate military assistance to Pinochet altogether at this point? It was not for lack of consideration of stiffer measures: Senator Kennedy originally floated a much tougher resolution. The Senate leadership, however, forced him to offer a milder substitute.[45] Furthermore, heading into the debate, the Nixon administration unequivocally stated that it would not terminate aid on the basis of human rights.[46] If Capitol Hill, indeed, felt a deep, unequivocal resolve about the Chilean situation, foreknowledge of Nixon's disdain for legislative concerns leads one to expect more, not less, decisive action by Congress.

The answer lies with the lack of activist pressure, which meant that credible information leading up to the congressional debate on the foreign aid bill was lacking. Consequently, the legislature adopted a wait-and-see attitude.

Given the tight government controls on movement and information in Chile, available evidence on early post-coup developments was almost exclusively anecdotal. There existed few, if any, eyewitness accounts of summary executions or reports from individuals who had actually been tortured. One of the most publicized reports, for instance, came from an American couple imprisoned at the national stadium; they estimated four to five hundred murders during their time in detention, although they admitted only to hearing shots and did not witness any of the killings themselves.[47] Media sources consequently used terms such as "unconfirmed" and "unofficial" repeatedly to qualify their reporting of events. Furthermore, no single nongovernmental organization had published a detailed report based on firsthand evidence of political developments in the country prior to congressional action. Lars Schoultz notes that at the time, "none of the NGOs had placed major emphasis upon the still obscure question of human rights in Latin America."[48]

Informational uncertainty created uncertainty and hesitancy in the U.S. Congress. In a late September hearing that included testimony by witnesses presenting hearsay evidence, Senator Kennedy himself admitted the need for credible information. The following exchange with Assistant Secretary of State for Inter-American Affairs Jack Kubisch in a 28 September 1973 hearing highlights this point:

> Kennedy: We hear from these witnesses this morning and although they are not eyewitnesses, at least they reported serious accounts of mistreatment and they described the situation which they saw. What value do you put on any of this testimony? . . . I mean, if it is going on . . . then we really ought to be raising all kinds of holy hell about it. . . . There is certainly enough evidence to send up some storm signals.
> Kubisch: Yes. You are right. There are storm signals. . . . We do not have all the facts now but we are tracking down everything we can. . . . It has so far been hearsay, shot's heard, people do not return, et cetera.[49]

For most, unconfirmed storm signals meant policy restraint. Allowing that alarm was justified, Senator Lawton Chiles said, on September 21, "We need to adopt a careful attitude of watchful waiting while keeping our hands off." Senate Foreign Relations Committee Chair William Fulbright expressed his disgust at developments yet also cautioned that given "unconfirmed" reports the United States should "keep . . . [its] policy open and flexible."[50] Schoultz sums up the 1973 situation in Congress well, "Timing was one reason for the weak language [in the resolution]: the legislation was completed two months after the coup, before the full human rights implications of the Pinochet government's policies had been documented." As a result, he continued, "Concern over the abuses of the Pinochet junta was more unfocused outrage than an organized attempt to alter United States policy."[51]

Termination of Military Credits and Loans: December 1973–July 1976

Throughout 1974, Chile's strategic importance was a constant theme. In congressional hearings, top Nixon administration officials pressed the importance of supporting Pinochet's effort to restore economic and political order in the wake of the "trauma" under Allende. Some on Capitol Hill sounded the same themes.[52] Statements to this effect were not mere public justifications. National Security Advisor Henry Kissinger warned in private policy meetings that a communist Chile "would undermine our position in the entire Western Hemisphere," noting that "because it was a continental country, Chile's capacity for doing so was greater by far than Cuba's." Kissinger pictured falling dominoes with far-reaching implications. "Chile bordered Argentina, Peru, and Bolivia, all plagued by radical movements," he said, "success [for the Communists] would have implications also for the future of communist parties in Western Europe, whose policies would inevitably undermine the Western Alliance."[53] Concerns mounted over U.S. strategic losses due to the underpreparedness of Chile's military and Peru's military purchases from the Soviet Union.[54]

As a whole, Congress turned a deaf ear to these concerns in 1974. Human rights took center stage instead. NGO pressure emerged as the major difference from a year earlier.

Highlighted by the western media, human rights abuses continued at a rampant pace in Chile throughout 1976 and beyond. In this period, an estimated one hundred and forty thousand or more were detained for political reasons without charges or trial. Many were tortured as well. By the end of 1974, as many as five thousand political murders occurred.[55] Approximately one thousand people disappeared between 1973 and 1978, while six thousand individuals faced trial before military tribunals, which lacked all elements of due process and fair trial procedures.[56]

At the same time, a new factor entered the policy debate beginning in late 1973: NGO reports based on extensive interviews with government officials and Chilean prisoners. Each report painted a picture of widespread government-orchestrated human rights abuses. In early January 1974, AI published a report from a mission to Chile in November 1973. The report claimed that "torture has taken place on a large scale" and that the army had committed "many summary executions."[57] Other NGOs followed AI's lead, creating a cascade of reports over the next several months. Based on a spring mission undertaken with the ICJ, AI released preliminary assessments of abuses in the summer of 1974 that became part of an eighty-page report on the first anniversary of the coup in September 1974. Detailing case-by-case accounts of torture by the regime, AI estimated that to that point, between five and thirty thousand had died at the hands of the regime, and another six to seven thousand remained prisoners.[58] The ICJ and USCC independently reported similar findings.[59]

NGO activity pressed Congress to terminate the U.S. pledge of security assistance to Chile in 1974 (credits, grants, and loans) and 1976 (cash sales). I focus greater attention on 1974 since activity that year represented the first and most important step since Chile (like most Latin American states) traditionally received nearly 90 percent of its military hardware through grants and direct aid.

NGO information was at the center of the legislative movement against Chile. Schoultz grants special attention to AI, which "created a receptive attitude in Congress" by contributing "significantly to a change in the nature of the debate over U.S. policy."[60] Of the approximately thirty-three floor statements opposing continued assistance made by members of Congress in 1974, twenty-nine cited NGO reports as a basis for action. The other four cited human rights generally with no reference to information sources.[61] In eight committee hearings on Chile in 1974 and 1975, members of Congress vigorously challenged administration witnesses. Setting aside his ambivalence of the prior year, Senator Kennedy, for instance, lambasted the deputy assistant secretary of state for inter-American affairs, Harry Schlaudeman, in July hearings:

> The International Commission of Jurists has gone down there and has indicated that they have received most convincing evidence . . . The Catholic Bishops say that there are interrogations with physical and moral pressures. When you have wave after wave of findings that there is systematic torture then we become interested in what our Embassy is doing down there. . . . I gather a remarkable sense of a lack of urgency about . . . violations of human rights.[62]

The next month Kennedy introduced the amendment to terminate Chilean aid on the Senate floor, citing no fewer than four different NGO reports as his body of evidence for action.[63] In House hearings, Representative Fraser took on administration policy with reference to NGO information, calling Schlaudeman "a great apologist for an authoritarian regime." Committees, furthermore, included reports by the ICJ, AI, Fair Trial Commission and various other organizations in the appendices of the printed hearing texts.[64]

In mid-1974, the House and Senate foreign affairs committees took the first step against Chile with a reduction of military assistance. In contrast to Chairman Fulbright's hesitancy the year before, the House Foreign Affairs Committee Report justified the move on the basis of NGO information: "The committee is deeply concerned by reports that indicate that the Chilean Government has engaged in practices which violate internationally recognized human rights of its own citizens and of other persons."[65] Members of Congress in the full House and Senate, however, wanted more decisive action, namely full termination of military aid.[66] In October 1974 the main debate occurred, again, in the Senate with an amendment by Kennedy to a continuing resolution for 1975 foreign assistance funding. The discussion offered a stark contrast to that of the prior year.

Senator Kennedy initiated the debate. He detailed the end of Chilean democracy with the coup and then launched into a litany of NGO evidence. Senator Harold Hughes, a nonparticipant in the 1973 Senate debate, delved into the same body of activist reports in stating his support for the amendment. "The evidence is abundantly clear," Senator Hughes stated. "The record has been spread of what this Government has done and is continuing to do." As an opponent of the measure, Senator Gale McGee argued against the pressure of moral activists that he saw driving the support of aid termination: "We are demeaning the role of this body in projecting a policy for the United States that can have an impact and gain respect all over the world, not among lobbying groups."[67]

The measure passed by a 47–41 vote. The vote was not as close as the tally suggests. Not only were several senators absent, but a number of the no votes were cast on the parliamentary grounds that a continuing aid resolution was not the appropriate place for new policy departures, regardless of the merits of the motion. A better indication of support came the next day, when the Senate attached the same measure to the Foreign Assistance Act of 1974 by a voice vote.[68] The Senate Foreign Relations Committee adopted the Kennedy amendment in conference, and President Ford reluctantly signed it into law.[69]

Congressional action did not stop there. Continued Chilean repression in 1975 and 1976 plus a pair of reports by the Inter-American Commission on Human Rights (IACHR) spurred new initiatives.[70] For instance, congressional pressure forced Secretary of State Kissinger to cancel a stopover in Chile during a spring 1975 visit to a number of southern cone countries.[71] Military assistance also came to the fore again. Citing NGO information, House and Senate committees adopted provisions preventing loans and credits to Chile for military hardware.[72] The Ford administration countered with claims of Chile's strategic value, themes that some on Capitol Hill echoed. "We have a friend in Chile," Senator Barry Goldwater said. "I think it is rather inconsistent to find this body willing to cut off help to a friend while breaking our backs to do everything to help our enemies."[73] Yet in a debate nearly identical to that of 1974, the Senate adopted the measure to add a termination of all military sales to Chile in February 1976.[74] House members agreed in conference. The termination of all security assistance to Chile became law later that year.

THE UNITED STATES AND ARGENTINA: 1974–77

If U.S.-Chilean relations demonstrate the importance of interest group pressure, the Argentina case illustrates the centrality of partner behavior. Across most of the 1970s, NGOs documented and disseminated information on human rights abuses in Argentina. Yet the U.S. Congress did not punish Argentina, largely because liberalizing developments pushed Congress to a wait-and-see posture. When norm-violating behavior and interest group pressure finally converged in late 1976 and early 1977, Congress responded by ending military assistance.

Liberalization and Congressional Restraint: 1974–Spring 1976

In the late 1960s, attacks by well-organized Marxist insurgents, namely the Montoneros and People's Revolutionary Army, against the ruling military government became a standard feature of Argentine politics. After years of unsuccessful attempts to end the violence, the military agreed to presidential elections. In 1973, longtime populist leader Juan Perón, returned to Argentina from exile and won the presidency; his wife Isabel became vice president. The military's hope in elections proved elusive, however. Perón's austerity measures to shore up the economy created labor unrest across Argentina. Terrorist attacks by Marxist insurgents resumed with increased vigor. Chaos intensified all the more when Isabel assumed the presidency upon her husband's death in 1974. In response to leftist violence, right-wing terrorist groups, especially the Argentinean Anticommunist Alliance (AAA), organized and practiced their own brand of brutal political assassinations and torture. In desperation, Perón turned to the military, approving far-reaching operations against leftist groups. In November 1974, she imposed a state of siege that suspended all constitutional rights of citizens.[75]

The situation worsened from there. Noting the daily bombings in Buenos Aires and the increase in disappearances and assassinations, Joseph Tulchin claimed that the violence reached the "intensity of civil war" by late 1976.[76] In March 1976 General Jorge Videla, commander in chief of the armed forces, led a coup against the hapless Perón government. By late 1977, the military made substantial strides against the People's Revolutionary Army, but the larger Montenero group remained active. Reports of daily insurgent attacks in the capital, clandestine arms factories, and "Vietnam-style warfare" by the insurgents peppered the headlines of leading news outlets.[77]

Between Isabel Perón's ascension to the presidency in mid-1974 and the summer of 1976, various sources indicate a pattern of human rights abuses in Argentina. In the eighteen months prior to the coup, an estimated six hundred people died at the hands of rightist death squads, with three to four thousand jailed for political reasons. When one includes political murders by leftists, the number killed reaches into the thousands. Within weeks of the coup, approximately eighty five hundred were detained; most were tortured with electric shock, sexual abuse, and psychological torment.[78]

Major media sources conveyed information about the poor human rights situation in Argentina. From the start of Isabel Perón's presidency to three months into the post-coup government, the *New York Times* alone published 108 articles and editorials that detailed or discussed specific cases of individual and mass political assassinations, torture, kidnappings, detentions, and restrictions of fair trial procedures.[79]

Furthermore, international NGOs avidly highlighted the political chaos under Isabel Perón and General Videla from 1974 through 1976 and assigned the brunt of responsibility to the Argentine government. Following initial praise for the transition to democracy, the ICJ issued a harsh report on the situation in Argentina under Isabel Perón in 1975. Based on the visit of an ICJ mission, the twenty-page report detailed cases of torture and arrest as well as assassinations of defense attorneys, all undertaken by right-wing paramilitary groups with the government's support.[80] AI echoed the same themes. Seeking unambiguously to raise the profile of abuses in Argentina, AI criticized the imposition of the state of siege in November 1974 and reported vast increases in political murders (anywhere from 450 to 2000 cases), detentions (4000 people), and a large, though indeterminate, number of abductions. Indicting the government, the NGO in 1976 claimed, "There is strong evidence to suggest that highly placed officials have condoned or selectively supported right wing acts of terrorism."[81]

The U.S. government, including Congress, remained entirely unresponsive to NGO concerns into the early Videla period. Relative to the Chile case, this indifference to NGO claims about Argentina seems surprisingly contradictory. There were no congressional committee hearings on Argentina until late 1976. Furthermore, while Congress vociferously protested Kissinger's 1975 proposed trip to Chile, not a single legislator complained that the same tour included a stopover in Argentina.[82] The lack of attention to the Argentine case by the most ardent human rights legislators in the United States seems particularly startling. The 1975 IACHR report on human rights, cited at length on Chilean abuses by so many of these legislators, also included, for instance, a stern section on government abuses in Argentina. Congress ignored it.[83]

Liberalizing developments in Argentina under Perón and during the first several months of the Videla government appear to explain legislative inactivity best. To the extent that it was involved, the Argentine government at first appeared far from the sole or most heinous violator of human rights. Of the 108 *New York Times* articles detailing rights abuses in this period, 68 discussed actions for which left-wing insurgents took direct responsibility and 34 detailed actions for which right-wing death squads took responsibility.[84] These articles and others carried both general numbers of abuses and case-by-case examples: 138 political assassinations in the two months after Isabel Perón took office, a rightist political leader murdered with a suitcase bomb (February 1974), a Mercedes-Benz executive kidnapped and killed by the left wing (June 1974), the disappearance and murder of a dozen or more university students by the AAA (March 1975), and so on.[85] Latin American experts testify to abuses on both sides. Iain Guest highlights cases of the Monteneros assassinating factory managers as well as AAA death squads and kidnappings. "The killings and disappearances increased on both sides through 1975 and 1976," wrote Tulchin.[86]

Second, Perón and the military took steps to curb state-led violence and protect democratic liberties, even amidst the state of siege. In mid-1975, for instance, the government prosecuted José López Rega for his role in directing the activities of the AAA from his post as interior minister. In fact, General Videla drove this move. A military study accusing López Rega of belonging to "the general command" of the AAA became the basis on which the government filed charges.[87] In late 1975 and early 1976, prior to the coup, the military took additional steps to support the democratic process. Videla and other military leaders pledged, for instance, to support the existing government and constitutional process in late 1975. The general demonstrated this posture when he helped stem an alleged coup in December 1975. Finally, Videla took the reigns of government in March 1976 with great reluctance. He staved off pressure to lead a coup earlier in the hopes that the democratic system in Argentina might rectify itself.[88]

After the coup, the three-man junta took steps, initiated by Videla—the most moderate member—in a similar direction. In his first major speech, Videla committed to increase respect for human rights and bring both right- and left-wing violence under control. At the time, he publicly expressed disdain for Pinochet's model in Chile. The regime also allowed freedom of movement and a high degree of press freedom. While the government banned certain extreme left-wing parties, other political organizations continued to operate. Videla appointed civilians to the government in preparation, as he said, for an eventual return to democracy and reorganized the security apparatus in order to monitor the treatment of prisoners more effectively.[89] Scholar Barry Rubin recognized Videla as leader of "the moderate military faction" seeking to deal with the "many abuses . . . from groups and factions not under the control of the central government."[90]

All of these steps kept the U.S. Congress from sanctioning Argentina in this period. During the Perón years, the only congressional statements on Argentina expressed support for the government against leftist violence.[91] Videla's coup did raise some legislative concerns about human rights, but the centrist actions of Videla and the persistence of the left-wing violence led to a wait-and-see attitude.[92] Leading human rights supporters reflected these impressions as well. Following a long statement about the potential illiberal consequences of the coup, for instance, Senator Kennedy in July 1976 spoke just as harshly against left-wing violence as the conservative, pro-Videla members of the U.S. Senate. "The political violence from the right has been matched by terrorism from the left," said Senator Kennedy. "Both must be stopped." At the time, Kennedy made no reference to penalizing the Argentine government with security assistance termination.[93] Other human rights advocates on Capitol Hill spoke of the predominant congressional impression of Videla's moderation as a driving force behind congressional policy. At a hearing before the House Foreign Affairs Subcommittee on International Organizations, for instance, Representative Fraser prefaced a question to a witness by saying, "It is argued that President [Videla] would like to curb these excesses, but that he has trouble." To another he said, similarly, "Well, it is argued . . . that General Videla lacks the ability in a political sense to bring the more right-wing elements under control. . . . But, it is argued that he would like to do it, and perhaps is moving in a position to begin to moderate some of the violence." Indicative of its impact on the policy process, several witnesses and other House members at the hearings spoke at length about their impression of Videla as a moderate.[94] On the House floor, Representative Koch, who had championed the severance of security assistance to Uruguay on human rights grounds, similarly noted that "there is considerable debate as to exactly who is responsible for this campaign of terror being waged" in Argentina.[95]

In the end, Congress imposed no restrictions on Argentine security assistance in either the 1974 or 1976 foreign assistance bills, the same ones in which the United States sanctioned Chile. When considering these measures, in fact, no member of Congress even introduced an amendment to limit aid to Argentina.

The Termination of Argentine Security Assistance:
Summer 1976–1977

Starting in late 1976, an increase in human rights abuses in Argentina and new NGO pressure turned the congressional tide entirely. Despite General Videla's promises, from the late spring of 1976 summary executions, instances of torture, and violations of due process increased rapidly in Argentina. In addition to the numbers already cited on detentions and torture in the months after the coup, scholars estimate fifteen to thirty thousand disappearances across the life of the Videla regime, most of them ending in execution, presumably. Almost all of those came in the first eighteen months of the junta. Scholars also note the absence of all forms of due process, with judges both refusing to investigate torture cases and acquiescing to false sentences for fear of reprisal from the regime.[96]

The western media reflected these trends. From the end of May through the end of December, the *New York Times* published 77 articles on various aspects of human—especially, political—rights abuses in Argentina. Nearly all of those articles mentioned right-wing and government violence, with roughly half mentioning activity by leftist guerillas.[97] These articles pointed to increased abuses, especially against leftist intellectuals, church leaders, and refugees. In July, right-wing terrorists assassinated three Roman Catholic nuns, three priests, and two seminarians. At the same time, reports began to emerge on almost a daily basis of bullet-ridden bodies found in empty fields and parking lots across the country: on 5 July, fifteen bodies near Buenos Aires; on 20 August, forty-six near Pilar, sixteen in Banfield, and fifteen near Cordoba; and a few days later, thirty outside of Buenos Aires. In many of these cases, the AAA took direct responsibility. Media sources also detailed arrests and disappearances (three to five thousand in late July) as well as the inability of citizens to gain information about detained and missing family members.[98]

The increased violence caught the attention of Congress. Citing an apparent lack of "will" by Videla to stem right-wing activities, Senator Kennedy introduced a resolution calling on the Ford administration to allow Argentine refugees easier entrance into the United States. Representative Koch introduced the same measure in the House.[99] Complaining that "violence continues unabated," Representative Fraser held hearings in September 1976: "The subcommittee is holding these hearings in view of the appalling level of violence existing in Argentina. . . . Serious allegations have been raised . . . that certain elements within the government have . . . been directly engaged in such violence." Over the next two days, the committee heard testimony from the USCC, the Anti-Defamation League, and several Argentine nationals. Each party expressed the opinion that Videla's government stood as a direct and willing accomplice to the activities of the right-wing death squads.[100]

These testimonies represented the first bits of NGO information, which eventually led to case-by-case accounts of government acts of violence. The leading groups included AI, the USCC, the NCC, WOLA, and the ILHR. In all, AI and the USCC provided, by far, the most important information. Through the network of Catholic churches and several research missions to Argentina, the USCC generated a detailed list of hundreds of cases involving political rights abuses, including torture and assassinations. On this basis, the organization concluded that a "systematic and gross pattern of human rights abuses" existed in Argentina at the hands of the regime.[101]

Amnesty International's report was the most visible. In February 1977, AI released the findings of a November 1976 mission to Argentina that claimed "irrefutable evidence" of rights abuses. Furthermore, the report included detailed incidents that placed the government at the center of the deteriorating human rights situation in Argentina.[102] AI found the government holding at least five thousand political prisoners who had never been charged or tried, many of whom had been tortured. It offered cases of summary execution, noting, for instance, seventeen known cases over a few months in 1976 at Cordoba Penitentiary alone. Eighteen pages of the report provided places, dates, and times of specific cases of disappearances (somewhere between two to five thousand) at the hands of the regime.[103] Guest claims that the AI mission represented "one of the most significant human rights missions" ever undertaken by an NGO.[104]

In an attempt to stem the tide against Argentina, the Carter administration responded to the reports with a 50 percent reduction in the request for Argentine security assistance. The administration then appealed to Congress not to make further cuts. National Security Advisor Zbigniew Brzezinski as well as the Latin American bureau at the State Department privately warned that the United States would jeopardize naval cooperation with Argentina in the South Atlantic, where the Soviets had recently increased activity; harm an ally dealing with internal civil war whose military was dependent on the United States for spare parts and equipment; and lose vital influence in a country with "1,000 miles of coastline" that had long followed an independent foreign policy that was disruptive to U.S. interests under various Perón governments.[105] In addition to concerns over Marxist insurgents, various congressional sympathizers raised identical themes in the debate over Argentine aid throughout 1977.[106]

Human rights, however, dominated the congressional agenda. Senate and House committees terminated all military credits and loans to Argentina in the 1977 foreign aid bill. The full Senate followed by negating all cash and commercial military sales. Late in the year, the House terminated the last vestiges of the U.S. military aid pledge when it deleted a $700,000 military training program from the appropriations bill.

NGO information played the critical role at each juncture. In fact, Schoultz notes that members with little interest in foreign affairs worked with "some enthusiasm against aid to Argentina" on the basis of NGO pressure in 1977.[107] The House Committee justified its actions, for instance, on "a number of hearings on human rights" at which the USCC, NCC, and other groups testified. Statements by several members mentioned the AI report as well.[108] As to full House and Senate action, each of the twenty statements in support of terminating aid cited Argentine abuses and at least one NGO source as the only reason for action. In the Senate, Senator Kennedy detailed the junta's poor record on human rights as justification for an end to all cash and commercial sales. On the latter point, he cited the AI report extensively, in addition to appeals from the NCC and USCC. Senator Frank Church endorsed the amendment, referencing the personal stories of torture victims that WOLA brought to his office. The Senate approved the amendment by voice vote.[109]

In the House, debates on Argentine aid followed the same lines. Representative Gerry Studds discussed the 1976 coup and then cited portions of the AI report as well as a USCC letter written to each member of the House. Others made similar comments.[110] At the time of the coup, "We did not know which way the government was really going to go" said Representative A. Toby Moffett. "The situation is much clearer today than it was 2 years ago and it is a situation to which we should not be contributing arms."[111] Representative Edward Roybal referred to the long history of repression, citing the AI report. Representative Koch, who was on the Appropriations Committee, did the same. Representatives William Lehman and John Krebs spoke of the "ample evidence" and "adequate record" of abuses as a basis for the measure. Representative Don Bonker detailed his meeting, presumably arranged by an NGO, with a young girl tortured by the regime. "In fact, the girl told me that she had heard about the military training which they got, most of it from the United States," he said.[112]

The House terminated the training program by a comfortable 223–180 margin. The Senate later adopted it in conference committee, and both houses passed the full appropriations bill in late October. When President Carter signed the measure on 2 November, the United States completed its termination of all military assistance to Argentina.[113]

Washington soon faced strategic fallout from its decision. In addition to canceling naval exercises with the United States, Argentina began purchasing weapons from several Warsaw Pact countries and increased trade with the Soviet Union. The greatest perceived damage came with the 1980 U.S. grain embargo against the USSR. Argentina made the resumption of U.S. security assistance a condition for joining the embargo. An interagency review recommended the move, but faced with continued human rights violations in Argentina and congressional pressure, the Carter administration retained the ban. Argentina subsequently helped the USSR weather the blow of the U.S. embargo by increasing grain sales to the Soviets from 1.4 million tons in 1978 to 7.6 million tons in 1980. As Guest observed, "Washington watched and agonized."[114]

The United States and Nicaragua: 1975–78

One day after terminating assistance to Argentina in 1977, the House debated the future of military aid to Nicaragua. Unlike in the Argentina case, Congress chose to sustain assistance. Despite NGO pressure, liberalizing developments in Nicaragua at the time of the debate kept Congress at bay. Increased repression the next year resulted in legislative pressure against aid, which President Carter heeded with a ban on military assistance in late 1978.

Repression, Liberalization, and Congressional Restraint: 1975–77

From the early 1950s, the Somoza family in Nicaragua stood as a firm anticommunist ally to the United States. Consequently, across the first two decades of the Cold War, Nicaragua received more than $300 million in military assistance alone.

By the mid-1970s, Anastasio Somoza Debayle's dictatorial regime faced growing discontentment at home. Widespread government corruption brought complaints from the business community and other opposition figures, many of whom boycotted the fraudulent presidential elections in 1974 that gave Somoza an overwhelming victory and reinforced his near-total political control in the country. Resistance beyond the established political elites and outside the cities took a different form. Especially in the countryside of north-central Nicaragua and among leftist intellectuals, an armed insurgency led by the Sandinista National Liberation Front (FSLN) by mid-decade had shown impressive growth.[115]

Following a declaration of martial law, Somoza initiated a brutal campaign to root out Sandinista violence in 1975 and 1976. The National Guard entered the mountain villages of Nicaragua and conducted a campaign of abuse, torture, and execution of anyone suspected of affiliation with the Sandinistas. The most brutal accounts involved innocent and unarmed women, children and families. There were so many stories: the slaughter of five peasant families, including twenty-nine children, in Varilla; the mass execution of eighty-six civilians in Matagalpa; the killing of forty-two women and children in Kaskita; and the uncovering of mass graves near numerous villages.[116] Due to the remote locations of most of these villages, news of the abuses reached the United States slowly. In 1975, the *New York Times* published nine articles on Nicaragua; in 1976, only one. None detailed human rights abuses.[117]

In early 1977 developments inside Nicaragua during the previous two years became more widely known, largely due to NGO activity. After collecting details from local priests and its own investigatory missions, the Catholic Church in Nicaragua produced a report with case-by-case accounts of abuses. WOLA used this information with other sources to produce a report on abuses, which it presented to the OAS. The report detailed hundreds of cases of torture, summary executions, and rape prior to 1977. In August, AI released a report that covered similar abuses, including information on dozens of political prisoners, from 1974 to 1976.[118]

At the same time that NGOs began to publicize developments in Nicaragua, Somoza's regime initiated a series of liberalizing steps to curb human rights abuses. New procedures succeeded in bringing National Guard abuses under control.[119] Somoza also lifted the state of siege and reinstituted previously suspended constitutional provisions, including freedom of the press.[120] The precipitous decline in reports of abuses across the spring and summer of 1977 caught the attention of a *New York Times* correspondent in Nicaragua. "All last year and until February this year, we were getting regular reports of mass executions or disappearances of peasants," observed Alan Riding. "Since March, we haven't received any reliable reports of a massacre. The National Guard has definitely been told to clean up its act."[121] The Catholic Church in Nicaragua confirmed these conclusions. It gave a cool reception to the AI report, noting that conditions had changed since 1976. Latin American scholar Bernhard Diederich concluded that "conditions had improved greatly since the beginning of 1977 and the killings . . . had been brought to a halt."[122]

The debate over Nicaraguan military aid began in the Subcommittee on Foreign Assistance of the House Committee on Appropriations in April 1977. Church and NGO reports sparked the committee's initial concern.

Yet from the very start, liberalizing developments in 1977 plagued the subcommittee hearings, eventually derailing the termination effort in the full House.

In the April hearings, the State Department and a host of pro-Somoza witnesses brought the reality of human rights improvements and reforms in Nicaragua to light. The deputy assistant secretary of state for inter-American affairs, Charles Bray, admitted, for instance, that the bishops letter carried some efficacy. He confirmed significant human rights abuses during December 1975 and January 1976. At the same time, Bray pointed to liberal improvements in the situation since that time. He noted "a marked decline in reports of human rights abuses attributed to the National Guard since mid-1976. He then proceeded to mention that Nicaraguan courts remained in civil hands, exiles returned to live normal lives, and freedom of association continued with little state interference. A host of business leaders, U.S. citizens living in Nicaragua, and academics testified to much the same state of affairs.[123] On the other side, two nationals testified to extensive human rights abuses, and a representative from WOLA discussed that organization's findings from 1975 and 1976.

Subcommittee members expressed frustration over the conflicting reports. Representative Clarence Long, the subcommittee chair, noted at the conclusion of the hearings: "The chair must state that he is at least confused about what the real situation is in Nicaragua. . . . We have had statements on the one hand from people who look very reputable and sensible, who have stated an extreme condition. We also have people on the other hand who look like quite responsible, sincere citizens who have denied these accusations completely."[124] Despite the ambiguity, in May 1977 the Appropriations Committee added an amendment to the appropriations bill to terminate all military loans, credits, and sales to Nicaragua. The committee adopted the measure by a narrow 21–20 margin.[125]

But the full House of Representatives took a different position. When the bill reached the House floor on 23 June, Representative Charles Wilson introduced an amendment to restore Nicaraguan military aid in full. Representative Wilson noted the necessity of aid in order to shore up a Nicaraguan government that was facing "continuous confrontations with Castro-trained guerillas." Other members pointed to Nicaragua's long-term friendship to the United States.[126]

The big difference from the Argentina debate, however, was the extent to which supporters of the Wilson amendment cited liberalizing development. Representative John Ashbrook outlined the very brief amount of time allotted to the pro-Somoza witnesses relative to anti-Somoza witnesses in the hearings. "I can not help but wonder how much knowledge we deduce" from the hearings, he said. "That sounds like a kangaroo court." Representative Robert Dornan drew attention to the lack of NGO reporting on more recent developments: "I notice that many of the Members of our body can give an up-to-date report on Paris or London, but nobody has taken advantage of an opportunity to go to Nicaragua to get an in-country briefing there or who has any first-hand evidence to give the House." Representative Bob Eckhart echoed Dornan in complaining about the lack of a "comprehensive study" of Nicaragua relative to other Latin American countries in recent months.[127]

Dornan's comment sparked a lengthy discussion about certain positive, reformist steps taken by the Somoza government in the area of human rights. Representatives David Bowen and Ralph Metcalfe gave positive assessments from recent trips to Nicaragua. Bowen cited his recent discussions with Nicaraguan opposition leaders and newspaper editors, saying that they were "amazed at the progress that was being made in that country." Bowen then asked, "Why should we punish them when they are substantially reducing the use of force in dealing with their internal problems and showing greater respect for human rights than in recent years?" Representative George O'Brien agreed, saying that he "understood on good authority that the National Guard's questionable activities have been cut back" and that "we should encourage this trend" by preserving the aid commitment. Several other members seemed swayed by reports of positive change in Nicaragua.[128]

The House voted to preserve the U.S. commitment to Nicaragua, passing the Wilson amendment by a 225–180 margin.[129] Schoultz captured the difference from other cases: Nicaragua "was free from the reputation of extreme brutality that the Argentine and Chilean governments had earned." The decision represented a "wait-and-see" posture in the truest sense. Following the House vote, the State Department persuaded Senator Kennedy to withdraw his proposal to terminate military assistance with a promise that no funds or weapons would be released until Nicaragua made significant progress on human rights. The Carter administration made a similar pitch to members of the House prior to the floor debate.[130] With an unambiguously poor record of human rights abuses brought to light by NGOs, the post-1977 plight of Nicaraguan assistance hung on the future actions of Somoza himself.

Abuses and Termination: 1978

Citing liberalizing steps, the Carter administration signed a new MDAA with Nicaragua in September 1977, as the old agreement was up for renewal. In doing so, the State Department released $800,000 in funding that was left over from the Ford administration for the purchase of five thousand M-16 rifles.[131] It also allowed military training grants approved under Ford to go forward. In deference to Congress, the State Department decided to wait on further human rights improvements before scheduling the delivery of military hardware recently approved by Congress.[132] The administration also presented a military aid request, albeit substantially smaller than previous years, for Nicaragua to Congress for FY1979.[133]

As political opposition to Somoza increased throughout 1978, the human rights situation in Nicaragua once again began to deteriorate. With it, the United States faced a growing strategic challenge as well. During the congressional debate in 1977, the State Department confessed the minimal challenge to U.S. national interests presented by the Sandinistas. Somoza's crusade from 1975 to 1977 nearly eradicated the Marxist movement, State concluded. The assessment of Sandinista strength shifted substantially in 1978, however. By mid-year, Sandinista attacks expanded nationwide and became more sophisticated. Furthermore, strong evidence surfaced of increased Cuban aid to the movement. In August, National Security Advisor Zbigniew Brzezinski and other high-ranking U.S. officials warned in internal memos that the collapse of Somoza's regime would result in a pro-Soviet government in Nicaragua. On these grounds, a contingent within the administration pressed for continued military assistance.[134] In short, by late 1978 terminating aid made little strategic sense.

Across the first part of 1978, Somoza lashed out violently against all sources of opposition to the regime, including those with no apparent ties to the Sandinistas. In February, the National Guard killed more than two hundred protestors in Monimbo; in July another fourteen were killed at a rally; and by the summer, reports of increasing numbers of political arrests had emerged.[135] The worst repression came in August and September following extensive Sandinista gains across the country. Somoza reimposed martial law on 13 September. The National Guard began a crusade to recapture lost territory; it was told to take no prisoners. More than five thousand unarmed civilians were killed, many by summary execution. Others died as the military used the air force and tanks to bomb and strafe villages with gunfire.[136] The U.S. media documented the violence at length. Of the ninety-eight articles on Nicaragua in the *New York Times* alone during 1978, thirty dealt with attacks by the National Guard and human rights violations therein.[137]

Various NGOs released details of the violence and abuses as well. During the September violence, WOLA distributed information gathered by the Catholic Church in Nicaragua to members of Congress.[138] Given their immediate access, the Red Cross also produced accounts of abuses by the National Guard.[139] Throughout October and November, AI, the IACHR, and an ecumenical group of church organizations published scathing reports on Somoza's activities.[140] Noting specific cases, the IACHR report charged the National Guard with violation of human rights "in a grave, persistent and widespread manner," including the "indiscriminate bombing" of civilians and use of "summary and mass executions."[141]

The U.S. Senate moved in late September. In two separate measures, it terminated all military and economic assistance to Nicaragua. Senator Mark Hatfield introduced the amendment to terminate military aid. He noted "the mindless violence and atrocities" committed by Somoza as the basis for action, citing several newspaper articles that relied on figures from the Red Cross. Senator Frank Church discussed the indiscriminate killing by the National Guard across the country. Senator Kennedy drew attention to a report of American Jesuits who undertook a study mission to Nicaragua in August in his report of "wholesale slaughter" at the hands of the Somoza government. While the economic assistance amendment drew greater dissent from some members, the Senate adopted both measures by a voice vote. The Senate's military assistance measure was accepted in House-Senate conference and became law, but the conference removed the economic assistance measure due to complaints from House members.[142]

The Carter administration adopted the Senate's provision on military assistance before the House-Senate conference on the foreign aid bill. It announced the suspension of all new military shipments and training to Nicaragua in addition to limits on economic assistance in accord with the Senate provision. Sound evidence indicates that Carter moved both in response to and in order to preempt the rising tide on Capitol Hill. For starters, the announcement came on 22 September, the same day as the Senate votes.[143] Furthermore, in his comments during the debate, Senator Hatfield mentioned that he and his co-sponsors in the Senate had informed the State Department of his amendment and "were able to elicit from the administration a commitment to put a hold on everything in the pipeline [that is, items already approved by Congress] of a military character."[144] Perhaps the most telling evidence to Capitol Hill's influence came from former Carter administration officials. "It was clear that going easy on Somoza would contradict the president's emphasis on human rights and alienate his foreign policy allies in the Senate," wrote National Security Council staff member Anthony Lake. "When Senators Kennedy and Cranston or Congressman Koch pushed for action on Nicaragua, a president and administration that put human rights at the center of its foreign policy had to act or suffer political embarrassment."[145]

Absent U.S. support, Somoza's domestic strength deteriorated rapidly; he yielded power to the Sandinistas in July 1979.[146] "Another Cuba" soon emerged in Central America.

THE UNITED STATES AND PERU

U.S.-Peruvian relations in the 1970s offer a particularly poignant comparison to the cases of Chile and Argentina. In 1968, the military replaced a democratically elected government with an authoritarian regime. The junta held power in Peru throughout the 1970s. Yet unlike in the cases of Chile and Argentina, the United States never severed its longstanding military aid commitment to Lima. The reason for this lies with certain liberal steps taken by the Peruvian government. On the one hand, the junta avoided the repressive extremes of its counterparts in Chile and Argentina. On the other hand, it agreed to democratic elections in the late 1970s. These liberal reforms helped preserve U.S. foreign assistance.

Commitment Consistency in the Decade of Human Rights: 1974–81

Following a period of extended economic decline, the Peruvian military took power in 1968.[147] Unlike past military interventions in Peruvian politics, the government of General Juan Velasco Alvarado sought to do more than simply set the stage for a return to democratic elections. Velasco intended to carry out extensive economic and political reforms during a lengthy period of military rule.

Toward this end, the regime pursued a uniquely leftist reform course. Grounded in the lower-middle-class nature of the military, a mixed capitalist-nationalistic economic plan emerged. Internationally, Peru took the dubious step of initiating an arms purchasing arrangement with the Soviet Union, becoming only the second state in the Western Hemisphere behind Cuba to import weapons from the USSR.[148] This dramatically elevated the strategic importance of U.S. military assistance to Lima. As one State Department official noted, "We are in a competitive situation . . . with the U.S.S.R."[149] According to a National Security Council assessment, continuing and even increasing military aid was critical to weaning Peru away from foreign sources as a means to countering "extrahemispheric influences, namely the USSR, inimical to U.S. interests from seeking to gain entry into these areas."[150]

By the mid-1970s, the human rights issue emerged in U.S.-Peruvian relations. Like other military regimes in Latin America, Peru received increased NGO attention in the 1970s and 1980s. In May 1974, AI, for example, reported on the plight of labor unions—the most frequent target of mass arrests by security forces in Peru—and the disturbing state of prison conditions.[151] A change of power in Peru in 1975 only intensified NGO criticism. General Francisco Morales Bermúdez unseated the Velasco government in a bloodless coup. Morales implemented an IMF-supported austerity plan that resulted in popular unrest and a July 1977 nationwide strike. The government responded with a wave of arrests and eventually imposed a state of siege.[152]

Of the NGOs monitoring the situation and publicizing developments, AI was the most active. In 1977 and 1978, it protested to the Peruvian government on a number of occasions about the arrests of labor leaders and workers. In March 1979, an AI mission published a report following a visit to Peru. It described a variety of human rights abuses, including specific cases of arbitrary arrest and torture. Finally, in 1983, AI issued a report on human rights abuses in Peru that the democratically elected president of Peru, Fernando Belaúnde Terry, publicly ridiculed.[153]

Relative to its impact in the Chile and Argentina cases, NGO pressure in the Peruvian case fell on deaf ears in the U.S. government, including Congress. The reason lay with certain liberalizing steps by the Peruvian government during the 1970s. During the Velasco years, the unusual leftist bent of the regime diffused U.S. congressional activism. Unlike other military regimes in Latin America, the close association of the Peruvian junta to the peasant class restrained the military from a massive campaign to exterminate the political left, especially Marxists political elements, across Peru. The human rights landscape in Peru thus lacked cases of widespread torture and summary execution.[154]

Furthermore, because the regime sought to act as a teacher to the nation and not to rule by force, a high percentage of Peruvians accepted the suspension of democracy and saw the regime as legitimate. The posture of churches and political parties in Peru proved especially important here. As a catalyst for international reprimand in the cases of Chile and Argentina, the Catholic Church in Peru emerged as an important supporter of the Velasco and Morales regimes. The leading leftist political party also supported the regime. "This being so, the military government between late 1968 and early 1976 could rule most of the time," wrote Frederick Pike, "with only a moderate use of coercion, even while excluding national majorities from real participation in high-level decision-making."[155] Even on this point of political participation, the junta proved different than its southern cone neighbors. Even though the state outlawed political parties, a variety of political organizations flourished under the Velasco regime.[156]

Members of the U.S. Congress and even NGOs recognized Velasco's unusual moderation on human rights. Despite concerns over arrests, AI and the ICJ both placed Peru in a different category from many of its neighbors, like Chile. In a 1976 article on the surge of military regimes in the southern cone, for instance, the ICJ repeatedly noted the "exception" of Peru.[157] AI articles and press releases often recounted cases of arrests—only to praise Peru in the next sentence for progress in prosecuting suspected torturers within the security services and military.[158]

On Capitol Hill, Peru's moderation received attention.[159] Representative Michael Harrington, for instance, noted the importance of drawing "distinctions between totalitarian societies of the right and the left." He and others then contrasted the Chile case and Peru's record. Reflecting the impact of liberalizing developments in Peru, other congressional discussions in this period often revolved around the lack of information that seemed to exist on human rights conditions in Peru. Conservative opponents of military aid to Peru tried to use this to argue that liberal human rights supporters in Congress overlooked left-leaning regimes. What they missed were the unique features of the Peruvian regime that limited the fodder for human rights outrage in the United States.[160]

After Velasco's 1975 departure, a different set of liberalizing developments explains the continued abeyance of the U.S. Congress. The promise of a return to democracy and a 1980 presidential election emerged as the two core events in Peru that offset the growing tide of NGO criticism of the country during the mid- to late 1970s. Following the nationwide strike in 1977, the Morales regime grabbed international headlines with the surprising announcement of a transition to democracy. From that point forward, liberal moves by the junta repeatedly diffused the controversial steps by Morales that NGOs sought to accentuate. Morales, for instance, freed all the prisoners of the 1977 strike, undoing a prime piece of NGO evidence in the case against the regime. Furthermore, despite the continued unrest that resulted in the 1979 state of emergency, the Morales Government never wavered from its pledge to return Peru to democracy. Constituent Assembly elections were held to draft a new constitution in June 1978. The Assembly completed the constitution in 1979, and Peru elected Fernando Belaúnde Terry to the Presidency in 1980.[161]

Within the U.S. Congress, the transition to democracy effectively drowned out NGO criticism of Peru. Even before the 1977 democratization pledge, Morales had received praise for progress on steps toward individual freedom. In a 1976 report, the State Department lauded the Morales government for granting amnesty to all political prisoners in Peru; "the appointment of civilian ministers for the first time in 8 years"; and "intensified government discussion of popular participation in the political process at lower administrative levels."[162] Congress followed with its own positive assessments. In September 1977, Senators Ernest Hollings and William Scott wrote a Senate report on Peru following a trip to several Latin American states in which they noted the following:

> Among the military governments in Latin America today, Peru stands as an exception to the rule. . . . Despite all of the immediate problems, and in many respects they are truly overwhelming, the Peruvian military is planning for the day when the troops go back to the barracks. On July 28 of this year, President Morales Bermúdez told the people of Peru that a new constitution will be drafted and that elections will be held in 1980.[163]

A 1978 report by Senator George McGovern following a visit to Peru struck much the same tone.[164] Congressional human rights supporters also sang the praises of Peruvian democracy. Senator Kennedy said, for instance, "I know that the Congress and the people of the United States join me in congratulating the Peruvian government and people for their very positive step toward restoring human rights and democracy in their important Andean country."[165]

While Belaúnde's untarnished image did not survive indefinitely— Congress ended military aid amidst human rights abuses later in the decade[166]—the unusual military regime under Velasco in the mid-1970s and the reality of democratization in Peru during the late 1970s and early 1980s stood as critical liberalizing factors. As a result, the U.S. military aid commitment to Lima remained intact in an era when the U.S. Congress was terminating assistance to Peru's more anticommunist, pro-U.S. neighbors, Chile and Argentina.

The Alternatives: Realism and Domestic Institutionalism

The 1970s were a turbulent time in U.S. politics. One might especially wonder if political fallout from the Watergate scandal explains the above cases. Specifically, Watergate may have emboldened Congress to assert its will on foreign policy more forcefully against a weakened executive branch. Partner behavior and activist pressure would matter much less than I contend.

While plausible, this argument is problematic in explaining the cases detailed in this chapter. Congress terminated or reduced bilateral security assistance in several cases prior to Watergate—Cuba under the Batista regime stands out, especially. So to say that anything new came out of Watergate seems an overstatement. Furthermore, the Watergate argument offers a poor explanation of variation within and across cases in the 1970s. This is especially poignant in the case of Chile during the Nixon and Ford administrations, when executive weakness following Watergate could not have been more pronounced. Congress made its 1973 decision to sustain aid to Chile late in the year, when the Nixon presidency was already in a precipitous decline. The battle for White House tapes was well under way, several of Nixon's top aides had resigned, and public confidence in the president was slipping dramatically.[167] A weak, scandal-wracked executive cannot explain both congressional abeyance in 1973 and aggressiveness in 1974. Along these same lines, the Watergate argument offers no explanation of why some states and not others were sanctioned at different points across the decade. In sum, the domestic turmoil of Watergate seems to have mattered little in these cases.

If not Watergate, perhaps the Vietnam War played a major role. Vietnam undoubtedly influenced U.S. foreign policy in dramatic ways in the 1970s. Among other things, Congress claimed greater control over foreign policy, slashing defense spending and trimming direct U.S. military involvement abroad.[168] Vietnam alone proves insufficient, however, for reasons similar to Watergate. It can not account for why the United States took so long to act against certain violators as well as why it chose to punish some and not others. Furthermore, the Vietnam explanation cannot attest for cases of congressional security assistance termination before the war, most conspicuously, again, the severance of aid to the Batista regime. Overall, while one cannot deny that Vietnam and Watergate deeply influenced the U.S. policy process, the humanitarian norms explanation seems to supply a clearer picture of the forces at work in specific decisions regarding U.S. security assistance during the 1970s.

Realism

Given the vital role that security assistance played in U.S. competition with the Soviet Union during the Cold War, these types of pledges should be strong cases for realism. As with other regions, the United States viewed aid to Latin America as serving one of several goals: to bolster pro-U.S. regimes against communist insurgency movements or social elements; to preclude and counterbalance Soviet influence gained through arms transfers; and to sustain influence with friendly regimes for cooperation and coordination of broader Cold War objectives, both in the Western Hemisphere and beyond.[169]

As we have seen, the United States believed that security assistance to partners in each of the cases analyzed in this chapter fulfilled these objectives. The Chilean, Argentine, and Nicaraguan governments each faced sizable pro-communist resistance movements that gained funding from the Soviet bloc at the time of U.S. assistance termination. Washington saw these movements as a threat to its security goals in the region. Of equal strategic importance to the United States, a strong post-coup Chile served the purpose of countering perceived regional gains by the Soviet Union. In 1973, 1975, and 1978, the leftist regime in Peru bought military hardware from the Soviet Union. Like Cuba, a contingent of Soviet advisors came with these weapons.[170] Deep concerns about lost strategic position due to these developments hung over U.S. policy debates on Chile from 1973 to 1976.[171]

Realism anticipates that the United States ended these and other pledges in the region due to one of two potential geopolitical changes: an increase in partner dependence on Washington or the lessening of old threats/emergence of new ones. These two conditions, however, face problems in many Cold War cases. To begin with, aid termination often occurred with little or no change in the level of partner dependence on the United States. Of Chile, Nicaragua, and Argentina, none witnessed a major decrease in power requiring it to lean more heavily on the United States for greater assistance. Most notably, all states refrained from direct military conflict with another country at any point prior to U.S. action.

Consistent with the second realist alternative, some might argue that détente made U.S. security assistance less relevant. In reality, the opposite occurred for U.S. policymakers. While détente marked a reduction in nuclear tension and brought change to U.S. relative power, Cold War competition continued apace via other means across the 1970s, especially in the developing world.[172] Security assistance was chief among these means for the United States, a strategic rationale encapsulated in the 1969 Nixon Doctrine.[173] In response to domestic pressure to avoid another Vietnam, the doctrine involved a drawdown of U.S. forces and a call for allies to rely more on their own defenses.[174] Representing "a philosophy of invigorated partnership," security assistance was to ensure allied defense preparedness as the United States withdrew.[175] The doctrine, furthermore, outlasted the Nixon administration. Domestic pressure to keep military budgets low coupled with perceptions about the growing intensity of competition in the developing world (witness the 1973 Arab-Israeli War as well as Angola, Mozambique, and Ethiopia soon after that) kept security assistance at high levels across the 1970s.[176]

Congressional appropriations reflected the rationale of the Nixon Doctrine.[177] Funding for Foreign Military Sales (FMS) agreements worldwide increased from $3.5 billion to $19 billion between 1971 and 1975, averaging about $10 billion each year for the remainder of the decade. In Latin America, FMS grew from approximately $40 million to $269 million in about the same time period.[178] Not surprisingly, assistance to Chile and Argentina increased substantially when anticommunist military regimes came to power in each country during the 1970s.[179] Overall, at the time of Chilean, Argentine, and Nicaraguan aid termination, security assistance was perceived as a more vital tool for U.S. Cold War competition than at any point since World War II.

In light of the security assistance logic, aid to Peru probably offers the strongest case for realism: assistance continued in order to regain a lost strategic advantage to the Soviets. This seems questionable as a primary determinant of U.S. action, however, when one considers that nobody in Congress ever mentioned it. Furthermore, this strategic argument loses ground when the congressional discourse on human rights in Peru is compared to similar discourses in the Argentine, Nicaraguan, and Chilean cases. In sum, humanitarian norms offer a better account for these cases, taken as a whole.

Others might argue that détente created the necessary space for human rights to matter in U.S. foreign policy. This might be true to some extent, but it does not explain specific cases very well. In the congressional push to restore U.S. moral prestige after Vietnam, the relaxation of Cold War tensions probably helped create policy space for the passage of several bills that institutionalized human rights in U.S. policy.[180] Even putting this aside, the common international structure of détente cannot account for the timing of decisions to terminate aid within cases or the selection of some human rights violators for reprimand and not others across the 1970s, most notably Chile and Argentina relative to Peru.[181] On the other hand, détente fails to explain U.S. humanitarian action before and after the 1970s. Cases here include aid termination to the Batista (1958) and Somoza (1978–79) regimes in addition to congressional refusal in the 1980s to lift earlier human rights restrictions on aid despite strong lobbying on strategic grounds from the Carter and Reagan administrations.[182] Overall, détente offers limited explanatory leverage over specific policy decisions to terminate or preserve security assistance.

Domestic Institutionalism

The cases assessed in this chapter should be strong ones for domestic institutionalism. As noted at the outset of this chapter, security assistance was well institutionalized in Mutual Defense Assistance Agreements (MDAAs). As we have seen, aid existed with little or no controversy for decades before termination.[183] Based on the discussion in chapter 1, institutionalists anticipate termination under one of two conditions: a negotiated agreement to end the assistance or unilateral steps by these partners in violation of MDAA responsibilities to the United States.

While making contributions, these institutionalist explanations do not adequately account for security assistance termination and preservation in many cases.[184] On the one hand, cooperatively negotiated termination rarely, if ever, marked U.S. decisions to end assistance during the Cold War. Argentina, Chile, and Nicaragua fall into this category.[185] The Argentine government, in fact, regarded U.S. termination in 1977 as an "arbitrary . . . immoral and unilateral" severance of the 1964 MDAA between the two countries.[186]

As to partner defection, the Rio Pact and the MDAAs with Chile and Argentina stipulated that military assistance was for defense of the Western Hemisphere against an external Soviet attack. The use of aid by the Chilean, Argentine, or Nicaraguan governments to repress leftist insurgencies and political movements at home might be considered by institutionalists a violation of these restrictions, which led to U.S. desertion.

There are two problems with this argument. First, due to the success of Fidel Castro's 1959 insurgency-based revolution in Cuba, the use of assistance domestically against communist movements in Latin America became acceptable under the rubric of hemispheric security.[187] The United States increasingly allowed—even promoted—the use of aid for internal purposes as consistent with attempts to prevent communist gains in the region. This definitional shift is probably the main reason that no member of Congress pointed to any "violation" of the inter-American accords as a reason for ending the pledges assessed in this chapter.

When we use this more historically consistent definition of hemispheric security, domestic institutionalism, in fact, expects the opposite of what occurred in the cases studied in this chapter. As discussed above, Chile, Argentina, and Nicaragua were in the midst of unambiguous efforts to solidify control over Marxist, anti-U.S. elements within their borders at the time of assistance termination. Aid should have been continued. If any state came close to violating inter-American accords, it would have to be

Peru. Peru's violation of hemispheric defense revolved around its use of U.S. military equipment for mild forms of regional balancing against neighboring states, especially Chile and Colombia.[188] This point was not lost on Congress, either. Numerous members complained of Peruvian arms buildups for these reasons.[189] Despite these potential MDAA violations, U.S. assistance continued all the same.

Second, even if one holds to the original definition of hemispheric security, institutionalism cannot explain variation in U.S. behavior. The Argentine government used U.S. aid for domestic purposes for years before Washington ended assistance. In Peru, military governments repeatedly used force to clamp down on the opposition from 1968 to 1980, but U.S. assistance continued. Likewise, the Batista regime in Cuba long utilized assistance to repress domestic opposition before the United States finally took action. It appears that we need to look at factors outside of or, as in the case here, in addition to the institutionalist framework in order to deepen our understanding of U.S. decisions to terminate and preserve security assistance.

CONCLUSION

The United States entered the 1970s with military aid commitments to a large number of Latin American states. Across the decade, it abandoned pledges to some of them and not others. Why?

Realist and institutionalist explanations lack explanatory leverage over the problem. Realism's best explanation revolves around détente and the waning of U.S.-Soviet bilateral tensions. In reality, détente made security assistance more strategically vital in the minds of U.S. policymakers than ever. Further more, realism fails to explain case-by-case variation in U.S. behavior. Institutionalism faces the same problem.

Humanitarian norms, by contrast, offer a powerful explanation of inter- and intra-case patterns of U.S. action. The theory expects the United States to end pledges when two individually necessary and jointly sufficient conditions exist—illiberal partner behavior and activist pressure. In the absence of this scenario, the theory anticipates commitment consistency. The broad overview of U.S. military commitment relations to Latin America presented in Table 3.1 demonstrates correlations that appear to validate these expectations. Detailed case studies further reinforced these findings. The combination of inhumane behavior by the Chilean and Argentine regimes and strong NGO pressure resulted in U.S. congressional termination of pledges to both countries. The history of commitments to

Table 3.2. Humanitarian norms by decision point: The U.S.–Latin American cases

Congressional decision point	Illiberal behavior	Activist pressure	Commitment outcome
Chile (1973)	Yes	No	Preserved
Chile (1974)	Yes	Yes	Terminated
Chile (1976)	Yes	Yes	Terminated
Peru (1973–81)	No (liberalizing)	Yes	Preserved
Argentina (1974–76)	No (liberalizing and dispersed responsibility)	Yes	Preserved
Argentina (1977)	Yes	Yes	Terminated
Nicaragua (1977)	No (liberalizing)	No	Preserved
Nicaragua (1979)	Yes	Yes	Terminated

Peru across the 1970s and Nicaragua in 1977 offered stark contrasts. In each of these cases, commitment consistency resulted amidst liberalizing steps, uncertainty over who was to blame for inhumanity, or a lack of NGO pressure.

The structure of the Chilean, Argentine, Peruvian and Nicaraguan stories allows us to assess the argument from another angle as well. Each case offered multiple decision points, effectively increasing the number of observations available for analysis. Table 3.2 details the presence or absence of the two variables in the humanitarian norms argument in addition to outcomes at each point. The intersection (or not) of illiberal partner behavior and activist pressure captures the course of events within each case. In tandem with the inter-case comparisons, these intra-case findings vastly expand the explanatory leverage of the argument. Overall, humanitarian norms offer the strongest and most plausible explanation of patterns in U.S. security assistance relations with Latin America during the 1970s.

[4]

Apartheid in U.S.–South African Relations

Cold War perceptions dominated patterns of U.S. engagement in postwar southern Africa. Not surprisingly, U.S. pledges of trade privileges, economic aid, and export promotion assistance to countries in the region came with expectations. These included the responsibility to use assistance for agreed-upon development goals and projects as well as more general expectations of loyalty to Washington's strategic objectives against the Soviet Union. Castro's Cuba, Sandinista Nicaragua, and Marxist regimes in Angola and Ethiopia knew all too well the cost of challenging the United States on this point: all witnessed full or nearly full termination of economic aid by Washington as they strayed into the Soviet orbit.

This chapter assesses the very different courses that U.S. commitments took to two specific states in southern Africa: South Africa and Mozambique. The tales of U.S. relations with each country share a strategic starting point. From the early postwar period, South Africa was perceived as a vital Cold War ally to the United States, especially in the late 1970s and early 1980s. Pretoria provided between 40 and 100 percent of the U.S. supply of eight of ten designated critical strategic minerals. That the other major suppliers of many of these minerals were communist regimes and that the U.S. experienced shortages in its strategic mineral stockpiles during the late 1970s heightened the perception of U.S. mineral dependence. Beyond minerals, South Africa also offered protection over sea routes that the United States viewed as important for Middle East oil and stood as its proxy in supporting pro-western rebels in Angola, a communist country occupied by a large contingent of Warsaw Pact troops.[1]

While considered much less vital to U.S. policymakers, Mozambique gained strategic importance in the 1980s as well. After an initially close relationship with the Soviet Union following independence in 1975, Mozambique became a critical player for the United States in bringing peace to southern Africa in the 1980s as a pretext for elimination of the communist presence in Angola and the region in general. Specifically, by signing the Nkomati Accord with South Africa in 1984, Mozambique gave U.S. President Ronald Reagan's policy of constructive engagement its first victory in the region.[2]

The United States provided economic assistance to expand and develop the strategic advantages that it perceived in each of these relationships. Among other arrangements, South Africa gained access to Export-Import Bank (ExIm) funding facilities, Most Favored Nation (MFN) Trading status through the General Agreement on Tariffs and Trade (GATT), and an annual sugar quota.[3] The result was an economic explosion in South Africa that ushered in substantial U.S. corporate investment in leading industrial sectors of the South African economy (oil, automobiles, banks, computers, heavy engineering, and technology) starting in the late 1950s. Richard Hull contends, "South Africa had become a keystone of Cold War strategy, with the [United States] government and private sector working hand in hand."[4] With respect to Mozambique, the United States awarded an annual economic assistance package to Maputo in order to meet pressing development needs in 1984. The pledges came with the condition that Mozambique liberalize its economy and continue to loosen ties with the Soviet Union and move further toward non-alignment.[5]

The similarities between U.S. relations with Mozambique and South Africa, however, end there. The mid-1980s brought very divergent paths. The major change was in U.S.–South African relations. In 1985 and 1986, the United States abruptly imposed consecutive rounds of punitive economic sanctions against South Africa. Each major strategic commitment, including ExIm, MFN, and the sugar quota, was terminated. Washington also violated a 1947 international air service agreement with Pretoria by revoking the landing rights of South African Airways in U.S. terminals.[6] By contrast, U.S assistance expanded substantially to Mozambique. In 1984, U.S. food aid to Mozambique increased ninefold, making Maputo the largest recipient in the world.[7] By the end of 1988, it had received more than $220 million from the United States in development assistance, making it the largest recipient of U.S. development aid in sub-Saharan Africa.[8]

On the face of it, these outcomes are not merely different but seem quite puzzling, especially in light of realist and institutionalist explanations. Both schools offer poor explanations of U.S.–South African relations. In sanctioning South Africa, the United States turned its back on a historically ferocious anticommunist ally viewed by U.S. policymakers as being at the peak of its strategic value to the United States. In Mozambique, the United States willingly established ties with a Marxist regime that welcomed the presence of ten thousand Soviet and Warsaw Pact military advisors on its soil through the 1980s. Even more puzzling, Mozambique's turn to the United States emerged in large measure because of the military success of the Mozambique National Resistance Movement (MNR or Renamo), an anticommunist guerilla organization much like those that the United States directly aided as "freedom fighters" in neighboring Angola as well as Nicaragua, Afghanistan, and Cambodia starting in 1985.

This chapter demonstrates that the humanitarian norms argument developed in chapter 1 best explains U.S. policy toward these two strategic partners in the mid-1980s. It also explains the timing of sanctions against South Africa after thirty-six years of close cooperation.

SOUTH AFRICA

Outside of a handful of members of the Congressional Black Caucus (CBC), the system of government-sponsored racism in South Africa known as apartheid was far from a burning issue for U.S. policymakers as the 1970s opened. Attention focused primarily on Pretoria's strategic value to Washington. Official U.S. policy turned a blind eye to apartheid, contending passively that U.S. corporate engagement offered a liberal example of equity that could encourage long-term change to the system.[9]

By 1980, the position of Congress, in particular, on apartheid had changed substantially. The 1970s human rights movement along with three events converged to spark the congressional shift. These include the emergence of black majority rule in Angola and Mozambique following Portuguese decolonization in 1975; the riots in Soweto, South Africa, in 1976; and the end of white supremacist rule in Rhodesia in 1978. Each event pointed to a common conclusion for many lawmakers in the United States: a tide of change in favor of greater egalitarianism seemed to be sweeping across southern Africa.[10]

The Ford and Carter administrations reacted to these events with greater rhetorical pressure for reform in South Africa. President Carter went the farthest in this respect by encouraging U.S. corporations operating in South Africa to adopt new standards, known as the Sullivan Principles, for fair employment practices.[11] Carter, however, shied away from punitive actions against South Africa; for example, he refused to advocate making the Sullivan Principles mandatory for U.S. corporations.[12] Perceived strategic interests came first. The "Cape route . . . [for] Middle East oil" and concern for the "enormous southern African reserves of minerals" for the U.S. defense industry dominated the administration's thinking," according to Hull. Panic over reports of low stocks of minerals, in fact, led Carter to shuttle the National Materials and Minerals Policy, Research and Development Act through Congress in 1980.[13] South Africa stood as the major supplier of minerals designated for re-stocking in the Act. In the years to follow, President Ronald Reagan accentuated Carter's policies all the more, as his administration further deepened ties with Pretoria.

The U.S. Congress was a different story. A movement emerged on Capitol Hill for an end to institutionalized racism in South Africa—that is, the political and social system of white rule and exclusively white political rights and representation. Lawmakers also desired an end to the inhumane methods of torture, political arrests, and political executions that helped preserve the system. In the late 1970s, these values came to the fore in several legislative initiatives. Following the brutal government response to the Soweto riots, the House of Representatives easily passed a resolution condemning the South African government's use of violence and arrests of black political protestors. Debate on the measure reflected growing indignation over apartheid. Representative Charles Diggs detailed recent actions by the South African government and then noted, "South Africa is the only country to base its repression and denial of basic rights exclusively on race." Representative Cardiss Collins said, likewise, "These tragic events are but a small part of an institutionalized pattern of the repression of human rights that has characterized the Republic of South Africa since the adoption of the apartheid system as official policy in 1948." Representative Edward Markey called abuses in South Africa "abhorrent to the instincts of every American."[14] The resolution marked the first time that either house of Congress passed a measure related to apartheid.[15]

A year later, Congress took further action, despite opposition from the Carter administration, in the form of the Evans Amendment to the Export Administration Act of 1945. It imposed some restrictions on ExIm funding, which contributed to apartheid. While far from terminating South African access to ExIm facilities, these new conditions contributed to a decrease in the overall amount of ExIm lending to Pretoria.[16] In the months before and after the adoption of the measure, members of Congress sounded off about apartheid. Representative Ronald Dellums referred to the "intolerable apartheid policies." Representative Andrew Maguire noted, "What we have in South Africa is a police state with respect to that majority of 22 million persons who are not permitted to participate in making the decisions in society." The concerns crossed party lines, as members of the Republican Party spoke out as well. Representative John Buchanan observed that combating apartheid in South Africa involves "what we most basically are as a nation."[17]

The Reagan administration's policy of constructive engagement for southern Africa deepened congressional expectations for change in South Africa. While it would have the effect of bringing the United States closer to the government in Pretoria, a stated goal of constructive engagement was to create the regional context for inter-state peace and induce political reform in South Africa. From the outset, Assistant Secretary of State for African Affairs Chester Crocker, the Reagan administration architect of the policy, was explicit about the latter. "One might have thought that this new approach represented a cozy relationship with apartheid," wrote Crocker. "In fact, as I articulated the concept before entering public office, it represented an ambitious *regional* strategy linked to a purposeful and interventionist *bilateral* strategy" toward South Africa.[18] Before a committee in the Senate, he echoed that the future of U.S.–South African relations depended largely "on the extent to which the policy of constructive engagement produces positive, measurable results" away from apartheid.[19]

Congress zeroed in on these pronouncements. For members of both parties, apartheid reform became the litmus test for constructive engagement. As a result, members of Congress, especially in the House, were quick to stand against any U.S. policy that drifted too closely to South Africa and failed to address apartheid. In Reagan's first term, the strongest statement to this effect came in 1983. Following the administration's approval of a $1.1 billion IMF loan to South Africa—the largest loan to Pretoria in IMF history—Congress passed a measure that directed the U.S. representative at the IMF to vote against all future loans to the South African apartheid regime.[20] "Certainly no justification is necessary for opposing South Africa's apartheid system," Representative Stephen Solarz said. "I know my colleagues would all agree that any system of institutionalized racism is incompatible with fundamental democratic principles and human rights."[21] Representative Peter Rodino made an increasingly familiar argument: "As a nation committed to racial equality and human rights, we can no longer justify increasing American investment to nourish the economic growth of a regime that denies the majority of South Africans the right to participate fully in the social, political, and economic life of that nation."[22]

Vocal criticism came from Republicans as well. The chair of the Senate Foreign Relations Subcommittee on Africa, Nancy Kassebaum, wrote that Republican Party principles "are, in fact, in direct contradiction to apartheid." She claimed that the Republican platform was far more consistent with the positions of many Marxist regimes in southern Africa and ANC principles than the values of the South African government.[23] The Republican Chair of the Senate Foreign Relations Committee, Richard Lugar, later wrote, "The majority of Americans empathize with the sufferings of South African blacks."[24] In other activity by Senate Republicans, Larry Pressler and Rudy Boschwitz joined a handful of Democratic senators in condemning Reagan administration decisions to loosen export restrictions to the South Africans. Senator Paul Tsongas introduced a resolution on the issue intended to "demonstrate to the administration how strongly Congress feels about South African apartheid." In support of the resolution, Senator Edward Kennedy lambasted the administration for their decision to export goods for use by the South African police, who "enforce the abhorrent apartheid policy."[25]

Congressional Abeyance: 1977 to mid-1984

Given its obvious concerns about apartheid, why did Congress not impose sanctions against South Africa in the late 1970s or early 1980s? Two factors help answer this question. First, liberalizing steps by the South African government contributed to congressional abeyance. Second, activists used information alone in this period against an ally perceived as vital. As discussed in chapter 1, this lower-end pressure expectedly failed to alter the status quo.

In the years after Soweto, the western media and NGOs documented the illiberal moves of the South African government. Media reports through the early 1980s captured daily developments: police open fire in 1980 on a demonstration to honor the Soweto victims, killing 50 and wounding 174; state bans on all political meetings critical of the government; two blacks shot and killed by police at a funeral; the closing of all black newspapers in 1981; the arrest and permanent detention of thirty leading black trade union leaders in early 1981, followed by the same against fourteen others later in the year; several reports of anti-apartheid political prisoners dying mysteriously while in police detention; reports by more than sixty former detainees of torture by electric shock and other methods while in prison; and the arrest of 289 black protestors in early 1983.[26]

Activist groups aggressively lobbied Capitol Hill, demanding stiff economic sanctions. In July 1976 and January 1978, Amnesty International (AI), for instance, produced reports with case-by-case details of torture, political imprisonment, and other human rights abuses.[27] The Washington

Office on Africa (WOA), the American Committee on Africa (ACA), and TransAfrica, a new black lobbying organization, also produced numerous issue briefs and aggressively pressured Congress. TransAfrica and WOA became important actors in the anti-apartheid cause. They gave activists a more coherent presence in Washington for the first time.[28]

Scholars agree that along with events in South Africa, activist pressure contributed to both greater rhetoric against apartheid by the Carter administration and the Evans Amendment in Congress. Overall, though, the impact of the activist movement was negligible at best. Many congressional staff members noted that the main problem was the lack of pressure from constituents. Into the early 1980s, the average member of Congress received fewer than ten letters per year on apartheid. One staff member of the Senate Foreign Relations Committee noted, in fact, that there "was no significant lobby" on South Africa. Of WOA and TransAfrica, he contended that "their influence is nil." Following the lead of the executive branch, he further noted that members of Congress felt deep unease about apartheid but recognized, in the end, the prevailing strategic rationale for continued U.S. cooperation with South Africa.[29] As we shall see in the next chapter, in this respect South Africa through this period mirrored U.S. relations with the likes of South Korea, the Philippines, and Iran: the illiberalism was well known, information activists were present, but perceived strategic value trumped both.

In the early 1980s, another factor—signs of liberalization—also seemed to encourage U.S. congressional restraint. Along with warming relations with Mozambique under Reagan's constructive engagement policy, the white regime in South Africa introduced a set of liberal reforms. The most important was a much-heralded tricameral legislature, intended to increase minority representation at the federal level of government and expand voting rights to certain minority groups.[30] Debate over the new legislature dominated South African politics from 1981 through early 1984. The plan gained the support of some liberals within South Africa, while others hailed it as a potential first step toward dismantling the entire apartheid system.[31] Senator Richard Lugar captured the impact on Congress: "Many important changes in government policy had been adopted in 1981, when the Reagan Administration entered office. More important, South Africa's Prime Minister P. W. Botha, had raised hopes for even greater reforms as he jettisoned the intellectual and political baggage he inherited from his predecessors." Lugar was not alone. As a leading Democrat on the South Africa issue, Senator Paul Tsongas said, "I have sought as one Senator to temper my criticism of . . . [constructive engagement] so as to leave the administration with both time and political space to conduct their experiment."[32] The core commitments that underwrote the U.S.–South African relationship remained, therefore, unscathed: bills introduced in the House to take the extreme steps of imposing sanctions against Pretoria were turned aside in 1980, 1981, and 1982.[33] The Senate remained even more patient. No such measures were introduced in that chamber until 1985.

Round One of Sanctions: Late 1984–1985

The tide of liberalization did not last forever, nor did the low levels of activist pressure. These developments set the stage for sanctions. Political tension increased progressively in South Africa in 1984. The economy was faltering, so the government announced increases in rents and electric rates in South Africa's black townships in September. This led to an outbreak of protests in the townships that coincided with ongoing black boycotts of the new parliament under Botha's reformed constitution. The parliament angered blacks. Its segregated tricameral structure included so-called whites, Indians, and Coloreds—Africans were totally excluded.[34]

As in the case of the Soweto riots (and other riots as well), South African security forces responded with force. They killed twenty-nine and injured more than three hundred blacks in the September riots. The violence only escalated from there. By the end of the year, the police had killed more than 160 protestors in townships across the country. In November, black trade unions joined the United Democratic Front (UDF), a black movement organized to protest the constitution, in a mass strike across South Africa. The strikes were the deepest and most expansive in apartheid history. The government panicked, for the first time ever deploying the army to control black townships. By December 1984, the government in Pretoria had banned all black trade unions and placed thousands of civil rights activists in preventative detention.[35] Media outlets in the United States reported extensively on all of these developments.[36]

Whereas the Reagan administration responded with mild statements of concern, Congress moved more dramatically. The Senate had taken no action on South Africa since the IMF bill. In fact, since 1980, it had repeatedly shelved resolutions intended to criticize South Africa or Reagan's constructive engagement policies directly. September and October 1984 witnessed a distinct shift. The Senate passed a series of nonbinding resolutions, including one that condemned the recent arrests, detentions, and killings following the introduction of the new constitution. Members of Congress pointed to government actions in justifying these measures.

"We have observed events unfolding in South Africa in recent weeks and we are quite frankly shocked at what we have seen," said Senator Tsongas, in his opening remarks upon introducing one of the resolutions. Likewise, Senator Charles Percy noted, "Our newspapers have been full of reports of unrest and violence in South Africa's black ghettoes. . . . Peaceful demonstrations by government opponents have led to beatings and detentions." Senator John Glenn detailed recent events and concluded that apartheid is "appalling, inhumane, and unjust."[37] As an illustration of the importance of Pretoria's brutality in late 1984, consider this: two Senate resolutions had been languishing with no scheduled activity in committee. Within days of the initial violence in September, the Foreign Relations Committee as well as the full Senate scheduled and passed the resolutions—and by a voice vote, no less.

For its part, the House approved similar resolutions around the same time. The concern over events in South Africa mirrored the Senate. Representative Gerald Solomon admitted, for instance, that he had opposed the resolutions earlier due to progress by the South African government in releasing political prisoners. In September he changed that position, noting, "Such progress has since reversed . . . with a wave of detentions last month in connection with the Parliamentary elections for coloreds and Asians." Many others echoed similar themes.[38]

Republican lawmakers also began to pressure the administration to change its policy. In late November, Senators Lugar and Kassebaum sent a letter to Reagan citing the September events in South Africa as grounds for a review of constructive engagement. Of the letter, Lugar noted, "While I had been a skeptical supporter of . . . constructive engagement in 1981 and 1982, believing it deserved the opportunity to prove itself, it was clear from the news from South Africa that a rethinking of the policy was now needed."[39] In December, a group of forty young conservative Republicans in the House wrote a similar letter to the South African Ambassador calling for steps "toward complete equality for all South Africans." The letter reinforced developments in South Africa as justification for change.[40] Crocker acknowledged the domestic pressure: "We warned the South Africans that the growing township unrest and their response to it were becoming a more serious political issue in the United States."[41]

Despite all the sound and fury, Congress refused to take punitive steps against South Africa in 1984, especially the Senate.[42] That posture changed the following year with a TransAfrica-led grassroots social movement in the United States that demanded sanctions. The roots of the movement lay primarily in tactical decisions made by activists in the early 1980s. Mobilization here mirrored the stages discussed in chapter 1. Frustrated by the lack of progress under the Carter administration and the support that Reagan's constructive engagement initially enjoyed on Capitol Hill, anti-apartheid activists turned decisively toward advocacy at the state and local levels of government. Initiated by a 1980 conference dubbed the Campaign Against Investment in South Africa, activists began pressuring state and local government to divest from pension funds that included corporations with investments in South Africa. The movement grew progressively during the decade. By mid-1985, eleven states and thirty-five cities, including New York City, had passed divestment measures.[43]

For the national debate, the campaign produced an invaluable benefit beyond divestment: constituencies. As a spokesperson for TransAfrica noted, "Our objective on the state level . . . [is to] get as many states as we can to address the South Africa issue in any limited way so we can broaden our education network." Debate at the state level, in short, spread the word about the brutality of apartheid and Reagan's tacit support for it. It also served as a means for networking. TransAfrica organized hundreds of meetings with groups and individuals that might potentially support the cause. One activist noted that the grassroots initiative meant that "we are beginning to reach outside our boundaries and our traditional support groups." With the help of other activists, TransAfrica built a nationwide network and "action alert" system in congressional districts across the country with 10 percent or more African-American representation. A key component of the network was the more than three hundred African-American officials that the group contacted at the state and local levels to hold local meetings and sponsor divestment measures.[44]

The impact of the constituency-building initiative was felt in Washington, D.C., in 1985. Desperate to press the legislative debate from rhetoric toward sanctions, TransAfrica Director Randall Robinson and two others entered the office of the South African Ambassador to the United States on 21 November 1984. They refused to leave until the South African government released more than one hundred members of the UDF. The three were quickly arrested. On their release from prison, Robinson announced the formation of the Free South Africa Movement (FSAM), a group that organized a daily vigil of protests at the South African Embassy as well as intense lobbying of Congress for sanctions against South Africa.[45] This was TransAfrica's call for its nationwide network to take action.

Leaders of the FSAM linked its consistent message of racial equality to America's own struggle during the civil rights movement. U.S. business and government aid to South Africa, it argued, contributed to oppression. Apartheid in South Africa therefore became connected to domestic politics in the United States. Aided by extensive media attention and continued oppression in South Africa, the FSAM grew rapidly in Washington, D.C., and beyond in 1985. Protests and arrests outside the Embassy also grew.[46] House members, Senators, professors, and celebrities were arrested daily. By July 1985, more than twenty-nine hundred people had been taken into custody outside the South African Embassy.[47] More importantly, the protests sparked a groundswell of activity in cities across the United States. Protests quickly spread to twenty-three major metropolitan centers, including New York, Chicago, and Los Angeles where South African consulates were located. Demonstrations also erupted on college campuses nationwide. In early 1985, American colleges and universities joined numerous states and cities across the United States in divesting from U.S. corporations in South Africa.[48] According to one scholar, "Never before in history had South Africa been so completely in the public eye. . . . The antiapartheid movement had made racial discrimination in South Africa a major domestic American issue."[49]

As the FSAM grew, the South African government did little to help its own cause. The government's violent crackdown against black opposition intensified across the early months of 1985. The first major event came in March. In the midst of a five-night sequence of broadcasts by Ted Koppel on *Nightline* from South Africa, the South African police killed twenty-one people and wounded twenty-seven others. It was the single worst police massacre since the Sharpeville riots in the 1960s. In April, the government banned meetings by the UDF, detained hundreds of its members, and charged half a dozen of its leaders with treason. Pretoria also lashed out against ANC targets in neighboring states. In May, defense forces raided Angola, followed in June by action in Botswana. Topping off these developments, on 20 July the government intensified its crackdown by imposing a state of emergency. Within four days of the declaration, 665 people were detained under the new authority given to the police.[50]

While the Reagan administration refused to bow to sanctions pressure, the FSAM pressed Congress into action. From his State Department post, Crocker castigated Republicans on this score. "A locomotive was headed down the track at their [Republican members of Congress] president," Crocker wrote, "and they had no intention of standing in its way. They also had no intention of letting the 'race' issue within the burgeoning South Africa debate go by default to the Democrats."[51] Lugar admitted as much, noting that the FSAM had drastic "implications for the country and the Republican Party." Following the brutal actions of the government in Pretoria in 1984 and 1985, Lugar observed, "The South African apartheid issue became a rallying point for black and white Americans who wanted to make a more dramatic statement about racism in the political dialogue of this country."[52] Republicans and Democrats in Congress joined the tide.

Legislative activity on South Africa subsequently ballooned. In the first three months of 1985, four different sanctions measures were introduced in the House. For the first time in history, stand-alone sanctions legislation was proposed in the Senate—in fact, there were six different bills under consideration by June. By mid-summer, the Lugar-Kassebaum bill was the lead version in the Senate, while a more radical measure offered by Representative William Gray was the lead legislation in the House. Gray's bill, which paralleled a proposal introduced in the Senate by Senators Edward Kennedy and Lowell Weicker, called for the elimination of new U.S. investment in South Africa, computer sales to South Africa, and the importation of South African Krugerrand coins. The Lugar-Kassebaum bill would impose sanctions only if apartheid did not disappear in two years. On 5 June, the Gray bill easily passed the House, despite strong objections from the State Department.[53] Under the weight of events and interest group pressure, Lugar amended his bill in committee. He adopted immediate bans on computer sales, bank loans to South Africa, and nuclear cooperation with Pretoria.[54] On 11 July, the full Senate passed the measure by a wide margin, 80–12. In conference committee, Lugar again caved in and accepted the House ban on Krugerrand imports, one of the main commodities exported to the United States by South Africa.

A closer look at the House and Senate debates reveals the deep influence of South African government action and the FSAM. Sixty-eight percent of those who spoke in support of the Lugar-Kassebaum bill on the Senate floor mentioned events in South Africa or the failure of constructive engagement. The same percentage of supporters discussed the role of public opinion or activists, like the FSAM. In the House debate on the Gray Bill, approximately 88 percent of those that supported the bill discussed events in South Africa or the failure of constructive engagement. Thirty-six percent mentioned activist pressure—this lower number relative to the Senate probably reflects the greater time constraints and, hence, shorter comments during legislative debate in the House.[55]

Congressional statements make the point. "The recent actions of the government of South Africa have made it crystal clear that the U.S. policy of constructive engagement is an empty facade, a policy in fact not producing results," said Senator Paul Sarbanes. Others pointed to events contrary to strategic factors. As a Republican, "perhaps . . . I am supposed to swallow my distaste for apartheid on the grounds that the South African government is pro-Western in its sympathies, an anti-Marxist state . . . I think not," Senator William Roth said, "Western societies do not attempt to rob their citizens of their citizenship . . . [or] shoot peaceful demonstrators in the back." Senator Frank Murkowski, another Republican, talked of "the growing consensus in Congress today that recent events in South Africa . . . justify some congressional action."[56] Detailing one illiberal action after another by Pretoria, House statements were particularly critical of constructive engagement. Representatives noted that the Reagan policy had "done virtually nothing," does not "seem to be bringing about the necessary reforms," and has "not produced desired results." Constructive engagement has "proven to be neither," noted one speaker.[57]

Comments praising the work of activists, like Randall Robinson, as well as state and local divestment drives were equally prevalent. "The recent protests in this country are testimony to the concern men and women of conscience have regarding this issue," Representative Willis Gradison stated. "My colleagues, the protests in front of the South African Embassy in Washington and on college campuses across the Nation . . . are as much about our country as they are about South Africa," claimed Representative Hamilton Fish. "These voices and our legislation are about what we stand for and what we will stand against."[58]

Interestingly, the comments of sanctions opponents help bring to light the powerful impact of the FSAM. Generally more concerned about strategic issues, opponents often criticized their counterparts for making foreign policy on the basis of domestic politics. "I used to drive home every afternoon and watch these people parading up and down in front of the South African Embassy," said Senator Barry Goldwater, for instance. "The thought often went through my mind, I wonder if any of them know what they are up to." Senator Jesse Helms mocked, "So today we hear all of the pious protests about apartheid. . . . Oh, it is fine to go and picket and parade. . . . The common and popular political procedure is to beat one's breast and say, 'I am against apartheid,' and, 'I am for racial justice.'" Conservatives also made similar statements when commenting on the duplicity of not applying similar measures to communist or black majority states in Africa or elsewhere in the world. "There are some cases in Africa . . . where there is black oppression of blacks," one Senator noted. "Yet, there has been no national outrage in the United States to condemn that." Another said that in these cases, it is not "chic" domestically for the United States to take action.[59]

The House passed the conference report by a 380–48 margin on 1 August. By the end of the month, the Senate was prepared to do the same. As if impetus in this direction was not strong enough, South Africa's imposition of a state of emergency in late July only accentuated the congressional impulse for sanctions.[60] Both House and Senate Republicans warned Reagan that the votes were there to override a presidential veto of the sanctions bill.[61]

Following a combative speech by Botha, now the President of South Africa, the White House moved to accommodate Congress. In doing so, the administration unambiguously deserted its own preferred course and bowed to congressional demands for sanctions. On 9 October, the administration issued an executive order containing the sanctions in the conference report.[62] "The Secretary [of State, George Shultz] said, 'This is your bill in executive-order form,' " wrote Lugar. "Senate Majority Leader Bob Dole and I agreed that the executive order meant the acceptance by the President of our bill, and we should declare victory."[63] Reagan himself admitted bowing to congressional pressure: "I respect the goals that have motivated many in Congress to send a message of U.S. concern about apartheid. . . . Therefore, I am signing today an executive order that will put into place a set of measures designed and aimed against the machinery of apartheid."[64] Of the major U.S. commitments to South Africa detailed at the outset, the Krugerrand import ban broke the pledge of nondiscriminatory MFN status to South Africa. The coming months would reveal this to be just the beginning.

The Collapse of Liberalization and Additional Sanctions: 1986

The rise of the FSAM was crucial to explaining the timing of the first round of sanctions against South Africa. The move to a second round of sanctions by the United States in 1986 proved equally dependent on events inside South Africa. Reagan's executive order in 1985 did not end the public debate over apartheid. In fact, the success of the FSAM seemed only to fuel the drive on U.S. campuses, in boardrooms, and at the state and local levels of government for further action. The peak of this new surge came in the last two months of 1985 and early 1986. The media regularly reported this growing trend—one source noted that the wave of campus activism was greater than it had been in the previous decade. University divestment paralleled student activity. By March 1986, one study found that one hundred universities had divested a total of $410.9 million of their holdings in U.S. companies operating in South Africa.[65]

Beyond college campuses, the FSAM took several steps to intensify the campaign for further action against apartheid. In October, the group organized National Anti-Apartheid Protest Day, which drew huge demonstrations across the country and led to scores of arrests. At the one-year anniversary of the movement in November 1985, Randall Robinson promised "a recommitment" to the goal of equality in South Africa.[66] In early

1986, the FSAM organized a three-week tour of the United States by the popular South African archbishop Desmond Tutu. The activist group also initiated a boycott of Shell Oil, a major provider of petroleum to South Africa. The AFL-CIO, the National Association for the Advancement of Colored People (NAACP), and the United Mine Workers of America joined the boycott as well. In March, the AFL-CIO sponsored a "Day of Solidarity With Victims of Apartheid" rally in Washington, D.C.[67] In the *New York Times* alone, coverage of South Africa grew to a record eleven hundred articles in 1986—an average of 2.3 per day.[68]

Amidst the continued wave of activist pressure, Congress remained surprisingly quiet during the first half of 1986. Early in each new congressional term since 1977, there had been at least one bill introduced by a member related to apartheid. Ironically, in the midst of the most fervent public outburst on apartheid to date, there was no such measure brought forward in the House for the first part of 1986. Even legislative speeches and comments on South Africa were limited. From mid-October 1985 to May 1986, Senators and Representatives made only a handful of statements.

Why was the legislature so docile? The reason lies with a series of liberalizing developments in South Africa during early 1986. The author of the 1985 House sanctions bill, Representative Gray, explicitly noted the central role that developments in South Africa would play after the executive order: "Events will dictate what happens next, events that are beyond Congress' control and beyond the President. The Senators and the Congress will see if there is any movement away from apartheid in South Africa. . . . Remember that in the Congress there is bipartisan support for something stronger than what the President did."[69] True to Gray's expectations, congressional steps were, in fact, delayed in early 1986, as the South African government showed signs of genuine reform.

The trend began in early February when President Botha gave a reformist speech to the South African Parliament. He said that the country had "outgrown the outdated concept of apartheid."[70] This was followed the next day with a proposal from Botha for sharing power with blacks under a new national statutory council and a pledge to equal education by June. In early March, Botha lifted the state of emergency; 327 people were subsequently released from prison. In April, he took a big step by rescinding the pass laws, which determined where South African blacks could live and work. One of the most hated aspects of apartheid, the law accounted for an estimated two to three hundred thousand arrests between 1980 and 1986.[71] Finally, in the spring, the South African government agreed to allow a group from the British Commonwealth, the Eminent Persons Group (EPG), to open negotiations between it and the ANC.

These moves received a warm welcome in the United States. The most vocal anti-apartheid voices in Congress praised each step. Representative Howard Wolpe called the pass law termination "a significant development." The former chair of the Africa subcommittee and longtime sanctions supporter, Steven Solarz, said that the move was "probably the single most significant step the Government of South Africa has taken in dealing with the problem of apartheid."[72]

Liberalization was short-lived, however. The positive trends of early 1986 all but disappeared in May. U.S. congressional action soon followed. The reversal began in the midst of EPG negotiations in May. Without warning, the South African Defense Force (SADF) raided ANC targets in Zambia, Zimbabwe, and Botswana on 19 May. Shortly after, the SADF attacked ANC targets in Swaziland. Crocker compared the rash acts to those of a "caged animal," which "set off big waves in the United States." The EPG promptly called off its mediation. Black protests quickly escalated in South Africa. On 12 June, Botha reimposed a state of emergency, which led to the detention of scores of opposition leaders.[73]

Sanctions legislation soon followed on Capitol Hill. The pretext for doing so was South African government actions. Of his new sanctions bill, Kennedy said, "To those who see faint signs of progress and ask us to hold off, we say, 'Read the morning headlines.'" He continued, "The sanctions we have are not strong enough—and the raid on South Africa's neighbors is now exhibit A in the case for strengthening them."[74] Suddenly, the rising public movement for action during the previous six months gained newfound political leverage. Republicans in Congress, especially, felt the pressure. The day after the EPG report and the reimposition of the state of emergency, Kassebaum called on Crocker to offer political cover for Hill Republicans. She specifically demanded that the President take "a visible lead" and "do something" on South Africa.[75]

Over the next four months, the Reagan administration was anything but helpful to congressional Republicans. The president issued recriminations that lacked substantive steps. He isolated most congressional Republicans with a nationally televised speech in July in which he pledged no sanctions against South Africa and defended the white regime in Pretoria. According to Lugar, "It became clear that Africa policy issues were not getting the attention at the Presidential level they needed in light of events in southern Africa."[76] He subsequently introduced a sanctions bill in the Senate.

Legislation against South Africa moved quickly on the Hill. On 18 June, the House passed by voice vote a bill that required total U.S. divestment and a full trade embargo on South African products. In the Senate, the milder Lugar bill again became the lead sanctions measure, passing by an 84–14 margin on 12 August. In order to build a veto-proof measure, Senate leaders convinced colleagues in the House to adopt the Lugar bill. On 4 September, the House overwhelmingly passed the Lugar version, called the Comprehensive Anti-Apartheid Act (CAA), and sent the measure to the president. Reagan vetoed the CAA on 26 September. The House quickly overrode the veto. On 2 October, the Senate did so as well, by a 78–21 margin.[77]

Looking inside the debate, the events of May were critical. In the initial House debate in June, approximately 76 percent of those speaking in support of sanctions mentioned the failure of constructive engagement or the 1985 executive order in light of specific recent events in South Africa. In the Senate's initial debate of the Lugar bill, the number of statements in the same category was approximately 65 percent. The importance of South African illiberalism seems all the more important given the relatively low references to public opinion or activist groups among the statements of sanction supporters—approximately 8 percent in the House and 37 percent in the Senate.[78]

Domestic political pressure mattered, however. Commentators, media analysts, and, most importantly, legislators pointed repeatedly to the crucial role of grassroots pressure in 1986. Nearly 62 percent of those speaking in favor of sanctions during the Senate override debate mentioned domestic political pressures. Republican Senator Mitch McConnell, for instance, cited "activist . . . [and] anti-apartheid group" material in making his appeal that the president stands in opposition to an "overwhelming majority of the citizens of this country." Senator Christopher Dodd noted the important role that the "grassroots anti-apartheid movement has played . . . in bringing us to the point we are today." Senator George Mitchell argued that the "American people already have spoken out against apartheid. Cities, towns, universities and States across the Nation have taken action."[79]

Beyond the congressional debate itself, legislators admitted the importance of public opinion and the upcoming November elections. A House Republican noted that a Reagan veto would "have some impact" on congressional elections in the fall.[80] Following the Senate's override vote, Senate Majority Leader Bob Dole described the vote as a "litmus test" of how lawmakers feel about civil rights in America.[81] Dole sounded a similar theme when asked about the FSAM in 1985: "Well, it focused on the problem. And I think from that standpoint, those who had the responsibility, Chairman Lugar and others at the hearings, made modifications. . . . Not only the focus, not being arrested and all that, but the fact that they were very actively visiting the different people on the Hill. Let's face it: some see it as a big civil rights issue that's important down the road."[82] The day after the Reagan veto, a Republican senatorial candidate was defeated in an early Senate election in Louisiana, due to higher than expected black voter turnout. This, implied Lugar, was a harbinger of things to come for Republicans seeking to maintain control of the Senate if the party decided to follow its president and resist sanctions.[83]

The CAA foisted a foreign policy agenda on the president that led to the termination of several longstanding commitments by the United States to South Africa. These included, notably, MFN trading status through an embargo of selected products from more than 150 South African firms; all export financing, especially ExIm Bank funds; the sugar quota; and landing rights for South African Airlines. The United States lifted these provisions only after South Africa began to dismantle apartheid in the late 1980s and 1990s.

MOZAMBIQUE

Mozambique became one of the largest recipients of U.S. economic assistance in Africa in the years following the aid agreement instituted in 1984. Aid flowed on the basis of Maputo's cooperation with the United States in brokering the Nkomati Accord, which brought peace with South Africa and anticipation that Mozambique may move farther from the Soviet sphere. This surge in U.S. aid came with some controversy. Several NGOs initiated a determined effort to end aid to Mozambique. The climax came with the 1987 Senate debate on a new ambassador to Mozambique. In the end, Congress decided to do nothing. The reason lay with developments in Mozambique that cast the supposedly "freedom fighter" Mozambique National Resistance Movement (MNR), not the Marxist Frelimo government, as the most inhumane political group in the country.

Humanitarian Norms and Freedom Fighters Values in the U.S. Congress: 1980–84

Explaining U.S. and, especially congressional, policy toward Mozambique begins with an understanding of the unique mix of humanitarian and freedom fighter norms in Congress during the 1980s. With the surge of the Cold War into Africa and Central America following détente in the late 1970s, Congress followed the lead of the Reagan Doctrine and developed clear interests in supporting anticommunist insurgency movements, or "freedom fighters," in developing regions across the globe. U.S. government policy pursued, in this respect, a two-pronged strategy: terminate aid to Marxist regimes with close ties to the Soviet Union and open lines of direct military and economic assistance to pro-western insurgencies within those states. Sparked by pressure from conservative activist groups, like the Heritage Foundation and the Conservative Caucus, the United States pursued this two-track policy with Afghanistan, Nicaragua, Cambodia, and Angola into the late 1980s.[84]

On Capitol Hill, these freedom fighter values contained a unique humanitarian wrinkle. Congress expected that the insurgency movements it supported would be more than a means to defeat a communist regime. Consistent with the humanitarian proclivities within Congress as demonstrated in chapter 3, members of Congress showed a strong desire for freedom fighters to express actual support for democracy and thereby demonstrate a respect for the values of individual liberty and human rights. In a discussion of U.S.–Latin American policy, one scholar described it this way:

> In 1984 and 1985 the Reagan Administration clearly played on . . . reserves of anticommunism in order to gain congressional backing for its policies in El Salvador and Nicaragua. . . . The reverse of the negative consensus against communism in Central America was a positive consensus [in Congress] on what was desirable there, based on the American political values of democracy, electoral government, and individual liberty. . . . Elected representatives in the United States—themselves products of the electoral system—exhibit a deeply held faith in these principles.[85]

Rooted in a deep humanitarian tradition, in effect Congress took the *freedom* in the term *freedom fighters* quite seriously in decisions on aiding anticommunist insurgency movements in the 1980s. The case of Nicaragua offers one of the best-known examples of this. Here, Congress severed all military assistance to the Contra rebels with the Boland Amendment after revelations of extensive inhumanity by the insurgency movement. Complicity by the CIA fueled the congressional initiative all the more.[86]

Given its proximity to Mozambique, Angola offers an even better example of freedom fighter norms at work within Congress. Under extreme pressure from conservative lawmakers and in the shadow of the Reagan Doctrine, Congress repealed the Clark Amendment, a measure that denied aid to the UNITA rebel movement in 1985.[87] The move came against the administration's will, as Crocker argued that the Reagan Doctrine was not applicable to the complex reality of politics in southern Africa.[88] Aid to UNITA was not the end of legislative activity on Angola. In the wake of the Clark repeal, a number of activist groups formed the Coalition to Restore a More Benevolent Order (RAMBO), a lobbying initiative to sever all economic ties with Angola. The group convinced Congress to terminate ExIm funding and suspend Angolan MFN trading status. The Reagan administration opposed each of these moves as well.[89]

The Clark Amendment debate in particular revealed the strategic-humanitarian focus within Congress when it came to dealing with anti-communist resistance movements and the governments that they were fighting. On the one hand, the Cold War context was an undeniable part of the decision-making process. "By repealing Clark, we will be saying that the President should have the flexibility and the leverage available to respond to Soviet and Cuban adventurism in the Third World," said Representative Samuel Stratton. Representative William Broomfield, along with other members, pointed out that "today, there are still 40,000 Cuban military and civilian advisers in Angola" as a justification to aid Savimbi. Equally prominent, however, were statements regarding the liberal essence of UNITA. Representative Stratton referred to repealing the Clark amendment as "removing a psychological barrier to all of those who wish to support democratic forces in Angola." Representative Robert Dornan spoke of aiding Jonas Savimbi as the "only chance for freedom to flourish." Representative Claude Pepper said, in this vein, "The Statue of Liberty invites men all over the earth to come to freedom—that includes Angola."[90] The congressional version of freedom fighter norms packaged the strategic and liberal humane together.

Mozambique and Commitment Preservation: 1985–86

RAMBO targeted Mozambique, as well, in hopes of turning U.S. policy in favor of the MNR.[91] It constructed a large coalition of groups to press Congress to alter the U.S. aid commitment to Mozambique.[92] The linchpin organization in this effort was the Mozambique Research Center (MRC), which was headed by Thomas Schaff. Schaff had a long history of experience with the MNR; his network of contacts with missionaries and church groups in Malawi and Mozambique provided extensive information on day-to-day developments inside the country. In this role, the MRC lobbied Capitol Hill and the international agencies of the U.S. government extensively, issued press statements, sponsored visits by journalists and academics to Mozambique, and raised funds for the MNR.[93]

The activist drive against Mozambique began in September 1985 with the visit of Mozambique President Samora Machel to the White House.[94] The welcoming of a Marxist head of state to Washington by the Reagan administration set off a firestorm. Activists sounded the message that the MNR was the liberal, humane alternative for Mozambique. At a press conference during Machel's visit, Senator Malcolm Wallop lambasted the Frelimo government of Mozambique as a friend of the Soviet Union and mass violator of human rights, noting especially the curtailment of free speech as well as arbitrary arrests and detentions. He then said, "We must support the democratic freedom fighters of Mozambique, those who stand for western values and governmental systems." He went on to talk of the MNR's "brave dedication to pro-western values." At the same press conference, Representative Dan Burton labeled Frelimo a "brutal client of the Soviet Union" and stated that the MNR "is a truly pro-western, pro-democratic government with a clear program and a good chance of victory."[95]

In 1986, the Heritage Foundation published a detailed report on developments inside Mozambique. Based in part on information from Schaff's network, the report detailed at length the inhumanity of Frelimo. It noted that Frelimo had killed thousands of political prisoners, especially in the late 1970s and early 1980s. An estimated two hundred thousand individuals had been sent to re-education camps during the tenure of the regime; many were tortured or killed. A State Department report corroborated these findings with details of extensive torture by the Mozambique government.[96] AI sent missions to Mozambique and detailed the brutal methods employed in re-education camps throughout the late 1970s and into the early 1980s. In 1985, it published a sixteen-page document on methods of torture in Mozambique. At the same time, AI noted some improvements on human rights by Frelimo: numerous amnesties of political prisoners by the government reduced the number of detainees in re-education camps from approximately one hundred thousand to between four and ten thousand; the government issued new guidelines to limit torture and summary executions; and repression against certain religious groups decreased substantially.[97]

While AI was more critical of the MNR, the Heritage Report celebrated the MNR. It noted the intentions of the rebels to restore "basic freedoms," create a "democratic constitution," and "hold elections" for Mozambique. Referring to the organization's leader, the report said, "It is reasonable to assume that a government led by a Christian president who promises religious, economic, and political freedom would be considerably better than an oppressive totalitarian regime supported by Moscow or Havana."[98] The conservative side of the movement was also clear about its policy proposals.[99] The Heritage report demanded a "stop to all U.S. aid to the Machel government," an "end to Mozambique's most favored nation trading status," and the initiation of "moral support and humanitarian aid . . . to the anti-communist forces" of the MNR.[100]

The lobby made its greatest inroads on Capitol Hill, as demonstrated most noticeably in the Senate debate over the nomination of Melissa Wells to be U.S. Ambassador to Mozambique in mid-1987. Wells was a strong proponent of retaining current ties to Frelimo and refusing official contact with the MNR. A small group of Republican senators initiated an effort to hold up the nomination on the Senate floor. In May, Majority Leader Bob Dole joined the ranks of those opposed to the nomination. His support generated a bipartisan coalition of twenty-eight senators that prevented the nomination from coming to a vote.[101]

The senators holding up the nomination demanded nothing less than a reversal of current policy toward Mozambique. When Dole joined the ranks against Wells on 1 May, he called Frelimo an oppressive Marxist regime and demanded that the administration initiate ties with the Mozambique resistance.[102] Senator Jesse Helms was the most outspoken:

> I have told the Secretary of State: "just say that you will meet with Renamo [or the MNR] and hear what they have to say." They say, "No, no way, Jose." Therefore, Mr. President, I say "No way, Jose" to the U.S. State Department in every effort to bring up this nomination. Until the State Department takes a look at its own dumb policy we are going to have a problem with this nomination.[103]

Senator Steve Symms echoed this sentiment, saying that the filibuster was "in the cause of the expansion of freedom and the cause of the Reagan doctrine."[104] For its part, the administration resisted the tide of congressional pressure. In May, Secretary of State George Shultz told Mozambique officials that he and the president were committed to the current policy. He said the same to Dole and Helms in July.[105] In mid-summer, a low-level desk officer at the State Department for the first time met with MNR representatives. The move was intended to placate the Senate. When the Senate failed to end the filibuster, the State Department ended its contacts with the MNR.[106]

On 9 September, a sea change in the congressional position on the nomination occurred. The cloture against the nomination was lifted, and Wells was confirmed by a comfortable margin. More importantly for our sake, there was no noticeable shift in Reagan policy. The administration continued foreign aid to Frelimo and even increased it some. The United States also remained as aloof from the MNR as at any prior point. In fact, on 6 October, President Reagan met with Mozambique President Joaquim Chissano at the White House.[107] What happened?

The answer lies with events in Mozambique, specifically the activities of the MNR in late 1987. Despite the activist surge, Congress was hesitant to embrace the MNR and cut ties with the Frelimo government as had happened in Angola. The reason lay with largely unconfirmed reports of brutal treatment of civilians by the MNR. From the early 1980s, AI increasingly highlighted MNR torture and summary executions, though it rarely discussed specific cases due to problems obtaining access to MNR forces and areas under its control.[108] In the United States, these reports cast doubt on the genuine commitment of the MNR to western values of human rights, freedom, and democracy.[109]

In the summer of 1987, these assessments of the MNR moved to the center of congressional debates. The cause was a spate of massive and, more to the point, *confirmed* MNR atrocities. It began when media sources reported that on 18 July, rebel forces in Mozambique conducted a ten-hour massacre of innocent civilians in the town of Homoine. In the streets of the city, 386 people were killed—some by machetes and others, purportedly, with U.S.-made weapons that were supplied to the rebels by South Africa. Another MNR massacre occurred on 31 July, in which thirty-two people were killed. On 10 August, seventy-two more unarmed civilians were reportedly killed by rebel troops in a town not far from Homoine.[110]

The Wells nomination process was immediately affected by these events, especially after the Red Cross, CARE, and several western eyewitnesses confirmed the rebel massacres. Compounding the case for the MNR, UNICEF released a study, entitled *Children on the Frontline* just after Homoine. The report estimated that the MNR had destroyed 25 percent of the health clinics in Mozambique and contributed to the deaths of approximately 325 children since the mid-1970s. Other international relief groups reported widespread atrocities by the MNR in 1986 and 1987.[111] In a matter of days, the MNR had gone from a plucky band of freedom fighters to a vilified terrorist organization, far removed from the beacon of humane and liberal values that its supporters both on and off Capitol Hill claimed it to be.

In September, debate in the Senate shifted demonstrably on this basis. MNR behavior proved so dominant that nearly each speaker, whether pro or con towards the Wells nomination, referenced the atrocities. MNR supporters tried to discredit the information. Senator Helms blasted the media for accepting the Marxist Frelimo regime's version of events as fact.[112]

He complained of a "malicious propaganda campaign by the *Washington Post* and similar media seeking to portray Renamo as perpetrators of massacres." Senator Symms claimed that the media was "giving people the wrong impression" about the MNR. The atrocities could not be overlooked, however. And, the coalition to suspend Wells's nomination crumbled. Senator Dole's change of heart was the most damaging for the pro-MNR forces, leading to the desertion of many moderate Republicans and Democrats. Of his decision, Dole said that if the nomination came to a vote, he would vote in favor. His reasoning was clear: "I am troubled by the State Department's policy toward Mozambique . . . [yet] the Administration is right to be leery of embracing Renamo politically, in light of legitimate questions raised about Renamo's goals, structures, and tactics." Others rebuked the MNR even more forcefully. "Organizations such as CARE and the International Red Cross state that RENAMO routinely strikes civilian targets and engages in human rights violations," argued Senator Allen Cranston. Senator Bob Kerrey juxtaposed the progress of government reforms with a list of atrocities and destruction resulting from the "immoral war being perpetrated by Renamo." Senator Claiborne Pell argued much the same way, adding that the Senate should not be pressing the State Department to meet with "a group, which is widely recognized as indulging in terrorist attacks against civilians."[113]

The summer atrocities of the MNR dominated the debate, eclipsing the opposition to Wells and paving the way for Senate approval of the nomination without any change to existing U.S. policy. The congressional door for MNR supporters and lobbyists shut even more tightly in 1988. In April, the State Department released an independent study, the Gersony Report, on Mozambique. The report consisted of extensive interviews with Mozambique refugees. It concluded that the MNR had killed at least one hundred thousand innocent civilians and was guilty of rapes, beatings, lootings, abductions, and mutilations.[114]

The report both crushed remnants of MNR support in Congress and virtually ended the activist campaign as a whole. As one pro-MNR activist admitted, Homoine and the Gersony Report "had an incalculably disastrous effect on Renamo's reputation in government and media circles."[115] Schaff admitted that favorable media coverage and fund raising became virtually nonexistent starting in late 1987.[116] In the end, Frelimo was, by no means, spotless in its human rights record, but amidst its economic reforms and the atrocities of the MNR, the Mozambique government appeared the lesser of two evils in the congressional discourse. Economic aid continued, as expected.

The Alternatives: Realism and Domestic Institutionalism

This section considers alternative explanations to patterns of U.S. aid relations with South Africa and Mozambique. Before moving to realism and institutionalism, I turn first to an alternative norms–based argument on the South Africa case. Audie Klotz claims that U.S. and European sanctions against South Africa emerged from anti-racism norms at the level of the international system.[117] This argument faces two problems in the U.S. case. If the United States acted on the basis of an international norm, we would expect discussion of the norm to have predominated in the sanctions debate. Since states as a whole are constituted by international norms, we would also expect the executive branch to have shared with Congress support for its norm-based behavior. Neither of these scenarios was the case, however, generating questions for Klotz about why the legislative branch in the United States was the lead actor and what role international norms played, if any, in the U.S. policy process. Second, Klotz posits that the anti-racism norm emerged in the 1950s and 1960s. Then why, in the case of South Africa, did it not actually matter until the mid-1980s? Klotz offers no systematic answer. These criticisms point back to the discussion in the first two chapters that we need to know much more about domestic political developments to understand where norms come from and how they matter in shaping actual policy outcomes.[118]

Realism

Realism anticipates that one of two potential geopolitical changes generated U.S. action against South Africa. First, the strategic environment might have changed to create an overwhelming new threat, making pledges to South Africa superfluous or less valuable to the United States. Second, South Africa may have lost power (most likely due to defeat in a conflict), which made the commitments more burdensome than beneficial to the United States. The lack of either of these types of changes explains commitment consistency to Mozambique, according to realism. Simply put, both propositions face problems explaining sanctions against South Africa but offer some leverage on the Mozambique case.

Both Mozambique and South Africa remained as important to U.S. strategic ends as in previous periods. In fact, geopolitical developments across the late 1970s and early 1980s made South Africa all the more valuable in the eyes of U.S. policymakers. Southern Africa continued to be a relatively safe bastion of anticommunist, western dominance into the early 1970s. Specific to South Africa, its bordering neighbors of Rhodesia, Angola, and Mozambique remained under the control of anticommunist allies, namely Britain and Portugal. That regional safety blanket, however, changed almost overnight for the United States in the middle of the decade. In 1978, Britain's final disengagement from Rhodesia (later Zimbabwe) resulted in Robert Mugabe's introduction of a Marxist government that immediately increased ties to the Soviet Union. All the more pressing was Portugal's departure from Angola and Mozambique. As noted already, Marxist regimes with close military ties to the USSR took over in both countries.

South Africa became Washington's military proxy in the Angolan conflict. Given congressional restraint on aid to Savimbi, Secretary of State George Shultz claimed that South African military supplies and support was "of critical importance" to the survival of the resistance movement.[119] This U.S. regional dependence on South Africa increased all the more with Reagan's policy of constructive engagement. A strong South Africa was critical to success. Crocker claimed, therefore, that sanctions against South Africa would damage "a sustained and nimble diplomacy" aimed at "competing regionally for influence with the Soviets and Cubans." Finally, South African sea lanes and minerals were no less valuable to the United States in the mid-1980s than at any prior point. Crocker, again, noted that administration officials believed that avoiding sanctions was critical in order to "keep South Africa's minerals and ports out of Soviet hands."[120] In sum, geopolitical shifts did not detract from South Africa's value in the 1970s and 80s; they enhanced them.[121]

Realism does better in the Mozambique case. Mozambique's move to non-alignment in the 1980s represented the first major triumph of constructive engagement. Crocker captured how the Reagan administration viewed Mozambique's strategic value: "Our priorities ... in encounters with Mozambique were ... to explore the readiness to abandon close Soviet and Cuban alignment. ... We came to view the Mozambicans as partners who wanted us to be successful in resolving the Namibian-Angolan wars. ... [They] could provide the context for cooperation in undercutting the Soviet position and eliminating Soviet military influence and presence" in southern Africa.[122] Like the humanitarian norms argument, realism expected commitment consistency toward Mozambique as well. This indeed transpired, giving realism some apparent leverage over this case. As to the second realist alternative, a change in dependence, realism again finds some success in explaining Mozambique but not South Africa. While the Frelimo government in Maputo clearly lost some ground to the internal opposition forces of the MNR following the initiation of U.S.

assistance, there was no demonstrable decrease in the external power of the state. Realism, thus, expects the commitment consistency to Mozambique that indeed transpired.

South Africa offers a different picture for this realist proposition. First, U.S. policy makers never doubted South Africa's ability to play a regional military role on behalf of U.S. interests. If anything, concerns existed in Washington that South Africa might become too overbearing as the leading regional power.[123] There were good reasons for U.S. confidence in South African power. With postwar industrialization and modernization, South Africa became far and away the overwhelming superpower among southern African states.[124] Across the 1980s, South Africa remained deeply engaged in Angola while simultaneously initiating numerous raids on neighboring Mozambique, Swaziland, Botswana, Zimbabwe, Zambia, and Lesotho.[125] Moreover, each of these raids occurred with no direct retaliation from the attacked states, all of which were generally too weak to effectively respond. Overall, South Africa's regional military power was unmatched, undaunted, and unchanged prior to sanctions.

As we have seen, the evidence in fact indicates that it was the United States, not South Africa, that perceived its strategic dependence to have increased prior to sanctions. The issue of strategic minerals stockpiling and sea routes appeared time and again in the sanctions debate. In 1985, Senator Strom Thurmond said the following: "South Africa . . . is strategically important to the United States because of its global location and vast mineral resources. It is a government friendly to the United States in a troubled and increasingly important area of the world, and this country should take care to ensure that it does nothing that would jeopardize its own security interests in the region."[126] On minerals, Senator Steve Symms echoed, "Clearly, we are engaged in a mutually beneficial trade relationship with South Africa. They are our allies and we do not have many in that region of the world."[127] In 1986, President Reagan called sanctions "an historic act of folly," because "strategically, this is one of the vital regions of the world." In addition to Persian Gulf oil passing around the Cape of Good Hope, Reagan said that South Africa is a "repository of many of the vital minerals—vanadium, manganese, chromium, platinum—for which the West has no other secure source of supply."[128] In sum, one could argue that U.S., not South African, dependence increased in the 1980s.

In short, realism offers a poor explanation of the South Africa case. On Mozambique, realism appears to present a viable picture of developments. Yet when one considers Mozambique and South Africa together, rather than as isolated cases, the scales tip in favor of humanitarian norms. Given that the United States faced the same geopolitical cues with respect to economic aid commitments to these two states in the same region, something outside of the realist paradigm has to explain why the United States terminated pledges to one and not the other. In effect, the common structure of the two cases cannot determine both commitment termination and consistency.

Domestic Institutionalism

Domestic institutionalism anticipates that the United States would terminate pledges to South Africa under one of two conditions: Washington and Pretoria negotiating an end to the various U.S. pledges or South Africa defecting on its commitment responsibilities as a prelude to U.S. action. The first of these scenarios seems highly unlikely. What state would ever agree to another imposing punitive sanctions against it? The second alternative seems more plausible in the South Africa case.

For both South Africa and Mozambique, unilateral violation of the terms of assistance deals could consist of two types. On the one hand, either might have violated the technical terms of the agreement on the proper economic/development uses of U.S. commitments. For ExIm funding or development assistance, this might have included the diversion of U.S. assistance or funding to projects or goals not agreed upon beforehand. In the case of MFN, South Africa might have increased tariffs or banned certain U.S. imports as a prelude to U.S. action. Under the trade norm of reciprocity, the United States would be justified in applying similar measures. The second type of unilateral violation is more generally strategic. Like many economic and trade assistance pledges during the Cold War, these commitments carried expectations that South Africa and Mozambique would continue to support or increase their support for U.S. strategic objectives. The purpose of these pledges was to build stronger friends and gain certain geostrategic advantages. For South Africa, unilateral violation along these lines would involve, most noticeably, reducing or ending U.S. access to strategic minerals or the termination of U.S. access to important ports that hampered or closed sea lanes around the Cape of Good Hope, if not both. In the case of Mozambique, Maputo's continued progress toward non-alignment through a reduction of Soviet and Warsaw Pact advisors in its country would stand as compliance with the terms of aid accords with Washington and explain the continued flow of assistance.

Institutionalism faces similar problems to realism in explaining U.S. action against South Africa. Furthermore, it does less well than realism or humanitarian norms at accounting for U.S. consistency to Mozambique. South Africa violated neither the technical nor the strategic terms of its commitment relations with the United States. There is no evidence that Pretoria used funds improperly or limited the access of U.S. goods to its markets. GATT standards do allow members to sanction other members who violate human rights. This explanation, however, offers no leverage over the central questions of the *timing* of U.S. action. South Africa had been a GATT member since the late 1940s, and the United States and European countries took punitive trade steps against it in the 1980s. One needs to look at factors other than GATT rules to explain why the United States acted.

From the above evidence against realism, South Africa's consistent anticommunism is obvious. First, South Africa never backed away from its responsibility to prosecute anticommunism in the southern Africa region prior to sanctions. The greatest testimony to this was, again, South Africa's continued support for Savimbi's UNITA freedom fighters in Angola. Pretoria was unrelenting in this respect. Second, South Africa also did not terminate U.S. access to important naval and intelligence facilities along its coastline prior to sanctions. The Simonston air base, specifically, remained as accessible to the United States as it had been when the basing rights were negotiated in the early 1970s. Third, South Africa did not sever exports of certain critical strategic minerals to the United States at any point in the first half of the 1980s. Most scholars point out that the South African economy was too dependent on exports of these minerals to take such a step.[129] If anything, South African mineral exports to the United States actually increased in the years prior to sanctions. This was especially true of chromium. With the 1978 ascension of Mugabe in Zimbabwe (southern Africa's other major chromium supplier), the United States increased chromium imports from South Africa from 31 percent to 55 percent by the end of 1983.[130] The congressional debate on South Africa is helpful here, as well. At no point did any member of Congress who supported sanctions justify his or her vote on the basis of Pretoria's failure to promote U.S. strategic interests. In fact, some members of Congress emphasized South Africa's status as an important ally for all of the reasons detailed above—and then in the next breath demanded the application of sanctions by the United States.[131]

The problem with the institutionalist explanation for Mozambique is straightforward. On the technical side, Maputo appeared to use U.S. development aid for its designated purposes. As to strategic expectations, however, Mozambique made little, if any, appreciable progress in the reduction of its dependence on Soviet military advisors and assistance after the Nkomati Accord. In fact, according to U.S. Government statistics, Moscow's role increased. Amidst growing tension with the MNR after the 1984 assistance package, Frelimo leaned all the more on the Soviet Union and other Marxist states, especially Zimbabwe. The Mozambique foreign minister and, later, president, Joaquim Chissano, was unabashed about aid from communist states. In early 1985, he declared, in light of MNR advances, "Mozambique may require more and more assistance from countries belonging to the Warsaw Pact." He added, "We are going to remain a socialist country."[132] The Soviet Union quickly moved to meet Mozambique's needs.[133] The U.S. Arms Control and Disarmament Agency claims that this was part of a growing trend following Mozambique's signing of Nkomati. In 1981, Mozambique received $70 million in military equipment from the Soviet Union. By the time of the U.S. commitment in 1984, the amount of Soviet military aid had risen to approximately $260 million. In 1985, it was anticipated that those numbers rose still higher and remained steady through at least 1987.[134]

Beyond increased Soviet funds, the number of Soviet and Warsaw Pact military and technical advisors in Mozambique remained unchanged after Nkomati. Even more so, Marxist Zimbabwe sent a large contingent of Soviet-trained and armed troops (estimated at between fifteen and twenty thousand by the middle of 1988) to Mozambique.[135] The seemingly close ties between Moscow and Maputo were confirmed in a three-day visit by the Mozambique president to the USSR in March 1986. Soviet President Mikhail Gorbachev and President Samora Machel confirmed, among other things, their strong support for the Marxist regime in Angola against UNITA.[136] A western observer appropriately summed up the situation just before the March meeting: "The Mozambican government remains more dependent than ever for its survival on Soviet and allied military aid."[137] In short, institutionalism would expect aid termination, not preservation, for Mozambique, especially when compared to the South Africa case.

CONCLUSION

This chapter focused on a simple puzzle: why did the United States end commitments to an ardent anticommunist ally in South Africa and sustain similar pledges to a neighboring Marxist regime in Mozambique during the mid-1980s? Through counterfactual evidence and process tracing, I demonstrated that domestic institutionalism and realism offer less than

Table 4.1. Humanitarian norms by decision point: The U.S.-African cases

Congressional decision point	Illiberal behavior	Activist pressure	Commitment outcome
South Africa (1977–84)	Yes/No	Yes (information only)	Preserved
South Africa (1985)	Yes	Yes (public opinion)	Terminated
South Africa (mid-1986)	Yes	Yes	Terminated
Mozambique (1985–87)	No (dispersed responsibility)	Yes	Preserved

satisfactory explanations. Domestic institutionalism anticipated outcomes that were the opposite of what actually occurred. Realism, likewise, offers no leverage on the reasons for U.S. desertion of South Africa. While realist predictions, indeed, hold for Mozambique in isolation, the theory falters when U.S. relations with South Africa and Mozambique are considered in tandem.

Humanitarian norms offer a better argument. I found that congressional human rights concerns drove the U.S. policy on South Africa. As demonstrated by table 4.1, the explanatory leverage of humanitarian norms expands all the more when we assess the various decision points across both cases. The argument expects termination in instances when *both* illiberal steps by the South African government *and* activist group pressure converge.

The ebb and flow of U.S. commitment steps followed this pattern. Specifically, sanctions in mid-1985 and mid-1986 came amidst the simultaneous occurrence of illiberal events in South Africa and FSAM pressure. The absence of one or the other of these factors explains why Congress did not terminate pledges in the late 1970s or early 1980s. South Africa initiated modest democratic reforms in the early 1980s that yielded a wait-and-see attitude in Congress. Even more pronounced in this period, information activists failed to generate congressional action. As expected in cases perceived as vital to security goals, it generally takes at least some form of public opinion support (garnered here by the FSAM) for activists to influence policy. The next chapter brings this to light all the more.

Partner behavior and interest group convergence proved critical to explaining U.S. commitment consistency in the case of Mozambique as well. A large coalition of anti-Mozambique activists engaged Congress around humanitarian and freedom fighter values beginning in late 1985. The activist effort to alter U.S. commitments failed, however, due to developments on the ground inside Mozambique. Namely, atrocities promulgated by the MNR against innocent civilians left the Mozambique resistance with a far from freedom-loving image in the U.S. Congress. As demonstrated by the Wells nomination, the legislative coalition against aid to Mozambique collapsed. In this case, Congress chose the lesser of two evils and elected to sustain pledges to the Marxist regime in Maputo.

[5]

Human Rights and Vital Security

This chapter focuses on humanitarian norms in cases where partners are believed to be especially vital, contrasting decisions by the United States to terminate aid to Turkey, Guatemala, and El Salvador with Washington's preservation of military assistance to South Korea, the Philippines, and Greece. Many of these latter cases are mentioned by critics as evidence that human rights matter little in great power politics. This chapter demonstrates, though, that under the conditions discussed in chapter 1, humanitarian norms played a critical role in all of these vital relationships. Above all else, the importance of both liberalizing developments and the nature of activist pressure come into sharp relief.

U.S. RELATIONS WITH SOUTH KOREA AND THE PHILIPPINES

South Korea and the Philippines were longstanding U.S. allies in the Cold War. Their perceived value to the United States was largely geostrategic. The 1952 Mutual Security Assistance Act that established the executive-legislative mechanism for providing countries with military assistance in the battle against communism was called into being by the Korean War. The United States was determined to protect states in the developing world against Soviet bloc aggression. Not surprisingly, South Korea quickly became one of the leading recipients of aid, with Seoul collecting nearly $13 billion in military and economic assistance by the late 1970s.[1] The Philippines represented another major aid recipient, signing a Mutual Defense Assistance Agreement (MDAA) with Washington in 1947. In return for U.S. assistance (approximately $876 million between 1946 and 1976), the Philippines served as a major outpost for the U.S. military in

Asia. It housed sixteen U.S. military bases, including the Clark Airfield and Subic Bay Naval Base. These outposts provided the best geostrategic location for the United States to act quickly in Southeast Asia, an advantage not afforded by other U.S. bases in Guam, Japan, and Hawaii due to their greater distance from the region.[2]

Like other allies of the United States in the developing world during the Cold War, South Korea and the Philippines faced growing internal political turmoil that eventually led to repressive, nondemocratic regimes by the 1970s. Until 1972, the Philippines was a relatively free but unstable democratic state. The situation worsened over time. As a result of deep and highly volatile ideological cleavages, the government faced daily bombings and work stoppages by the early 1970s. As the disorder reached crisis levels, President Ferdinand Marcos imposed martial law in 1972. It was the beginning of almost fourteen years of uninterrupted state-led oppression, including political arrests with long detentions, instances of torture, and summary executions. In the first few years of the martial law regime, approximately fifty thousand people were arrested for political reasons. Between 1972 and 1979, 250 demonstrations against the government occurred. Thirty-three of those ended with beatings and gun-fire from security forces.[3] By 1984, Fred Poole and Max Vanzi estimated that one hundred thousand civilians had died since 1972 in the battles between security forces and guerrillas; the Marcos regime became particularly infamous for its brutal treatment of prisoners: "Torture, rape and murder had become so prevalent in these new detention areas that the Philippines had moved toward the top of Amnesty International's list."[4]

The story of South Korea followed a similar trajectory, though with an even longer period of repressive rule. After the brutal government of Syngman Rhee fell during the widespread student protests of 1960, Korea's short-lived experiment with democracy over the next year ended with a military coup by General Park Chung-Hee in 1961. Under pressure from the United States, Park civilianized the regime and won consecutive rounds of relatively free presidential elections in 1963 and 1967. The 1971 elections brought a narrow victory for Park, however. Combined with concerns about the drawdown of U.S. troops under the Nixon Doctrine and U.S. normalization of relations with China, Park feared internal political problems and imposed martial law in 1972.[5] Extensive political repression followed. Most scholars agree that thousands of citizens "disappeared," and many thousands more faced torture at the hands of the regime. The most brutal violence was prosecuted against students, intellectuals, and religious leaders.[6] Abuses increased further when the Park regime became the victim of a coup by General Chun Doo Hwan.

[145]

Chun declared his commitment to martial law in 1980 amidst a growing democratic impulse in South Korean society. He imposed censorship on the press and closed the universities in South Korea. Under his rule, reports emerged of numerous police massacres, including the suppression of demonstrations in Kwangju in 1980 in which several hundred protestors were killed. Arrests of political opponents were common as well. In 1986, approximately thirty-four hundred people were arrested for political activities as part of a major government crackdown against student organizations.[7]

In both the Philippines and South Korean cases, human rights NGOs issued reports on developments and pressed the U.S. government to take action at numerous junctures throughout the 1970s and 1980s. With respect to the Philippines, Amnesty International (AI) and the International Commission of Jurists (ICJ) produced reports in 1976 and 1977, respectively. The Friends of the Filipino People and the Association of Major Religious Superiors in the Philippines also published reports around the same time. Each gave case-by-case details of human rights abuses in the Philippines. AI, ICJ, the International Committee of the Red Cross, and the United Church of Christ also published reports in the early 1980s.[8] The AI report in 1982 presented details of torture at eighty-four different prisons. It also pointed out that, with closer ties between the Marcos regime and the new Reagan administration, public summary executions in the Philippines increased threefold.[9] South Korea saw similar NGO activity. AI sent a mission and published a scathing report on martial law under Park in 1974. A representative from the mission also testified before Congress. The National Council of Churches published information on attacks directed against Protestant churches in South Korea. Human Rights Watch published a report in 1986 on the Chun regime.[10]

The United States government, especially Congress, was not entirely unresponsive to these events and reports. Congress took its most definitive action against South Korea. It cut the military assistance request for 1975 by more than a third and later withheld $20 million of the remaining aid for human rights reasons. It also reduced the ceilings on security assistance from 1976 through 1978.[11] On the latter, the House International Affairs Committee justified its action "because of the gross violations of human rights which continue in South Korea."[12] Congress also protested human rights abuses in Korea through various resolutions in the early 1980s coinciding with the close embrace of the Chun regime by the Reagan administration.[13] In the Philippines case, in 1977 Congress cut military assistance in half over the loud objections of the Carter administration. As repression increased in the early 1980s, Congress cut assistance again and passed several resolutions calling for an end to abuses and the beginning of a transition to democracy.[14]

Beyond these moves, strategic considerations dominated legislative and executive policy. One U.S. administration after another boldly announced that aid to both countries would not be terminated. Secretary of State Cyrus Vance said in 1977, for example, that "whatever the human rights violations" in the Philippines, the United States would not terminate aid because of "overriding security considerations."[15] Similarly, Ronald McLaurin and Chung-in Moon observed that despite all of the questions about Korean internal politics, "remarkably, for almost the whole of the period since World War II, security has been the dominant factor in U.S.-Korean relations."[16] In the end, Congress followed the same line. Military assistance levels tell the story: regardless of human rights pressure from activists as well as congressional complaints and measures to trim assistance, Congress approved major amounts of aid to both Korea and the Philippines during the period that human rights abuses were occurring.[17]

U.S. RELATIONS WITH GREECE AND TURKEY

In isolation, the Philippines and South Korea might convince one of the efficacy of the conventional wisdom discussed at the outset of this book. Other vital security cases in the 1970s and 1980s help dispel this impression. In 1952, Greece and Turkey joined the North Atlantic Treaty Organization (NATO), becoming the anchors of the alliance's southern flank, a role made all the more important by Colonel Mu'ammar al-Qadhafi's decision to terminate U.S. and British basing rights in Libya in 1969.[18] The United States established military bases in both countries early in the Cold War. From these, the United States sought to counter increased Soviet activity in the Mediterranean region and Middle East during the late 1960s and 1970s (especially as Moscow drew closer to Syria and Egypt), support Israel during the 1967 and 1973 wars, and gather intelligence on developments inside the USSR. Not surprisingly, the United States provided Turkey and Greece with major amounts of military assistance throughout the first three decades of the Cold War. Military sales and grants ranged from $150 to $250 million annually.[19]

Those commitments ran into difficult times in the 1970s, however, just as the Soviet Union was increasing its activity in the Mediterranean region. In the case of Greece, Congress allowed the Nixon administration to continue security assistance. In the case of Turkey, Congress terminated all military aid in late 1974. The embargo against Turkey remained in place until President Carter lifted it in 1978. The humanitarian norms argument helps us understand the different outcomes in these cases.

The United States and Greece

From the end of World War II, the United States and its European allies consistently had deep concerns about the potential for a communist or Soviet bloc–friendly regime in Greece. The Truman Doctrine, so important to the stance the United States took at the start of the Cold War, was initiated to preclude Soviet adventurism in Greece and Turkey, after all. By the mid-1960s, Greek politics had become highly unstable. The left-leaning government of George Papandreou had been removed from power by the Greek king. Amidst expectations that the next presidential elections would bring a communist to power, the military took over the government in April 1967.[20]

As with the Pinochet regime in Chile, the junta embarked on a campaign to restore political order and root out communist elements within Greek society. In the name of combating communism, the junta imposed martial law, suspending the constitution and banning press freedoms. Approximately eight thousand Greek citizens, many of them former government officials, were arrested in the early days after the coup and sent to detention centers. Torture was a common feature in the government's interrogation tactics. The government also prosecuted leaders of various political parties before military tribunals; many were imprisoned or executed.[21]

Various NGOs reported at length on the abuses under the Greek junta. AI sent a mission to Greece in December 1967 and published a report in January 1968. AI sent a follow-up mission and published a second report in April 1968 that further detailed the breadth of abuses.[22] A study by the U.S. Committee for Democracy in Greece confirmed in the spring of 1968 that Greek political prisoners had been denied due process; many had been tortured.[23]

The most important report came from the European Commission on Human Rights (ECHR). Sparked by the AI reports, the Council of Europe commissioned the ECHR to perform an exhaustive review of the Greek situation. In mid-1969, it produced a four-volume report that noted widespread ill treatment of prisoners, stating that the government "officially tolerated" torture within state facilities. It paralleled AI conclusions, noting that "the cumulative evidence of systematic, routine torture is striking." In Europe, the ECHR report generated public protests against the

Greek junta, eventually leading to the expulsion of Greece from the Council of Europe.[24]

In the United States, Congress took steps against security assistance to Greece, but the nature of activist pressure was a major factor in explaining why unequivocal termination never came. The congressional initiative started with developments in the immediate post-coup period. In the days that followed the coup, the Johnson administration imposed an embargo on all large military items, an embargo that would remain in place for three years. Just after the coup, several members of Congress expressed the need for even greater distance from the junta. The State Department and the Department of Defense responded by withholding certain amounts of small weapons for a while, but those deliveries resumed in August 1968 due to national security concerns. Mainly as a result of the large weapons ban, though, Greece received only 40 percent of the aid requested by Johnson for 1968 and 1969.[25]

The Nixon administration came into office in 1969 determined to resume aid in full to Greece. It repeatedly sounded the theme of Greece's strategic value but recognized the need to placate Congress. "The military, from the JUSMAGG mission in Athens to the Joint Chiefs of Staff in the Pentagon were screaming, 'Turn on the aid. Is there any reason not to? None at all, except the knuckleheads in Congress,' " a State Department representative recounted of a National Security Council meeting on Greece in 1969. President Nixon quietly increased assistance and eventually lifted the ban on large weapons, but in the process he impressed upon the junta the need to move back to democracy in order to preserve aid. In 1969, he told Henry Tasca, his ambassadorial nominee to Greece, "We've got to restore military aid; as far as the rest is concerned [Tasca here understood Nixon to allude to Greece's constitutional future], make it look as good as you can—but the priority is military assistance."[26]

The Greek junta took several steps in response to external pressure that at least raised the prospect of significant liberal changes on the horizon. In late 1968, it held a national referendum on a new constitution that was portrayed positively in the western media. In the spring of 1969, the junta also eased several martial law restrictions in response to international pressure. In accord with U.S. suggestions and in order to appease critics in the Council of Europe, the military government made additional modifications to martial law in the fall of 1969. In 1970, the regime also released approximately three hundred political prisoners.[27]

The administration's attention to encouraging changes that appeared reformist seemed well-founded. The mild steps taken by the regime probably helped stave off congressional activism in 1969. In the foreign aid bill before Congress that year, the Senate Foreign Relations Committee voted to terminate all security assistance to Greece. By a narrow margin, the full Senate removed the aid ban in December, inserting in its place a "Sense of the Senate" resolution demanding that the administration "exert all possible efforts to influence a speedy return to constitutional government in Greece."[28] In response, the Nixon administration promised that aid would be contingent on a return to democracy. Tasca told the junta directly that full aid could be restored if the regime held elections by the fall of 1971, when Congress would next consider foreign assistance.[29]

Two things raised the ire of Congress in the next round of foreign aid legislation. First, contrary to congressional wishes and its own promises, the Nixon administration restored full military assistance in September 1970. It cited a number of strategic reasons for the move, most notably the desire to strengthen NATO's southern flank as leverage in negotiations with Moscow and Beijing at the time. In making the announcement, the State Department stated that it hoped a return to democracy would come soon but that aid was not conditioned on that outcome. Second, congressional efforts to restrict aid came as the prospects for liberal change in Greece faded. Soon after its 1970 release of prisoners, for instance, the regime publicly arrested another ninety individuals for political reasons. It also refused to allow the Red Cross into the country to study the treatment and conditions of Greek political prisoners. All of this presaged a sharp increase in political violence, arrests, and torture in late 1971 and early 1972. Compounding the issue for the U.S. Congress, a U.S. Senate study mission determined in 1971 that not only was the Athens government "unquestionably repressive," but the Departments of State and Defense were helping to sustain the regime in power.[30] In sum, Greece was not moving closer to democracy, nor was the Nixon administration upholding its promise to press the junta toward that end.

In August 1971, the U.S. House of Representatives voted to terminate all military assistance to Greece. The Senate Foreign Relations Committee adopted a similar amendment in May. The full Senate voted down a measure to remove the aid termination in October, and the measure became law. In the Senate floor debate, the twin issues of illiberalism in Greece and activist information dominated the discussion. Senator Vance Hartke noted, for instance, "Those who predicted that the present Greek regime would quickly move to restore constitutional guarantees have been proven wrong." Senator Claiborne Pell also mentioned incidents of torture and "objective reports," including the ECHR and Red Cross findings. Opponents of the measure cited strategic considerations including NATO stability and the need to prevent a communist regime in Greece. "I am strongly opposed to undermining the deterrent effect of the NATO alliance as I believe all realists should be," Senator James Allen said, "I had thought that only communist nations wanted to weaken and destroy the NATO alliance."[31] The Senate vote of 49–31 to uphold the aid termination crossed party lines.

The legislation passed by Congress carried a significant loophole: it gave the president the authority to waive the termination in case of a national security emergency. The waiver was necessary because without it, supporters of sanctioning Greece felt they could not get the votes to pass the amendment. The Nixon administration did not hesitate to take advantage of the loophole. Soon after the bill's passage in December 1971, the administration issued a waiver on Greek military assistance and provided the junta with $72 million in military assistance in the first half of 1972.

Unlike vital security cases in chapters 2 and 4, the policy process surrounding U.S.-Greek relations included no identifiable public opinion pressure against the commitment. This probably accounts for the lack of resolve displayed by Congress to end military assistance unequivocally. Greek Americans, in particular, overwhelmingly supported the regime as a means for restoring political order in their ancestral homeland. The hierarchy of the politically influential Greek Orthodox Church in the United States endorsed the regime, even distributing pro-junta literature to its members. The largest Greek organization in the United States, the American Hellenic Educational and Progressive Association (AHEPA), was also a strong supporter of the regime.[32] The position of Greek Americans was not lost on the U.S. political process. As Clifford Hackett noted, "The generally complacent or even supportive attitude of the Greek-American community toward the dictatorship was cited regularly by the State Department in oral arguments to offset congressional criticism."[33]

U.S.-Turkish Relations

The role of public opinion as a turnkey factor in the Greek case becomes all the more vivid in light of U.S.-Turkish relations, where the Greek-American community took a far different posture, which led to a far different outcome.

The story of U.S. termination of military assistance to Turkey revolves around the question of Cyprus. The island of Cyprus was recognized as an independent state in a 1959 treaty involving Turkey, Greece, and Great Britain. The treaty granted each of the signatories the right to intervene militarily—if necessary, unilaterally—in order to enforce the stipulations of the agreement. The vast majority of Cypriots are of Greek origin, with

Turkish Cypriots comprising a minority that into the mid-1970s lived mainly in enclaves in cities across Cyprus.

In order to keep the growing domestic unrest to a minimum, the Greek military junta began to revive the socially popular topic of *enosis*, or unification of Greece and Cyprus. In the summer of 1974, the junta planned and assisted a coup on Cyprus. Nikos Sampson, an avid anti-Turk and a strong defender of *enosis*, became president. Turkey responded swiftly. It invaded Cyprus on 20 July. Quick Turkish military gains followed. Sampson's government collapsed, and Glafkos Clerides, a moderate member of House of Representatives of Cyprus who was respected in the Greek and Turkish Cypriot communities, became acting president. The two sides agreed to a cease-fire on 25 July. Negotiations opened in Geneva to find a better long-term solution to the Cyprus problem.[34]

The Turks wanted to abandon single government in Cyprus, pushing instead a proposal for Greek and Cypriot zones under separate governments. Turkey infuriated the Greeks with a request that the Turkish Cypriot region comprise 38 percent of Cyprus, an area more than twice as large as the Turkish share of the Cypriot population. The Turks, then, decided to take advantage of their greater military strength and expanded the range of issues under consideration at the Geneva talks. When Greece balked and asked for more time to consider the issues, Turkey refused and threatened war. The talks collapsed. On 14 August, Turkey invaded Cyprus for a second time.[35]

Turkey launched a brutal campaign, dislocating nearly three hundred thousand Greeks—approximately half of the island's population—in an effort to create separate Greek and Turkish zones on Cyprus by force. Greek refugees fled across the cease-fire line into what was now, according to Turkish fiat, "Greek Cyprus." The Turks also unleashed a reign of terror on the Greeks in their path. Media and, later, NGO reports offered case-by-case accounts of summary executions; the rapes of women from the ages of twelve to seventy-one; the torture and humiliation of hundreds of Greek Cypriots, including children; and extensive looting and plunder. The Council of Europe concluded that Turkey had violated seven articles of the European Convention of Human Rights. Findings from both the Red Cross and ECHR were at the heart of the Council's determination of Turkish inhumanity.[36]

Unlike the case of the Greek junta, the Greek-American community exploded in defense of Greek Cypriots. According to one scholar, the lobby quickly assumed "mythical proportions," rivaling the Jewish lobby in terms of influence in the U.S. government.[37] The breadth of both its campaign and its appeal seem most vital to explaining the success of the movement's impact on U.S. policy.

Greek-Americans have traditionally lived in tightly knit communities with a strong ethnic identity. The Greek Orthodox Church as well as AHEPA and the Pan-Hellenic Union (PHU) served as the major sources of Greek-American organization in the United States. AHEPA was formed in 1922 and PHU in 1907. Before 1974, the central missions of both groups, along with several additional Greek-American organizations, focused on preserving Greek heritage. In this sense, AHEPA and PHU were much like other groups in American society at the time, comparable to the Elks or Shriners. These organizations, and along with them the Greek community as a whole, had very limited political experience.[38] As discussed in chapter 1, civic organizations like these can become the basis for major constituency movements. In this case, that is exactly what happened.

The first Turkish invasion of Cyprus in 1974 upset many Greek-Americans. They shared that frustration and expressed it, but they did not organize politically. The second invasion brought into being an extensive grassroots movement coupled with a powerful new lobbying organization in Washington, D.C. The latter was a political action committee, known as AHIPAC, formed by the American Hellenic Institute (AHI) in the days following the invasion. The Greek Orthodox Church served as the other pivotal organization at the center of the movement. From the top of the church hierarchy in the United States, Archbishop Iakovos used the tight institutional structure of the church to move its 502 parishes in the country to action. As the "the moving force in the Greek community," the church worked hand in hand with AHEPA, AHI, and PHU to establish committees at the state and local levels across the country. Along with gathering humanitarian assistance, these committees assisted by local Greek Orthodox priests organized a nationwide petition and letter-writing campaign to pressure officials in Washington to terminate Turkish military assistance.[39]

The speed and force with which the lobby organized in a midterm election year probably gave it far more influence than one might expect from an ethnic group that comprised approximately two million people in the United States at the time.[40] Another key feature of its influence seems to have been the nature of its message. In its direct lobbying through AHIPAC, Greek-Americans focused almost exclusively on the injustice and illegality of Turkish action rather than the mere defense of ethnic kin in Cyprus. In 1974 testimony before Congress, Eugene Rossides, chairman of AHIPAC, said in the opening line of his prepared statement, "The basic overriding issue, of course, is the Rule of Law," referring to the illegal use of U.S. military equipment by Turkey in its invasion. Archbishop Iakovos testified as well before Congress, noting that, as a nation guided by "moral principles" and a "code of ethics in international politics," the United States was deeply obliged to help end the suffering of the Greek Cypriots. Greek-American activists pressed the point that the Greeks in Cyprus were victims. A House of Representatives report from a study mission to Cyprus in the fall of 1974 echoed the same themes.[41]

These arguments supported by the grassroots movement of Greek-Americans found ready listeners on Capitol Hill. Congressman Ray Madden claimed, "There is no bill pending that I've gotten more calls and letters on." A staff member on the House International Affairs Committee noted that "Congressmen were regularly inundated with communications from Greek American constituents" regarding the arms embargo legislation.[42] Representative Tim Foley claimed that he had never been subject to a campaign as intense as the one that he faced during the first year of the Greek-American lobby's push on Cyprus. Even members of Congress with few Greek-Americans in their districts returned from the summer breaks in 1974 and 1975 complaining about pressure from the lobby. "If it did nothing else, the campaign raised the level of congressional consciousness about a faraway island with no special historical, cultural or political links to the United States," wrote Laurence Halley of the broad impact of the lobby on Congress. "But, as the *Congressional Record* makes clear, and as participants in the debates remember, the lobby did a great deal more than that, instilling in members a partial view of the origin and meaning of the Cyprus events of 1974 and a consciousness, whether real or feigned, that it was Greece and the Greek-Cypriots who were uniquely the aggrieved party and worthy of congressional support."[43]

Despite significant pressure on strategic grounds, the White House was unable to stop the congressional decision to terminate all military assistance to Turkey in December 1974.[44] The vote was close in both houses; the lobby's pressure seemed the deciding element. In fact, various drafts of the measure against Turkey were cleared with representatives of the lobby in corridors on Capitol Hill.[45] "If we had not been able to put together a compelling case in terms of law, policy, and morality, we would not have been effective," said Congressman John Brademas. "But . . . without the kind of support we got from the Greek community, our case might not have been sufficient to win."[46] Congress loosened the embargo slightly in the summer of 1975, but the vast majority of aid restrictions remained in place until lifted through a lobbying effort by the Carter administration in 1978.[47]

Tellingly, the Greek-American community had largely lost interest in the embargo by that point. As discussed in chapter 1, long-term vitality and cohesion in grassroots movements proves difficult, especially when the movement draws its strength from generally apolitical participants. Dissolution can also be accelerated by a lack of success in achieving the movement's goals. It seems that both of these factors plagued the Greek lobby. Despite the U.S. embargo, Turkey refused to alter its Cyprus policy. The apparent ineffectiveness of the embargo created significant divisions in the lobby over whether to continue the same course. These divisions among the leaders contributed to growing disillusionment among Greek-Americans who lost interest in the issue when the lack of success became manifest. Many quit pressuring Congress directly. In sum, the lobby faded dramatically, giving Carter political space to revoke the embargo.[48]

UNITED STATES RELATIONS WITH EL SALVADOR AND GUATEMALA

By the 1980s, the Cold War moved with great vigor into Central America and the Caribbean Basin. The Sandinista government in Nicaragua declared itself a communist movement and established ties with Cuba. Evidence of Sandinista assistance to rebel movements in El Salvador and Guatemala began to emerge. Concerned about further losses, Central America quickly moved to the heart of Washington's strategic planning.[49]

In the 1970s, El Salvador and Guatemala faced similar fates in terms of military assistance from the United States. In both countries, political violence had been on the rise under military rule. El Salvador's violence was marked by state repression aided by a growing number of right-wing death squads, the most prominent being a group called ORDEN. The primary target was a small yet effective left-wing insurgency movement, found primarily in rural areas. Spurred by increasing human rights abuses, fraudulent elections in 1977, and NGO pressure (according to reports by AI, ICJ, and IACHR), Congress terminated military assistance to El Salvador after an initial reduction in aid by the Carter administration in 1977.[50] In Guatemala, the military regime faced a similar insurgency as El Salvador. State-led repression was widespread, at a pace of 175 to 200 political murders each month. Following fraudulent elections in 1974 and 1977 and extensive reports from AI and other NGOs on human rights abuses, Guatemala responded to U.S. criticism by declining further military assistance; Congress later terminated aid.[51]

In the late 1970s and early 1980s, as the Sandinistas consolidated power and rebel movements in Central America increased their activity, the

Carter and Reagan administrations began to push to reinstate assistance to both Guatemala and El Salvador. In the case of El Salvador in 1979, Congress acquiesced. All the same, aid remained very low relative to administration requests and strategic needs until after El Salvador's 1984 presidential elections. At the height of the rebel threat to Guatemala, Congress refused, however, to allow aid to resume. Patterns of liberal/illiberal developments in both countries as well as activist pressure help explain outcomes in U.S. behavior.

The United States and El Salvador

Following fraudulent elections in 1977, the human rights situation in El Salvador deteriorated substantially. The new regime of General Carlos Humberto Romero unleashed a reign of terror on the country. Trade unions, members of the political opposition, and human rights monitors, especially the Catholic Church, became major targets for the government. Various groups reported extensive political assassinations and torture under Romero. While the left-wing rebel movement carried out some violence, right-wing death squads and security forces were mainly to blame. It appeared that certain segments of the military had a hand in security force operations and death squad activity as well. It was estimated that in 1980 alone, ten thousand civilians were killed, many at the hands of death squads. In 1981, the Catholic Church in El Salvador recorded 12,500 deaths, with 2,644 of those coming in January of that year.[52] Another source placed the number at approximately one thousand per month in the early 1980s.[53] These killings paralleled more high-profile cases, such as the March 1980 assassination of El Salvador's Catholic archbishop, Oscar Arnulfo Romero, an outspoken human rights advocate, and the murders of four American churchwomen in December 1980.[54]

Numerous NGOs drew attention to the violence in El Salvador. In December 1980, for instance, various groups flooded offices on Capitol Hill with letters and phone calls after the murders of the churchwomen. The Lawyers Committee for International Human Rights produced a report on political assassinations later the same year. In 1981, representatives from AI and the Catholic Church testified on Capitol Hill about the poor state of human rights in El Salvador. In 1982, the Washington Office on Latin America (WOLA), Americas Watch, and the ACLU produced reports that publicized political murders and torture that year. In 1984, America's Watch published yet another report on the situation in El Salvador.[55]

Scholars widely agree that the United States was able to resume and continue assistance amidst these conditions due in large measure to certain liberalizing steps that the Salvadoran government adopted—under strong pressure from the U.S. government—beginning in 1979. "To U.S. policymakers the way to save El Salvador from the fate of Nicaragua was to pour in security assistance, after General Romero's replacement by a less unsavory government," wrote Michael McClintock. In 1979, high-ranking State Department officials made two visits to El Salvador, requesting that Romero resign. He refused. With the blessing of the United States, a military coup finally removed Romero in October. A junta comprised of young, reformist officers in the military and three civilians took control. A cabinet was also appointed that included members of several opposition parties. The junta quickly admitted major human rights violations under Romero and pledged to take steps not only to curb abuses but also to restore a constitutional order and hold elections. The leading right-wing terror organization, ORDEN, was also dissolved.[56]

The new junta proved unstable. It was reorganized three times before the end of 1980. As violence continued and right-wing military elements vied for control of policy, many civilians left the government. Under pressure from the Carter administration, the military continued to court civilians for government positions, however. In the final reshuffling of the junta in late 1980 following the murders of the churchwomen, José Napoleón Duarte, a civilian who headed the Christian Democratic Party, was appointed president. Constituent assembly elections were also scheduled for 1982.[57]

With these moves away from the Romero regime and the rebels in El Salvador beginning the "final offensive," the Carter administration appealed to Congress to reprogram $5.7 million in military assistance for delivery to El Salvador in early 1981. In addition to strategic concerns, the administration's pitch to Congress detailed the junta's liberalizing steps, painting the regime as the best chance for reform. This seemed to resonate with congressional human rights advocates. Senator Christopher Dodd, for instance, later in 1981 referred to the need to aid "President Duarte and the moderate elements in the government."[58] Congress agreed to the reprogramming, and the military assistance agreement to El Salvador resumed.

President Ronald Reagan took office in 1981 and immediately made funding for the El Salvador government a top foreign policy priority. Human rights and democracy promotion took a back seat to defeating the insurgency with force. In March 1981, Reagan used his special authority to circumvent Congress in times of a national security emergency to provide an additional $25 million in security assistance to El Salvador. Bolstered by a major public relations campaign emphasizing rebel ties to Cuba and

Nicaragua, the Reagan administration requested nearly $70 million in military assistance for 1982. Congress feared that too much military assistance would send the junta the message that it could do as it wished with little regard for human rights. In late 1981, Capitol Hill approved only $23 million for military assistance and required that the State Department certify progress by El Salvador on human rights improvement and economic land distribution reforms every six months as a condition for continued aid. The certification gained bipartisan support. "What we are looking for is progress," noted Republican Senator Charles Percy.[59]

Under considerable pressure from Congress—especially after certifying progress in January 1982 in the face of several NGO reports noting widespread abuses—the Reagan administration slowly began to change course.[60] In his current capacity, Duarte proved only a partial benefit to the Reagan administration in early 1982. As "the legitimator of the regime," he provided a superb "civilian figurehead" to characterize the regime as "almost democratic and so distract attention from the bloodbath."[61] But, in order to gain congressional support for higher levels of military assistance necessary to win in El Salvador, true liberal reforms had become necessary. The 1982 elections emerged as an important first step in a policy by the Reagan administration that increasingly came to emphasize democratization in El Salvador.

The outcome of the Constituent Assembly elections surprised the administration. In what was determined a free and fair election, the right-wing party of Major Roberto d'Aubuisson captured a surprising victory over Duarte and the center-left parties. Under extreme pressure from the Reagan administration, the right chose a moderate Christian Democrat as provisional president. But D'Aubuisson's party controlled the constituent assembly, and it quickly began to reverse certain aspects of the agrarian reform plan announced in 1981—a reform initiative of great interest to the U.S. Congress. Under still further pressure from Washington, which was intended to "present a convincing appearance of progress toward democracy and peace," the Constituent Assembly committed itself again to land reform and negotiated a seven-point agreement with other Salvadoran political parties. The agreement included plans to draft a new constitution in 1983, followed by presidential and legislative elections in 1984.[62]

Congress reacted cautiously to these developments. Several members noted that the 1982 elections were a positive step. But, given the right-wing victory, the continued violence, and the reversal of the land reforms, Congress remained unconvinced on the whole. The Senate Foreign Relations Committee reduced assistance to its 1981 level of $26.5 million (the administration requested over $100 million). The committee cited concerns over the direction of Salvadoran politics under the new Constituent Assembly. The House Foreign Affairs Committee did not even consider assistance, opting to wait on developments in El Salvador. "If the situation is not more promising, we'll put it over until next year," Committee Chair Clement Zablocki said in 1982.[63]

In El Salvador, 1983 witnessed a major increase in rebel activity.[64] Panicked by the situation, the administration made its strongest appeal yet for military assistance. It requested nearly $140 million for the following year. The appeal and publicity blitz that followed was a disaster for the president. Congress stood firm. Of the $140 million requested, Congress approved only $64.8 million in military assistance for FY1984. Furthermore, of that amount, 30 percent was dependent on the successful prosecution of the parties responsible for the murders of the churchwomen.[65] Congress also removed the president's emergency draw-down authority, whereby the administration could distribute military assistance without congressional approval.[66]

The Reagan administration now found it crucial to place democratization and human rights reform at the center of its policy on El Salvador. A study commissioned by the White House from a panel of high-profile policy experts, including former secretary of state Henry Kissinger, brought this reality to bear. The commission's report found that aid to El Salvador needed to be increased by at least 40 percent to achieve victory. But that level of aid required "bipartisan support," which meant that Congress would have to see "improved military and political performance in El Salvador" before providing the requisite funding. "It was not just that you had to have an election or those guys on the Hill would never shut up," noted Cynthia Arnson of policymaker assessments in Washington around mid-1983. "It was the key to winning the war."[67]

The Reagan administration responded with an aggressive push for liberalization in El Salvador. On the heels of a July announcement by the Salvadoran government that presidential elections would be held in 1984, U.S. Ambassador Thomas Pickering publicly delivered a blistering statement on the human rights situation in El Salvador and demanded government reform. Pickering's comments were followed in December by a visit of Vice President George H. W. Bush to San Salvador. He delivered a firm statement for reform, saying that "if these death squad murders continue, you will lose the support of the American people."[68] Bush then presented the government with a list of individuals in the military and security forces that as leading human rights violators needed to be brought to justice.[69] From that point, the Reagan administration hammered home the theme that the upcoming election had to be free and fair, or else Congress would terminate military assistance.

After the general election in March and a runoff in May, Duarte was declared the winner in El Salvador's presidential elections. By mid-1985, legislative and municipal elections occurred as well. While the human rights situation took time to amend, the violations and death squad activity declined substantially after 1984.[70]

Duarte's election had an immediate impact on the U.S. policy process, especially in Congress. Duarte visited Washington shortly after his election and promised extensive human rights reforms and steps to continue democratization. Congress moved decisively. It approved an additional $70 million in military assistance for 1984 and $125 million for 1985.[71] "Before 1984, [Duarte] was seen as a tool of the colonels," said Congressman Michael Barnes, chair of the Western Hemisphere Affairs Subcommittee of the House Foreign Affairs Committee. "Then [he became] a major democratic figure, a hero of democracy in the region." Many other members agreed. "I have seen this country of El Salvador go through the travail and the bright pangs of a democracy," said House Majority Leader Jim Wright during the assistance debate. "Let us not let that democracy be stillborn, nor die in its infancy." Congress never challenged policy on El Salvador after 1984. Observers of the process universally agree that the liberalization of democratic elections was the key turning point. The vote for more military assistance "thus testifies to the importance of events in the region as seen through the filter of U.S. political values and hopes," wrote Arnson. "Duarte's election signaled for many members that political reform was progressing in El Salvador in a peaceful, evolutionary manner, an antidote to violent revolution."[72]

The United States and Guatemala

The importance of El Salvador's liberal developments to the course of U.S. military assistance comes into greater relief when set against U.S. relations with Guatemala. By the early 1980s, the leftist rebel movement in Guatemala had made substantial strides. With evidence of support from Nicaragua and Cuba, the movement was operating in all regions of the country, of which it controlled at least two; had gained the support of many centrist political parties; and had seen its membership swell to the point that rebel forces were more than half as large as the Guatemalan army. By 1982, the situation had become so desperate that some predicted a rebel victory in a matter of months.[73] The Reagan administration castigated the human rights focus of Congress and the Carter administration and sought to turn attention to the strategic issues at stake. With repeated appeals to counter the "Cuban-supported Marxist insurgency," Reagan tried to lay the groundwork for congressional renewal of military assistance. In 1981, the administration even used its emergency draw-down authority to provide Guatemala with $3.1 million in spare parts and other nonlethal assistance.[74]

These efforts, which included attempts to paint Guatemala as reforming, failed miserably with Congress, due entirely to unabated repression by the Guatemalan government with no indication of liberalization. NGOs consistently brought all of this to light. As noted already, scholars estimate that by 1978 nearly two hundred civilians were being killed per month in Guatemala for political reasons. As the 1980s began, that number climbed still higher. The collapse of the Somoza regime in 1979 contributed to the heightened terror. A new paramilitary organization, the Secret Anti-communist Army, was formed in order to tighten state control further and to prevent a Sandinista-type victory. Along with other security forces, the organization took special aim at intellectuals and religious elements in Guatemala. The entire law faculty at San Carlos University, for instance, was abducted and never seen again. Labor leaders, students, priests, and lay religious workers were murdered by the thousands in 1979 and 1980.[75] These events were a prelude to the next four years. Between 1980 and 1984, scholars estimate that security forces were responsible for the vast majority of the 440 towns, villages, and hamlets destroyed during the civil war. That violence also displaced nearly a million people and saw between fifty and seventy-five thousand civilians killed.[76]

Unlike El Salvador, political developments in Guatemala during the early 1980s offered little hope that liberal change was on the horizon. For instance, Guatemala held a round of presidential elections in 1982 around the same time that El Salvador did. Civilians, however, were not allowed to run—all four candidates were generals in the Guatemalan military. More notably, the regime denied the popular Christian Democratic Party the right to put forward a candidate. Finally, the fraudulent elections were, in the end, themselves defrauded. General Angel Aníbal Guevara, the choice of the most conservative elements within the military, won the election. But he was prevented from taking office when the sitting president, General Fernando Romeo Lucas García, led a coup and appointed General José Efraín Ríos Montt as the new head of state. Under Ríos Montt, human rights abuses increased.[77] In short, Guatemala showed almost no potential for liberalizing.

NGOs aggressively detailed the inhumanity under the García and Ríos Montt regimes. In 1981, AI published an extensive report on Guatemala.

It proved particularly damning to the Reagan administration, which had just begun its pitch that Guatemala was on the path to liberal change. The IACHR, ICJ, and U.N. Human Rights Commission also published findings on Guatemala around the same time. These reports all attested to the abysmal human rights situation in Guatemala. In October 1982, AI released a second report detailing the government massacre of twenty-six hundred Indians and peasant farmers under Ríos Montt.[78]

Amidst the incessant repression in Guatemala and efforts to win aid for El Salvador, the Reagan administration held back from pushing Congress too far on aid resumption. Given the "appalling repression" in Guatemala, Edward Best noted simply, "U.S. military aid to the military regime in its brutal campaign against some six thousand guerrillas remained politically impossible."[79] Consequently, at no point in committee hearings or floor debates did Congress consider the option of resuming aid to Guatemala through 1985. Military aid, in sum, was a dead issue brought about by the extreme and unremitting brutality of the Guatemalan government and the pressure of human rights NGOs.

CONCLUSION

This chapter demonstrates several things that reflect and build upon the argument developed in chapter 1. First, it is difficult for human rights to influence policy in cases where great powers perceive vital security interests, as seen in the discussion of U.S. relations with South Korea and the Philippines. This is important because it demonstrates that my argument is falsifiable, at least in part. At the same time, they also validate certain internal dynamics of the humanitarian norms argument. Namely, to the extent that human rights were a part of the discussion at all in U.S. relations with South Korea and the Philippines, NGOs and Congress pressed the issue onto the policy agenda. In fact, this was the case in every instance discussed in this chapter.

A second finding of this chapter is that, difficult as it may be for human rights to play a role in vital security cases, it is not altogether impossible. The role of broad constituency and public opinion support proves, as it did with the British-Ottoman and U.S.–South African cases, a powerful force even in security relationships perceived to be of the greatest importance. The comparison of the Greek and Turkish cases brings this to light. Illiberal developments in Greece raised the ire of Congress, but not to the point politically that Congress terminated aid. The nature of activist pressure played a major role here. In the Greek case, NGOs that rallied against the security assistance commitment did so with information alone. As discussed in chapter 1, it is difficult for this type of pressure, absent public opinion support, to yield legislative steps to terminate pledges when vital security interests are believed to be at stake. The parallel case of Turkey makes this abundantly clear. In this instance, Congress severed all military assistance. The nationwide grassroots campaign against assistance to Turkey by the Greek-American community represented the major difference between the two cases. Along with British-Ottoman and U.S.–South African relations, Greece and Turkey also shed new light on the Philippines and South Korea. Activist pressure came exclusively from information NGOs in the Philippines and South Korea cases. One can only wonder if the outcomes might have been different if public opinion pressure had been brought to bear here as well. Finally, outcomes in the Turkish and Greek cases can not be chalked up to the declining strategic value of either U.S. ally. As discussed above, U.S. officials believed both to be of vital importance in the 1960s and 1970s.

For all the problems that information activists face in vital security cases, they show surprising influence in U.S. relations with Guatemala and El Salvador at a point when Central America was at the center of Cold War politics. As seen above, the liberalizing steps of the Salvadoran government in the early 1980s allowed the military aid that had been terminated in 1977 to flow again. But continuing problems with human rights brought to light by AI, the ICJ, and others kept aid relatively low until a transition to democracy could begin. The importance of these same groups is all the more evident in the instance of Guatemala, where brutality by the regime and activist pressure made the resumption of military assistance a political nonstarter in the United States throughout the 1980s.

In sum, even in the most critically valued of security cases, the politics that surround humanitarian norms in liberal states play an important role in determining commitment outcomes. The next chapter addresses the broader relevance of this book for the study of international relations.

[6]

The Implications of Enforced
Humanitarian Norms

Most international relations scholars assume that human rights matter very little in the foreign policy of great powers. This book demonstrates that such assessments are too pessimistic. The prominence of humanitarian concerns in the strategic commitments of Great Britain and the United States, two of the greatest powers in history, serves as the main body of evidence to support this claim.

The Explanations

In the cases of core British and U.S. strategic commitments assessed in this book, humanitarian norms better account for outcomes than two prominent alternatives, realism and domestic institutionalism. Table 6.1 offers a picture of the evidence that confirms this claim. The tables here demonstrate the prediction (either "preserve" or "terminate") for each case study on the horizontal access and the outcome ("preserve" or "terminate") on the vertical access.

Cases are placed in the various boxes in accord with the combination of the prediction and outcome of each individual argument for each individual case. Domestic institutionalism, for instance, expected U.S. termination in the case of Mozambique due to certain steps that the Mozambique government took in violation of its economic aid agreement with the United States. Because the United States, in the final outcome, sustained the commitment, the Mozambique case in the domestic institutionalist table is placed in the "terminate/preserve" box. From this example, one can see that a given school offers a good account when the cases line up in the "preserve/preserve" or "terminate/terminate" boxes. On this basis, humanitarian norms hold a clear advantage.

Realism

Realism anticipates that changes in the geopolitical context surrounding British and U.S. pledges increased the costs of those pledges, leading, in the end, to termination. Table 6.1 demonstrates, however, that this was

Table 6.1 Predictions and outcomes in British and U.S. commitment cases

	Prediction	
Outcome	Preserve	Terminate
Realism		
Preserve	(1) U.S.-Mozambique U.S.-Peru	(2)
Terminate	(4) U.S.-Chile U.S.-Nicaragua U.S.-Argentina U.S.-South Africa Britain-Ottoman Empire Britain-Portugal	(3)
Domestic Institutionalism		
Preserve	(1)	(2) U.S.-Mozambique U.S.-Peru
Terminate	(4) U.S.-Chile U.S.-Nicaragua U.S.-Argentina U.S.-South Africa Britain-Ottoman Empire Britain-Portugal	(3)
Humanitarian Norms		
Preserve	(1) U.S.-Mozambique U.S.-Peru	(2)
Terminate	(4)	(3) U.S.-Chile U.S.-Nicaragua U.S.-Argentina U.S.-South Africa Britain-Ottoman Empire Britain-Portugal

generally not the case in most of the instances in this study. In relations between Britain and the Ottoman Empire as well as U.S. ties with Latin
American and African states, no major geopolitical changes transpired.
Though weaker from the start than Britain and the United States, commitment partners uniformly sustained a relatively stable level of strength
across the course of the commitments. South Africa and the Ottoman
Empire carried out successful regional military campaigns in the 1870s and
1980s, respectively. Likewise, in each instance, adversary power remained
stable. The Ottoman case might be the slight exception with the emergence
of closer ties between Russia and Austria in the 1870s. All the same, Britain
could have precluded this relationship from affecting the Balkan issue with
more definitive steps to defend Constantinople in 1876 and 1877. Yet Prime
Minister Benjamin Disraeli was prevented from doing so by a
humanitarian-minded Parliament reluctant to authorize any moves that
even remotely appeared to be in defense of the "barbarous Turk." His Cabinet had to watch anxiously, therefore, as Russia attacked the Porte with no
guarantees that London's imperial interests would be protected.

Finally, Britain and the United States perceived no new threats that
might have made standing commitments superfluous and worthy of termination. Russia remained Britain's primary rival into the late 1880s.
Though Germany stood as a new power in Europe at the time of British
termination, the Anglo-German rivalry that culminated in World War I began more than a decade after Britain's 1877 desertion of Turkey. Across the
U.S. cases, Cold War competition remained steady in Latin America and
Africa. Realists might contend that détente decreased Cold War tension, allowing the United States to end unnecessary pledges in Latin America. Yet
U.S. presidents during the 1970s never re-conceptualized U.S. grand strategy in Latin America away from the Cold War. They perceived the pledges
in this study to be important for U.S. security. Moreover, U.S. commitment
termination in Latin America was prevalent in the 1950s, 1960s, and 1980s,
when the Cold War was at its most intense. In the cases detailed at length
in this study, therefore, realism expected the preservation of commitments.
Yet in most instances, termination occurred, indicating that Britain and the
United States clearly responded to something other than geopolitical impulses in these desertion cases.

Realism was not entirely irrelevant, however. In isolation, the Mozambique and Peru cases match realist expectations. Like all of the other instances under review, the various indices of geopolitical change remained
constant from the creation of these commitments. As realism expects, the
United States sustained its pledges. Yet even here realism's explanatory
strength comes into question when we bring other cases during the same

time period into the analysis. Most importantly, as detailed in chapters 3 and 4, the structural factors to which realism directs us cannot explain both commitment consistency and termination to neighboring states occurring at the same time. Why it was that Chile, Argentina, Nicaragua, and South Africa were selected for sanctions while Peru and Mozambique were not needs explanation. Here, humanitarian norms enter the picture. Activist groups attempted to move Congress to terminate pledges to both Peru and Mozambique around prevailing humanitarian norms. Yet liberalizing developments in the form of Peruvian reforms leading to a democratic system of government and the inhumane brutality of the Mozambique resistance (attested to by activists) led the U.S. Congress in both instances to retrench to the status quo and sustain existing pledges. Despite realism's predictions on Peru and Mozambique, counterfactual evidence indicates that humanitarian norms offer a better explanation in both cases.

This does not mean that realism is irrelevant to understanding strategic commitments. Humanitarian norms by no means explain all commitment outcomes. At times, realism's strategic rationale explains why states end pledges. The United States terminated its commitment to the ABM treaty in part due to the end of the Cold War.[1] The Reagan administration ended economic assistance to countries, like Sandinista Nicaragua and Robert Mugabe's Zimbabwe, as they moved into the Soviet orbit. In the late 1890s, London ended pledges to Italy and Austria with its revocation of the 1887 Mediterranean Agreements. The reason for Britain's move lay in the need to reorganize resources for the newly perceived challenge of German, rather than Russian, power.[2]

Depending upon the perceived value of available partners, the strategic logic of realism also dictates how and when humanitarian norms influence policy. In chapter 1, I mentioned that in cases involving partners perceived as vital, policymaking authority generally moves into the hands of the executive branch in democracies; as a consequence, policy tends to focus more on power-related considerations. Humanitarian norms should matter less here. Cold War cases like U.S. relations with the Philippines, South Korea, and Iran seem to validate this. At the same time, the findings in this book demonstrate an important point: even in perceived vital security cases, the political processes surrounding humanitarian norms still account for outcomes. The nature of activist group pressure seems most crucial here. On some occasions (for example, U.S. relations with El Salvador and Guatemala in the 1980s), information pressure can yield policy change in vital cases. But as seen with the Ottoman, South African, Greek, and Turkish cases, moral entrepreneurs that go beyond information and rally public opinion support increase the chances that norms will affect policy. This sheds new light on cases like U.S. relations with the Philippines and South Korea, where activist pressure consisted of information alone. Power mattered here, but commitment preservation also makes sense through the lens of humanitarian politics in democratic states.

Finally, a quick survey of nondemocratic commitment cases paralleling those in this study indicates that realism's strategic logic played a substantial role in determining numerous outcomes. Britain, for instance, was not the only power that violated the 1856 Treaty of Paris in 1877. Russia did as well. While Russia had longstanding economic and nationalistic interests in invading the Balkans, scholars agree that St. Petersburg violated Ottoman integrity and invaded only after it was certain that other European powers, namely Britain, would not oppose it.[3] Similarly, during the Cold War, the Soviet Union terminated economic and military assistance to both China (1960) and Somalia (1977) largely for strategic reasons. In the former case, for instance, ideological differences along with Moscow's concerns about strategic factors in Asia and relations with the United States were important causes of the Sino-Soviet split.[4] Finally, evidence indicates that China deserted an economic assistance accord with Vietnam in 1978 due to increasingly closer ties between Vietnam and Beijing's communist rival, the Soviet Union.[5]

To the extent that power plays a major role in nondemocratic commitments, one finds justification, at least for now, to retain the analytical distinctions in this study and others between democratic and nondemocratic commitment politics. But more research is certainly necessary here. Like liberal democratic states, nondemocratic regimes rely upon legitimating ideologies. We see this with pan-Slavism in the Russian case and Marxism with its varying interpretations in the China-Vietnam and Soviet cases. The processes by which factors like these matter in ending pledges is probably quite different—and might, in fact occur less frequently—in authoritarian states relative to democracies. Further work here could uncover some interesting findings.

Domestic Institutionalism

Of the three alternative explanations, domestic institutionalism appears to offer the least amount of explanatory leverage over the cases of British and U.S. commitment termination. Institutionalism expects that democracies end pledges when they negotiate either an end to a commitment with a partner or when the partner itself unilaterally reneges on the pledge. As demonstrated by table 6.1, the opposite of these expectations occurred in all cases.

Chile, Nicaragua, Argentina, and South Africa stood as some of the most ardent anticommunist states in the world, firmly entrenched in the western camp and solidly committed to the strategic objectives behind their relationship with the United States. Yet Washington terminated aid to each country anyway. Moreover, the United States did so in each case unilaterally. Termination was anything but cooperative. The same scenario applies to British desertion of the Ottoman Empire and Portugal. Each of these outcomes appears especially puzzling when compared to the U.S.-Mozambique and U.S.-Peruvian cases, where termination seemed far more likely than the above cases. In short, it is clear that London and Washington responded to something beyond institutionalist factors in making decisions to terminate or preserve commitments.

The forces that this study points to as producing these outcomes prove more problematic, in many respects, to domestic institutionalism than realism. The reason for this lies in the fact that legislatures and interest groups, the theoretical mainstays of commitment consistency for domestic institutionalists, proved to be the leading sources of commitment termination for democratic states in this study. On the one hand, this might cast doubt on the entire domestic institutionalist paradigm. If legislatures and interest groups prove more disruptive away from the negotiating table than institutionalists argue, then can the support of a commitment by these forces at the time of commitment formation really drive credible commitment signaling and the higher degrees of cooperation that apparently exist between democratic states? While a valid question, the implied criticism is probably too extreme. Domestic institutionalism appears to provide a helpful framework for understanding commitment credibility, especially at the bargaining table. What seems necessary is an exploration of subsidiary conditions or alternative factors that institutionalists have not yet uncovered in order to account for commitment politics away from the bargaining table. I turn to this issue below following a discussion of the humanitarian norms argument.

Humanitarian Norms

As demonstrated in table 6.1, humanitarian norms offer a strong explanation of the patterns of commitment consistency and termination in the cases of U.S. and British foreign policy assessed in this book. To this effect, the distribution of cases largely falls into boxes (1) and (3), indicating congruence between the argument's predictions and actual outcomes for each case. The resulting picture is a powerful one. Captivated by humanitarian concerns, the usually foreign policy–subdued legislative branch forced the termination of longstanding, strategically valuable commitments at the heart of the major foreign policy initiatives of the two most powerful democratic states in history.

The argument, as such, increases our understanding of why and how humanitarian values and legislatures intersect to determine the policy of democratic states at specific points in specific cases relative to others. To this end, with legislatures as the main repository for liberal humanitarian norms within democracies, two individually necessary and jointly sufficient conditions spark legislative initiative to overturn commitments: a pattern (absent liberalizing steps or dispersed responsibility for abuses) of illiberal partner behavior and activist group pressure to overturn the commitment. Since legislatures naturally defer to executive leadership on foreign policy issues, the presence of both factors proves necessary to generate commitment termination. The absence of one or the other usually results in commitment consistency.

Table 6.2 presents the individual decision points from each of the case studies on democratic commitments in chapters 3 through 5. The table

Table 6.2. Humanitarian norms by decision point: All cases

Legislative decision point	Illiberal behavior	Activist pressure	Commitment outcome
Black Sea Conference (1871)	No	No	Preserved
Berlin Memorandum (May 1876)	No (liberalizing)	Yes (information only)	Preserved
Constantinople Conference (December 1876)	Yes	Yes (public opinion)	Terminated
Russo-Turkish War (1877–78)	Yes	Yes (public opinion)	Terminated
Chile (1973)	Yes	No	Preserved
Chile (1974)	Yes	Yes	Terminated
Chile (1976)	Yes	Yes	Terminated
Peru (1973–81)	No (liberalizing)	Yes	Preserved
Argentina (1974–76)	No (liberalizing and dispersed responsibility)	Yes	Preserved
Argentina (1977)	Yes	Yes	Terminated
Nicaragua (1977)	No (liberalizing)	No	Preserved
Nicaragua (1979)	Yes	Yes	Terminated
South Africa (1977–84)	Yes/No	Yes (information only)	Preserved
South Africa (1985)	Yes	Yes (public opinion)	Terminated
South Africa (mid-1986)	Yes	Yes	Terminated
Mozambique (1985–87)	No (dispersed responsibility)	Yes	Preserved

tracks the ebb and flow of commitments at different points across cases in light of the two main variables in my argument. By dissecting each case into decision points, I increased the number of observations in the study, enhancing the external and, especially, internal validity of the theory.

Examples from table 6.2 help to demonstrate the argument. At numerous points in the study, a British or U.S. partner took inhumane steps in violation of humanitarian norms. Yet in the absence of activist group pressure, Parliament and Congress refrained from taking action. Congress expressed its disdain for developments in Chile following state-sponsored crackdowns against unarmed civilians in 1973, for instance. Commitment termination, however, emerged only after a wave of NGO information flooded the U.S. legislative policy process. In general, group pressure played the undeniable role of moving the provoked legislatures to the point of action. Prior to that pressure, Congress sustained commitments, even when the partners took inhumane steps.

On the other side of the ledger, we find that partner behavior proved just as critical as interest groups to the course of British and U.S. commitments. In numerous cases, activist groups engaged, yet legislatures sustained commitments due to events in a partner state. At various junctures in U.S. relations with Argentina, Peru, and South Africa, Congress refrained from sanctions because of the partner's liberalizing reforms.[6] Other cases demonstrated that ambiguity over the violator of legislative preferences within a partner state also stymied activist pressure. Despite a budding campaign based on entrenched freedom fighter values within Congress, activists opposed to U.S. aid to Mozambique lost all influence on Capitol Hill with the 1987 massacres of innocent civilians by insurgents in Mozambique.

A pair of counterarguments and boundary conditions deserves mention. First, some might wonder if divided government in the U.S. cases made Congress willing to pursue its interests against a president from the opposing party. Perhaps, this better explains outcomes than humanitarian norms. Party dynamics might have contributed marginally to the willingness of the Democratic Congress to give the Carter administration more time to press the Somoza regime to reform and the Republican Senate's initial willingness to wait on the Reagan administration's policy of constructive engagement toward South Africa. But even in these cases, in the end, divided government appeared to matter little to the outcomes in this book. When Democrats controlled the executive and legislative branches in the late 1970s, Congress terminated dozens of aid commitments despite opposition on strategic grounds by the Democratic Carter administration.

The same fate eventually befell Nicaragua. Many of these steps also came during the first hundred days of the Carter administration, that is, the strongest point for any U.S. presidential administration. The Republican controlled Senate, likewise, eventually moved against apartheid, despite Reagan's strategic appeals against doing so. As the case in chapter 4 indicates, many Democrats in the Senate also showed considerable patience toward South Africa in the early 1980s for reasons related to the humanitarian norms argument.

Beyond these examples, divided government does not appear to offer any explanatory power over intra- and inter-case variation in this book. If divided government mattered, for instance, why were some partners singled out for sanctions, while others were not? For example, human rights abuses were prevalent in Chile, Argentina, and Peru in 1973 and 1974 (a period of divided government), yet Congress punished only Chile. Furthermore, Congress chose to sustain aid to Argentina in 1976 (divided government) and terminate it in 1977 (unified government). These latter two cases run counter to the conclusions an argument about divided government would generate. Finally, it is worth noting that cases in the early to mid-1970s should be easy ones for divided government. If there was any point in U.S. history when we would expect divided government to matter most, it would have been during the years of high legislative-executive tension resulting from the Vietnam War and Watergate. In sum, divided government appears to have mattered little in the U.S. cases assessed in this book.

A second point relates to democracies that are not great powers. Are democratic superpowers more ideological and, hence, more prone to crusades for things like human rights than weaker liberal states? This is an interesting empirical question that needs further testing, a point made all the more evident by the fact that most studies of humanitarianism in international relations focus almost exclusively on great powers. Historically, it is likely that there are fewer incidences of weaker democracies terminating commitments to other states, mainly because they have fewer potential commitments to terminate than great powers. It took the rise of the United States to superpower status before it became enmeshed in a web of security commitments with the likes of Argentina, Iran, South Korea, and Nicaragua. Not only were these commitments absent at earlier stages in U.S history, they were not matched in volume by other democracies during the Cold War.

Regardless of differences in volume, there is good reason to expect similar humanitarian processes in weak and strong democracies. Cases in this book yield some evidence here. Like the United States, most countries of

Western Europe sanctioned South Africa for humanitarian reasons in the 1980s. The story of Great Britain is especially close to that of the United States. A reluctant head of state, Prime Minister Margaret Thatcher, was pressed to adopt sanctions by a Parliament inspired by public demonstrations.[7] Other European democracies faced similar domestic protests that moved them to action.[8] Greece offers yet another example. While the United States refused to act, European nations sanctioned Greece for human rights abuses in the 1960s and 1970s. Following an extensive report on the poor humanitarian situation in Greece, European countries voted to expel Greece from the Council of Europe. Several countries, including Germany, terminated economic assistance, and many passed resolutions calling for the expulsion of Greece from NATO.[9]

The Greek case, in fact, raises an intriguing point. It might be that weaker democracies are freer strategically than liberal great powers to end commitments. Even if liberal great powers are more ideological than weaker states, they still must balance ideational impulses against perceived threats, which are often viewed as more severe or vital (perhaps, even, overblown at times) for great powers relative to weak powers. This draws attention again to the important yet largely underanalyzed issue discussed in earlier chapters about the sources of collective beliefs regarding the strategic value of states. More to the point, weaker democratic states might be more prone to overturn commitments if those commitments are perceived as important rather than vital. According to the humanitarian norms argument, activists need much lower levels of domestic political pressure to succeed in these circumstances. The Greek case seems to demonstrate this well. European democracies, who might have seen Greece as less vital than the United States did, took more strident steps than Washington largely on the basis of information activist pressure. In sum, while more testing is necessary, it seems safe to assume, at the very least, a high degree of similarity between weak and strong democracies when it comes to the promotion of human rights internationally.

THEORETICAL AND PRACTICAL IMPLICATIONS

This book deepens our understanding of the domestic and international processes that determine when norms matter. Humanitarian norms have received considerable attention from constructivist scholars.[10] But without understanding how, when, and if norms matter in tough cases, questions about the relevance of this line of research persist.[11] Other schools of thought can be helpful here. In its attention to democratic politics, for instance, liberalism offers rich insights into institutions, domestic processes, and ideas. In turning to this literature, this book has advanced our understanding of humanitarian norms. Far from irrelevant or peripheral to international politics, humanitarianism often frames and determines policy choices in important strategic cases. One cannot understand this without exploring the nexus between norms and institutions in democratic foreign policy. Several implications follow from this for international relations.

The first of these relates to suggestions for activists seeking to raise the profile of humanitarian issues.[12] First, windows of opportunity within the foreign policy processes of democracies are vital to explaining the influence of nonstate actors.[13] Events intersect with *a priori* norms and expectations to produce these opportunities. Consequently, activists should closely monitor both partner behavior and legislative responses to that behavior in order to know when campaigns for policy change can best be initiated. Without these openings, group pressure proves far less significant—at times, even irrelevant—to the policy discourse. Activists, therefore, should become intimately familiar with the country-specific concerns of different legislators. Especially with smaller partner states, activists can also influence and broaden the range of those state-specific concerns among legislators prior to crises by sharing with legislators and executive branch officials their own political risk assessments of certain states. Overall, this regular engagement with policymakers offers familiarity and mutual understanding, which will be helpful in times of crises with certain partner states.

The research here also demonstrates that once openings exist within the legislature, groups must choose the method of group influence—whether information or public opinion—wisely. While rallying public opinion is always more likely to assure effectiveness, this type of pressure is most critical in cases believed to be of vital strategic concern to the democratic state. The first imperative, thus, for activists is to understand the perceived value of strategic partners. The breakdown of vital and important partnerships in chapter 1 is a good place to start. Activists, in short, should be able to determine the role that partners are believed to play in the overall grand strategy of liberal states by answering how policymakers view the partners with respect to the partner's role in forward defense, provision of critical natural resources, or protection over vital sea lanes. If a partner is not of high value in any of these areas, then activists can likely influence policy using information alone. Not all information is equal, though. Activists will be most convincing when they produce well-researched reports that detail multiple and specific cases of abuses. Firsthand information, especially when verified by other groups, is critical for credibility. On this point, groups would also be wise to coordinate with one another, since multiple reports by different groups increase the chances of catching the attention of policymakers. This type of coordination is already common among groups, to some degree. It should continue and expand as well.

If a partner is deemed vital, the task for activists becomes quite different. Information about abuses will still be an important tool for educating potential constituents in building a public opinion campaign. But much more is needed here. Activists face tough choices given the costs, time, and historical contingencies involved in building public movements. Above all else, activists need to find allies with constituencies and understand the broader values and beliefs within society as well as the groups that can facilitate (or hinder) the possibility for building a public movement. On the former, links to national organizations, like the U.S. Catholic Conference (USCC) or the National Council of Churches (NCC), with some degree of local representation provide a good starting point. For activists in the United States, there might be opportunities to branch out beyond traditionally liberal constituencies like these as well. Many conservative church-based groups in the United States, like the National Association of Evangelicals, have also become increasingly interested in issues of international justice. Alliances might be possible here. Overall, targeting groups with pre-established constituencies could be the quickest way to begin local discussions, meetings, and town hall gatherings that spark the formation of a group mentality for action. To the extent that it can be generated, media attention will also help convince core constituents and assist in the development of more expansive social movements.

Whether appealing to specific constituency groups or the public at large, activists will find themselves bound, furthermore, by developments within partner states and broader social values. NGOs have little control over the former. The best they can do is to draw attention to events that justify their cause. As to extant social values, activists need to be judicious in this area. Some cases will be more conducive than others to building a human rights argument. In addition to ideas about strategic value, there may be other layers of ideas that activists confront that will be more or less helpful to mobilization. In the introduction, I discussed the deep pro-Israeli sentiments in many quarters of the United States that make public support for action against inhumanity by the Israeli government difficult. Attacks by Palestinian terrorist groups in Israel do not help, as they seem to validate these sentiments all the more. Unless they are willing to invest in the long battle to alter these impressions, activists might find it more resourceful to focus attention elsewhere. This does not mean that all hope is lost in these types of cases. If that were so, slavery, colonialism, and apartheid would never have ended. But the costs can be high, and the benefits for the overall promotion of human rights globally should be thought through extensively. Greater success might come with attention to other illiberal allies (for example, Kazakhstan, Saudi Arabia, and Egypt) of the United States in the war on terror where these types of extant ideational barriers are less profound. In fact, debates in the United States over the intersection of Islam, politics, and oppressive regimes could present some interesting avenues for activists to insert human rights into the policy process.

The second major implication of this book involves potential avenues for synthesizing domestic institutionalism and arguments, like the one in this book, that focus on liberal norms. Domestic institutionalists claim that democratic states possess unique capacities, relative to nondemocracies, to send highly credible commitment signals to potential partners. This, in turn, facilitates cooperation and hypothetically explains why democracies appear to sustain their commitments better than nondemocracies away from the negotiating table. More specifically, these outcomes emerge when socio-legislative coalitions within democracies endorse the pledges of its executive when negotiating with leaders from other states. Socio-legislative endorsement effectively sends a credible signal by indicating to possible commitment partners that alternative sources of political power within the democratic state are both behind the pledge and will even defend the commitment if the executive branch tries to desert it. In rational choice terms, socio-legislative endorsement effectively reduces uncertainty by extending the shadow of the future—a vital factor to enhancing cooperation under the anarchy of international politics.[14]

As demonstrated by this study, institutionalism seems to face problems, in some instances, when we try to extend the argument beyond the bargaining table to democratic decisions on whether to sustain or desert pledges. The heart of the issue here lies in the argument's single-play rather than iterated approach to democratic commitment politics combined with the theoretical expectation of legislative powerlessness and the lack of independent initiative once pledges are domestically approved.[15] As discussed in chapter 1, the difficulty of legislative foreign policy rebellion is indeed real. Yet, institutionalist models rest on the premise that once a democratic legislature commits to a pledge, it effectively forfeits all independent capacity to raise questions later about, to reconsider, to debate the efficacy of, or to altogether negate existing international commitments.[16] While institutionalists would probably contest this as an overly rigid interpretation of their argument, one is left theoretically with this picture of socio-legislative processes in the absence of systematic attention to how institutions contribute to policy change.

In order to address this problem, the theoretical reintroduction of democratic pluralism is a necessary first step. It also raises a host of new questions for further research. To start, at least three analytical premises are important as building blocks. First, commitment politics must be conceptualized as an iterative, ongoing process within democracies even after the commitment-making stage. All foreign policy, including most commitments, faces points at which legislatures possess the opportunity for debate and reconsideration. As noted, the U.S. Congress reconsiders all foreign assistance and trade privileges on a biannual basis. It also has an extensive committee system to monitor executive branch foreign policy. The British Parliament possesses similar authority, although it is less formally structured. Legislatures, in effect, preserve the core function of overseeing executive policy, which affords opportunities to intercede in the policy process.

Second, legislatures possess the capacity to develop new, unique goals and objectives relative to the executive branch, which might conflict with prevailing policy. This book suggests that as the main repository of humanitarian values within democracies, liberal interest formation is not only possible but also likely within legislatures, especially with respect to international partners. Future work needs to explore what elements of these normative interests might be present at the point of commitment formation and how they evolve over time as they bring legislatures to end pledges at some points. This book offers some steps in this direction. Third, when interceding in the policy process, legislatures possess and preserve the authority to change policy, even above executive will. The cases in this study serve as examples. Congress and Parliament applied pressure that led to the termination of longstanding commitments to important strategic partners despite the expressed interest to the contrary of the executive branch. More systematic work into why and when executives respond to legislative pressure, especially when it is indirect rather than via the adoption of new laws, is especially important here.

These three premises offer the foundation for a more systematic picture of democratic commitments from start to finish. Along these lines, this book demonstrates that democratic states prove reliable at sustaining their commitments because legislative foreign policy is institutionally difficult to produce and is facilitated, furthermore, when a commitment partner avoids behavior deemed illiberal by the democratic legislature.[17] Furthermore, the findings here uncover at least one liberal pathway to the termination of commitments: when illiberal partner behavior combines with interest group pressure within the legislative policy process. Other liberal explanations for credible commitment signaling, democratic reliability beyond the bargaining table, and commitment termination within this broader framework need to be developed (or refined in the case of domestic institutionalism) and tested.

One final point on institutionalism is worth noting. Some might contend that my suggested changes to the institutionalist framework effectively negate the basis for credible signaling at the bargaining table. This would be the case if, in fact, *absolute* certainty of a partner's future behavior was necessary for states to enter cooperative relations in international politics. Yet absolute certainty rarely, if ever, exists in international politics—and states cooperate all the same. To this end, scholars largely agree that the reduction, rather than termination, of uncertainty is enough to produce cooperation. Neoliberal institutionalist scholars, who focus on the ways that international institutions expand the shadow of the future in enhancing international cooperation, admit this point. As Robert Keohane, for instance, notes of international institutions, "By reducing asymmetries of information . . . international regimes *reduce* uncertainty." At another point he writes, "In world politics, international regimes help to facilitate the making of agreements by *reducing* barriers created by . . . uncertainty."[18] Even if we incorporate the potential of future legislative defection into the institutionalist framework, we can expect that initial legislative endorsement of commitments reduces uncertainty to the point of enhancing credibility and facilitating cooperation. In the big picture, little appears lost in this synthesis of liberal institutionalist and liberal norms arguments. One gains, instead, avenues for exploring how norms and institutions combine to create change and, in the end, a better understanding of commitments politics as a whole.

Finally, this book speaks to the heart of contemporary international politics. The United States is fighting the war on terror with the same type of commitments that it used during the Cold War. Similar to the tactics of the Cold War, weeding out terrorism means intervening in the domestic politics of developing world states and alleviating the conditions under which terrorists thrive. Foreign military and economic aid stand as cornerstones in this initiative. States from Pakistan to the Central Asian regimes of the former Soviet Union, especially Kazakhstan and Uzbekistan, have benefited significantly. As the war moves further into the Middle East, Asia, and Africa, other states and governments will find themselves as the recipients of new or revitalized pledges from the United States.

If history serves as any guide, the course of these relations will not be dictated by the executive branch alone or the perceived strategic context in which these pledges were made. Driven by the legislative branch, liberal states face great pressure under certain conditions, outlined here, to be true to the liberal humanitarian values on which they as states are based. It may appear to some that this could hardly ever be the case in the war on terror. U.S. threat perceptions seem so high at present that America might appear less liberal today compared to the past. But hints of liberal concerns have already begun to emerge—in congressional posturing, no less. In recent years, the Bush administration significantly reduced military and economic assistance to Uzbekistan due to congressional concern over the poor human rights record of the Uzbek government.[19] Congress also took decisive action in the aftermath of the Abu Ghraib prison abuse scandal in Iraq, passing a strongly worded resolution and holding extensive hearings on the matter. Similarly, Congress remains very concerned and active on the issue of torture at the U.S. military base at Guantanamo Bay, Cuba.[20] Most notably perhaps, Congress has expressed increasing concern over illiberalism in Pakistan. In July 2007, it passed legislation that conditions further military aid to Pakistan on future parliamentary elections and a general return to democracy. Questions have also arisen in Congress about how vital the Pakistani regime of Pervez Musharraf is to combating al Qaeda on Pakistani soil. Consequently, if Musharraf reinstates martial law or stifles the democratic processes begun with the 2008 parliamentary elections, the stage could be set for Congress to seriously reduce or end assistance to Pakistan altogether.[21]

To its credit, the Bush administration has defused some of this pressure with reforms following Abu Ghraib and by adhering to congressional pressure on Uzbekistan.[22] But these steps have been responsive and haphazard in nature rather than proactive and systematic. This is not new, of course, in human rights policy. Historically, human rights policy in liberal states has been marked by benign neglect and extreme, sometimes rash, outbursts against strategically friendly governments. Democratic executives generally take up humanitarian concerns only to the extent that they are forced to do so politically at home, usually by legislatures. All of the cases in this book testify to that. Furthermore, when humanitarian action comes, longstanding executive resistance to sociolegislative concerns often leads to the most extreme policy steps, like severing cooperation with allies. Pent-up frustration from executive stonewalling often pushes legislatures to bypass milder options and adopt the most draconian of measures.

Neither of these outcomes—neglect or aid termination as a first step—is the most optimal when trying to build a policy that provides an effective approach to human rights while addressing important security concerns. Neglect of humanitarian issues results in inattention to the imperative of responding to human suffering. It can also be costly. During the Cold War, unabashed support by the United States for dictators in places like the Philippines, Iran, South Korea, and Nicaragua fueled deep anti-Americanism that, in some instances, later produced unfriendly regimes (for example, Sandinista Nicaragua and the Shah's Iran). Damage to highly valued U.S. interests followed. Likewise, the sudden termination of ties with partners can often produce unnecessary strategic losses. The ending of military assistance to Cuba and Nicaragua arguably contributed to the loss of both states to Marxist regimes. Great Britain suffered strategic losses in the Russo-Turkish War in 1878–79 after ending pledges to the Ottoman Empire that could have been far worse than they were in the end. As discussed at length in the literature on sanctions, the severance of ties can also prove highly ineffective at promoting goals, like human rights.[23]

A more forward-looking and carefully planned approach to policy offers the best chance for avoiding the pitfalls of benign neglect and an overly hasty severance of ties. Foreign assistance pledges, like those to allies in the war on terror, exist in a context of broader cooperation with partner states. Those states have a stake in assistance as well. It is important to use that assistance and context as leverage. As the chief actor in foreign policy, the executive branch needs to take the lead here institutionally, recognizing that liberal humanitarianism is a natural feature of the U.S. system. In doing so, U.S. presidents need to establish a cooperative partnership with Congress, something that is uncommon in U.S. foreign policymaking and certainly not a hallmark of the current Bush administration. In working with Congress on these issues, the president increases the chances of avoiding pressure from the legislature to take overly hasty or extreme measures. Executive initiatives for human rights must be sincere and include as a last resort the potential severance of aid and other cooperative commitments. Without this, Congress is likely to see humanitarian initiatives as a ploy to keep the focus on strategic concerns alone. Impressions like this could lead the legislature to cut aid in damaging ways. At the same time, Congress needs to recognize steps toward liberal change and be patient in allowing executive branch policy to work itself out before rushing to take action.

This human rights policy initiative in the war on terror should include several specific components. The National Security Council and State Department should first establish institutional mechanisms to generate a human rights risk assessment for each partner in the war on terror. At present, the only initiative that comes close to resembling this is the State Department's annual report on human rights in aid recipient countries. Risk assessments should be much more robust than this. The United States models various strategic scenarios that calculate risks related to specific allies and potential future situations. The same needs to be done with respect to human rights and war on terror allies. Assessments should include contingency plans in case of future collapses of government or political turmoil. In this way, assessments provide a set of readily available, forward-looking policy options tailored to specific cases. If humanitarianism is as important an issue as this study suggests, then it deserves attention comparable to strategic considerations. Human rights risk assessments, hence, seem natural and necessary.

Second, at the initiation and renewal of assistance agreements, it is imperative that diplomats impress upon partner states the need for continued or improved liberalization as part and parcel of cooperation with the United States. This might sound intrusive—and might even result in being so. One way to counter this impression with allies is for the United States to offer greater economic and development assistance for regimes that liberalize. Washington needs to demonstrate that it is committed to its allies and their longterm needs. Robust aid programs developed together with partners demonstrate this and help provide a more stable socio-political foundation for U.S. allies to begin liberalizing.

Related to the first two points is another important aspect of policy. If the human rights situation in a given country declines, the executive branch needs to create a timetable of expectations for partner reform. The timetable should be created in consultation with Congress. All timetables should include short-term steps for correcting abuses (institutional arrangements to bring abuses to an end plus the prosecution of those responsible for abuses) as well as long-term goals, including the encouragement of elections. This roadmap for change needs to be clearly delineated but also flexible by taking into account the possibility of unanticipated developments. As part of these initiatives, officials should outline the potential ramifications in terms of aid restrictions and termination if steps are not taken in a timely fashion.

Though rare, the carrot-and-stick engagement with partners along these suggested lines were not altogether absent in the Cold War. The Carter administration attempted a policy of this nature in its dealings with the Somoza regime in Nicaragua. It held out the offer of continued military assistance in return for liberal reforms. For a time, Congress gave the administration room to operate. Unfortunately, Washington's long history of unquestioning support for Somoza reduced the credibility of U.S. threats of aid termination. Somoza was certain that the United States would stand by him—Washington always had, why would it change course now? The subsequent anti-American backlash against Somoza also radicalized Nicaraguan politics to the point that finding a moderate alternative to Somoza became difficult. The Marxist Sandinista regime might never have come to power if the United States had initiated a more forward-looking, nuanced human rights policy before the late 1970s. In sum, by the time President Carter arrived, it was already too late.[24]

The closest situation that one might define as a success case along the lines outlined above was U.S.–El Salvador relations in the 1980s. In this instance, the constant badgering of Congress, which included pressure from the Republican Senate, forced the Reagan administration to apply substantial pressure on the Salvadoran government for liberal change. Congress kept aid very low until human rights abuses decreased and the country successfully held presidential elections. Consistent administration communication of the American legislature's position to officials in El Salvador helped bring that outcome about. Human rights improved, and longterm liberalization began. Though the Salvadoran case still lacked foresight and executive initiative, something approaching the policy proposals that I suggest above succeeded here. Namely, executive-legislative cooperation (though reluctant on Reagan's part) pressed El Salvador to reform. Unfortunately, cases like this have been rare in U.S. policymaking. The need now is to make this type of approach a higher priority and more institutionalized part of Washington's relations with allies in the war on terror.

In this set of policy suggestions for the war on terror, one finds the central theme of this book: humanitarianism is a deeply embedded part of liberal democratic foreign policy. With humanitarian norms framing decisions of both action and inaction in many instances, cases that appear on the surface as normatively inconsistent are often, in fact, quite consistent. Humanitarian norms shape and influence much more than standard approaches to international relations give credit. By demonstrating this in great power foreign policy, this book fills a large gap in scholarship on both norms and human rights. No doubt, many questions remain. What are the sources of humanitarian norms? How do international humanitarian norms matter in the formation of domestic level norms that affect policy outcomes? Why do different democracies adopt certain humanitarian norms at different times? For constructivist and liberal scholars alike, this book points to the greater value of pursuing these questions. It offers, furthermore, an analytical model that delves into each of these schools of thought for new discovery. Ideas and institutions often work together in shaping outcomes in the foreign policy of great powers. The questions are many, and the field of international relations is ripe for scholarship that continues in this vein.

Notes

INTRODUCTION

1. John Gallagher and Ronald Robinson, "The Imperialism of Free Trade," *Economic History Review* 6, no. 1 (1953): 1–15.

2. For the deliberations in Britain, see Richard Millman, *Britain and the Eastern Question, 1875–1878* (Oxford: Clarendon Press, 1979), 357–79.

3. Henry Kissinger, *The White House Years* (Boston: Little, Brown, 1979), 656–57.

4. George P. Shultz, *Turmoil and Triumph: My Years as Secretary of State* (New York: Scribner's, 1993), 1123; and Chester A. Crocker, *High Noon in Southern Africa: Making Peace in a Rough Neighborhood* (New York: Norton, 1992), 76.

5. On Cuba, see Thomas G. Paterson, *Contesting Castro: The United States and the Triumph of the Cuban Revolution* (New York: Oxford University Press, 1994), 125–38. On Nicaragua, see Shirley Christian, *Nicaragua: Revolution in the Family* (New York: Random House, 1985), 34–118.

6. This includes pledges that might be part of, and essential to, broader security commitment relationships to specific states, like military assistance by the U.S. to NATO allies or partners in the war on terror. For examples of broader commitments in contemporary U.S. foreign policy, see Robert J. Art, *A Grand Strategy for America* (Ithaca: Cornell University Press, 2003), 132–38. On the role of security assistance, see William H. Mott, *United States Military Assistance: An Empirical Perspective* (Westport, CT: Greenwood Press, 2002), 32–33, 87–92.

7. Philip A. Ray Jr. and Sherrod J. Taylor, "The Role of Nongovernmental Organizations in Implementing Human Rights in Latin America," *Georgia Journal of International and Comparative Law,* supplement to vol. 7 (Summer 1977): 477–506; and Arthur Schlesinger Jr., "Human Rights and the American Tradition," *Foreign Affairs* 57, no. 3 (Winter 1978/79): 512–26.

8. Dan Morgan, "Hill Faces Delicate Decisions in Assigning Foreign Aid," *Washington Post,* 2 November 2001; Helen Dewar, "Senate Backs Order on Prison Criteria," *Washington Post,* 17 June 2004; and "Elections, Democracy and Stability in Pakistan," *Asia Report of the International Crisis Group,* no. 137 (31 July 2007), 21.

Chapter 1. Humanitarianism and Commitment Termination

1. Jack Donnelly, *Universal Human Rights in Theory and Practice,* 2nd ed. (Ithaca: Cornell University Press, 2003), 46–49.

2. Ibid., 44–45. See also Rhoda E. Howard and Jack Donnelly, "Human Dignity, Human Rights, and Political Regimes," *American Political Science Review* 80, no. 3 (September 1986): 802–3.

3. Donnelly, *Universal Human Rights,* 44–45.

4. Paul Gordon Lauren, *The Evolution of International Human Rights: Vision Seen* (Philadelphia: University of Pennsylvania Press, 1998), 15.

5. John Locke, "Second Treatise on Government" (1690), in *The Human Rights Reader,* ed. Walter Laquer and Barry Rubin (Philadelphia: Temple University Press, 1979), 65.

6. Michael Joseph Smith, "Liberalism and International Reform," in *Traditions of International Ethics,* ed. Terry Nardin and David R. Mapel (Cambridge: Cambridge University Press, 1992), 129.

7. For an economic rights argument, see Henry Shue, *Basic Rights: Subsistence, Affluence, and U.S. Foreign Policy,* 2nd ed. (Princeton: Princeton University Press, 1996).

8. Michael Freeden, *Rights* (Buckingham, UK: Open University Press, 1991), 15.

9. Joseph Boyle, "Natural Law and International Ethics," in *Traditions of International Ethics,* ed. Mapel and Nardin, 123.

10. Howard and Donnelly, "Human Dignity"; Michael Ignatieff, *The Lesser Evil: Political Ethics in an Age of Terror* (Princeton: Princeton University Press, 2004); and Richard Ashby Wilson, ed., *Human Rights in the "War on Terror"* (New York: Cambridge University Press, 2005).

11. Martha Finnemore, *The Purpose of Intervention: Changing Beliefs about the Use of Force* (Ithaca: Cornell University Press, 2003), 157; on empathy, see Nancy Sherman, "Empathy, Respect, and Humanitarian Action," *Ethics and International Affairs* 12 (1998): 103–19.

12. Finnemore, *Purpose of Intervention,* 157.

13. Ibid., 52–84, 70.

14. Ibid., 71.

15. Paul W. Kahn, "American Exceptionalism, Popular Sovereignty, and the Rule of Law," in *American Exceptionalism and Human Rights,* ed. Michael Ignatieff (Princeton: Princeton University Press, 2005), 198–202.

16. Finnemore and Sikkink, "International Norm Dynamics and Political Change," *International Organization* 52, no. 4 (Autumn 1998): 886.

17. Finnemore, *Purpose of Intervention,* 142–58; Neta C. Crawford, *Argument and Change in World Politics: Ethics, Decolonization, and Humanitarian Intervention* (Cambridge: Cambridge University Press, 2002), chs. 1, 2; and Richard Price, "Reversing the Gun Sights: Transnational Civil Society Targets Land Mines," *International Organization* 52, no. 3 (Summer 1998): 613–44.

18. Neta Crawford, "Decolonization as an International Norm: The Evolution of Practices, Arguments, and Beliefs," in *Emerging Norms of Justified Interventions: A Collection of Essays from a Project of the American Academy of Arts and Sciences,* ed. Laura Reed and Carl Kaysen (Cambridge, MA: American Academy of Arts and Sciences, 1993), 37–61; Ethan Nadelman, "Global Prohibition Regimes: The Evolution of Norms in International Society," *International Organization* 44, no. 4 (Autumn 1990): 481–97; and Finnemore, *Purpose of Intervention,* 66–72;

19. Audie Klotz, *Norms in International Relations: The Struggle against Apartheid* (Ithaca: Cornell University Press, 1999), 94.

20. For a good theoretical treatment, see Jeffrey W. Legro, *Rethinking the World: Great Power Strategies and International Order* (Ithaca: Cornell University Press, 2005).

21. Crawford, "Decolonization as an International Norm," 39–40, 42, 47–48.

22. Klotz, *Norms in International Relations*, 95–97.

23. Finnemore and Sikkink, "International Norm Dynamics," 901–4.

24. Finnemore, *Purpose of Intervention*, 58–66.

25. Many human rights advocates claim that the balance tips too often toward the strategic. See Samantha Power, *A Problem from Hell: America and the Age of Genocide* (New York: HarperCollins, 2003).

26. Jean-Jacques Rousseau, *The First and Second Discourses*, ed. Roger Masters and trans. Judith Masters (New York: St. Martin's Press, 1964), 95; Jean-Jacques Rousseau, *On the Social Contract with Geneva Manuscript and Political Economy*, ed. Roger D. Masters and trans. Judith R. Masters (Boston: Bedford/St. Martin's Press, 1978), 213; and Steven Forde, "Classical Realism" in *Traditions of International Ethics*, ed. Terry Nardin and David R. Mapel, 78–80.

27. Rousseau, *First and Second Discourses*, 160–61.

28. Immanuel Kant, *Kant's Political Writings*, ed. Hans Reiss and trans. H. B. Nisbit (Cambridge, UK: Cambridge University Press, 1970), 80. See also David R. Mapel, "The Contractarian Tradition and International Ethics," in *Traditions of International Ethics*, ed. Terry Nardin and David R. Mapel (Cambridge: Cambridge University Press, 1992), 190–91.

29. Judith N. Shklar, "The Liberalism of Fear," in *Liberalism and the Moral Life*, ed. Nancy L. Rosenblum (Cambridge, MA: Harvard University Press, 1989), 36–37. See also John Gray, *Liberalism: Concepts on Social Thought*, 2nd ed. (Minneapolis: University of Minnesota Press, 1995), ch. 10.

30. Keith L. Shimko, "Realism, Neorealism, and American Liberalism," *Review of Politics* 54, no. 2 (Spring 1992): 301.

31. Ignatieff, *Lesser Evil*, 8.

32. See, for instance, James Bovard, *Terrorism and Tyranny* (New York: Palgrave Macmillan, 2003).

33. Fernando Teson, "Liberal Security," in *Human Rights in the "War on Terror,"* ed. Wilson, 62.

34. Zeev Maoz and Bruce Russett, "Normative and Structural Causes of the Democratic Peace, 1946–1986," *American Political Science Review* 87, no. 3 (September 1993): 624–38; and John M. Owen IV, *Liberal Peace, Liberal War: American Politics and International Security* (Ithaca: Cornell University Press, 1997).

35. John M. Owen, "How Liberalism Produces Democratic Peace," *International Security* 19, no. 2 (Fall 1994): 93.

36. Kant, *Kant's Political Writings*, 90–91, 100.

37. Michael W. Doyle discusses this in reference to the republican government. See "Liberalism and World Politics," *American Political Science Review* 80, no. 4 (December 1986): 1160–61.

38. Kant, *Kant's Political Writings*, 100–102. Some might argue that the U.S. administrations of Bill Clinton (Bosnia, Kosovo, and Rwanda) and George W. Bush (invasion of Iraq, promotion of democracy) represent major contemporary aberrations. For both, I admit that liberal executives do at times pursue humanitarian ends. More telling and consistent with my argument, Clinton acted at both a point of limited strategic threat to the United States and, at least in the cases of Kosovo and Bosnia, when some strategic concerns about the integrity of NATO were at stake. Bush's invasion of Iraq was undertaken less for liberal reasons than as a response to concerns about weapons of mass destruction and the war on terrorism.

39. Alexander Hamilton, Federalist no. 71, in Alexander Hamilton, James Madison, and John Jay, *The Federalist Papers* (1788; repr. New York: Penguin, 1961), 433; Alexis de Tocqueville, *Democracy in America,* vol. 1 (1835; repr. New York: Vintage Books, 1990), 234–35; and Hans J. Morgenthau, "The Conduct of Foreign Policy," in *Aspects of the American Government,* ed. Sydney D. Bailey (London: Hansard Society, 1950), 112–13.

40. Nadelman, "Global Prohibition Regimes," 479–526.

41. Price, "Reversing the Gun Sights," 613–44.

42. Mark Peceny, *Democracy at the Point of Bayonets* (University Park: Pennsylvania University Press, 1999).

43. Kant, *Kant's Political Writing,* 90–91, 100; and Owen, "How Liberalism Produces Democratic Peace."

44. Lisa Martin, *Democratic Commitments: Legislatures and International Cooperation* (Princeton: Princeton University Press, 2000), 29–30.

45. Alfred Stepan and Cindy Skatch, "Constitutional Frameworks and Democratic Consolidation: Parliamentarianism Versus Presidentialism," *World Politics* 46, no. 1 (October 1993): 1–22; Juan J. Linz and Arturo Valenzuela, eds., *The Failure of Presidential Democracy* (Baltimore: Johns Hopkins University Press, 1994); and Mathew Soberg Shugart and John M. Carey, *Presidents and Assemblies: Constitutional Design and Electoral Dynamics* (Cambridge: Cambridge University Press, 1992).

46. Helen V. Milner, *Interests, Institutions, and Information: Domestic Political and International Relations* (Princeton: Princeton University Press, 1997), 40.

47. Michael Laver and Kenneth Shepsle, "Divided Government: America Is Not 'Exceptional,'" *Governance* 4 (1991): 250–69, cited in Milner, *Interests, Institutions, and Information,* 39. See also Morris P. Fiorina, *Divided Government* (New York: MacMillan, 1992), 112–13.

48. Richard H. S. Crossman, *The Myths of Cabinet Government* (Cambridge, MA: Harvard University Press, 1972), 31–33.

49. Kenneth N. Waltz, *Foreign Policy and Democratic Politics: The American and British Experience* (Boston: Little, Brown, 1967), 56–59. See also, for example, Milner, *Interests, Institutions, and Information,* 41.

50. Though I add the important component of perceptions, the separation of policy issues into the categories of vital and important are most clearly fleshed out in Stephen D. Krasner, *Defending the National Interest: Raw Materials Investments and U.S. Foreign Policy* (Princeton: Princeton University Press, 1978), 55–60, 70, 82–90. See also Barbara Hinckley, *Less Than Meets the Eye: Foreign Policy and the Myth of the Assertive President* (Chicago: University of Chicago Press, 1992), ch. 3; Michael C. Desch, *When the Third World Matters: Latin American and United States Grand Strategy* (Baltimore: Johns Hopkins University Press, 1993), 10–11; and Theodore J. Lowi, "Making Democracy Safe for the World: National Politics and Foreign Policy," in *Domestic Sources of Foreign Policy,* ed. James N. Rosenau (New York: Free Press, 1967), 295–331.

51. These perceptions largely appear to be collective ideas, rather than the product of objective standards. Many realists, for instance, did not view the vast majority of the developing world to be of much value by objective standards of power or geopolitics during the Cold War. But U.S. policymakers often did feel such countries to be vital and acted on these collective perceptions. For more on these specific beliefs, see the realism section below. On ideas and strategic partnerships, see Mark L. Haas, *The Ideological Origins of Great Power Foreign Policy, 1789–1989* (Ithaca: Cornell University Press, 2005).

52. For a similar discussion on geographic regions focusing on Central America, see Desch, *When the Third World Matters,* 10–11, 138–41.

53. Krasner, *Defending the National Interest,* 70; and Lowi, "Making Democracy Safe," 300–301.

54. Owen, *Liberal Peace*; Keck and Sikkink, *Activists beyond Borders*; and Crawford, *Argument and Change*.

55. Herbert A. Simon, *Administrative Behavior: A Study of Decision-Making Processes in Administrative Organizations*, 4th ed. (New York: Free Press, 1997), 3. For others on creeds, see Jack L. Walker Jr., *Mobilizing Interest Groups in America: Patrons, Preferences, and Social Movements* (Ann Arbor: University of Michigan Press, 1991), 10; and Sidney Tarrow, *Power in Movement: Social Movements, Collective Action, and Politics* (Cambridge: Cambridge University Press, 1994), 4–5.

56. Pamela E. Oliver and Gerald Marwell, "Mobilizing Technologies for Collective Action," in *Frontiers in Social Movement Theory*, ed. Aldon D. Morris and Carol McClung Mueller (New Haven: Yale University Press, 1992), 252.

57. For examples of this, see James Ron, Howard Ramos, and Kathleen Rodgers, "Transnational Information Politics: NGO Human Rights Reporting, 1986–2000," *International Studies Quarterly* 49, no. 3 (September 2005): 557–87.

58. Relative to realist arguments, in particular, AI and others in the 1970s and 1980s published numerous reports on human rights abuses in countries like South Korea, Iran, the Philippines, and South Africa, where the United States had vital strategic interests.

59. Clifford Bob, *The Marketing of Rebellion: Insurgents, Media, and International Activism* (New York: Cambridge University Press, 2005), 18–19; and Lars Schoultz, *Human Rights and United States Policy toward Latin America* (Princeton: Princeton University Press, 1981), 84–85. For an example involving the Red Cross, see Price, "Reversing the Gun Sights," 620.

60. Bob, *Marketing of Rebellion,* 34–35. For further examples, see Schoultz, *Human Rights,* 74–88.

61. Neil J. Smelser, *Theory of Collective Behavior* (New York: Free Press, 1962), 277.

62. Bert Klandermans, "Mobilization and Participation: Social-psychological Expansion of Resource Mobilization Theory," *American Sociological Review* 49 (1984): 583–600.

63. David Snow and Robert D. Benford, "Ideology, Frame Resonance, and Participation Mobilization," in *From Social Structure to Action: Comparing Social Movement Research across Cultures*, ed. Bert Klandermans, Haspieter Kriesi, and Sidney Tarrow (London: JAI Press, 1988), 205.

64. See, for instance, ibid., 206; Smelser, *Theory of Collective Behavior,* 284–87; Doug McAdam, "Micromobilization Contexts and Recruitment to Activism," and Bert Klandermans, "The Formation and Mobilization of Consensus," both in *From Social Structure to Action,* ed. Klandermans, Kriesi, and Tarrow, 131, 178–79.

65. Smelser, *Theory of Collective Behavior,* 47, 81–82, 287.

66. McAdam, "Micromobilization Contexts," 132–38.

67. Ralph H. Turner and Lewis M. Killian, *Collective Behavior* (Englewood Cliffs, NJ: Prentice-Hall, 1957), 58–63, 65–74; Klandermans, "Formation and Mobilization," 175–77; and McAdam, "Micromobilization Contexts," 133–51.

68. Smelser, *Theory of Collective Behavior,* 295, 111–12, 271, 292. For a good example, see also Eric L. Hirsch, "Sacrifice for the Cause: Group Processes, Recruitment, and Commitment in a Student Social Movement," *American Sociological Review* 55 (April 1990): 243–54.

69. Klandermans, "Formation and Mobilization," 181.

70. Ibid., 174.

71. Gamson and Modigliani, "Media Discourse and Public Opinion on Nuclear Power: A Constructionist Approach," *American Journal of Sociology* 95, no. 1 (July 1989): 3.

72. Ibid., 6.

73. Turner and Killian, *Collective Behavior,* 336–37. For other examples, see Smelser, *Theory of Collective Behavior,* 299; Ralph H. Turner, "The Public Perception of Protest," *American Sociological Review* 34 (December 1969): 815–31; and Hanspieter Kriesi, "Local Mobilization for the People's Social Petition of the Dutch Peace Movement," in *From Structure to Action: Comparing Social Movement Research Across Cultures,* ed. Bert Klandermans, Haspieter Kriesi, and Sidney Tarrow (London: JAI Press, 1988), 41–81.

74. Smelser, *Theory of Collective Behavior,* 301.

75. Ibid., 306; and Turner and Killian, "Collective Behavior," 336.

76. See, for example, Cynthia Brown, ed., *With Friends Like These: The Americas Watch Report on Human Rights and U.S. Policy in Latin America* (New York: Pantheon Books, 1985), 107–8, 5–6. One can contrast, for instance, an isolated incident of police brutality against an orchestrated campaign of torture and arrest of multiple citizens from targeted groups within society. For the sake of this study, the latter constitutes a pattern of illiberal behavior, the former does not.

77. Aaron Wildavsky, "The Two Presidencies," in *The Two Presidencies Reconsidered: A Quarter Century Assessment,* ed. Steven A. Shull (Chicago: Nelson-Hall Publishing, 1991), 14; Richard F. Fenno Jr., *Congressmen in Committees* (Boston: Little, Brown, 1973), 29–30; and Mathew D. McCubbins and Thomas Schwartz, "Congressional Oversight Overlooked: Police Patrols Versus Fire Alarms," *American Journal of Political Science* 28, no. 1 (February 1984): 165–79.

78. Several factors might account for the absence of activist pressure at any given point in time. As discussed earlier, activists might be preoccupied with other cases where they perceive a greater chance to gain the support of policymakers. Furthermore, activists may not apply pressure at a certain juncture for organizational reasons. Information-gathering requires gaining access to a country, interviewing large numbers of individuals, and preparing reports. The entire process can take months if not years. Public opinion interest groups, likewise, require considerable time to get the message out to interested constituencies as well as organize rallies, demonstrations, and other expressions of broad opinion. Sometimes these delays matter little. In other cases, they can explain why groups miss certain windows of opportunity to bring policy change.

79. See, for instance, David Mayhew, *Congress: The Electoral Connection* (New Haven: Yale University Press, 1974).

80. The lack of a good exit strategy from Vietnam mattered here as well, of course.

81. Keck and Sikkink, *Activists beyond Borders,* 16, 23–25; and McCubbins and Schwartz, "Congressional Oversight Overlooked," 165–79.

82. This resembles processes in Jeffrey W. Legro, "The Transformation of Policy Ideas," *American Journal of Political Science* 44, no. 3 (July 2000): 419–32.

83. On the special credibility that NGOs often carry, see Bernard C. Cohen, *The Public's Impact on Foreign Policy* (Boston: Little, Brown, 1973), 98–100; and Keck and Sikkink, *Activists beyond Borders,* 6–24.

84. Cynthia McClintock, *Revolutionary Movements in Latin America: El Salvador's FMLN and Peru's Shining Path* (Washington, D.C.: United States Institute of Peace, 1998), 210–14; and Thomas G. Paterson, *Contesting Castro: The United States and the Triumph of the Cuban Revolution* (New York: Oxford University Press, 1994), 125–38. President Eisenhower took this step even though he felt that Batista was the best strategic option for the United States.

85. John Kingdon refers to events that "soften up" a target for interest group pressure. See Kingdon, *Agendas, Alternatives, and Public Choices* (Boston: Little, Brown, 1984), 76–94, 173–86.

86. Kenneth W. Waltz, *Theory of International Politics* (New York: McGraw-Hill, 1979), 33, 171; and Barry P. Posen and Stephen W. Van Evra, "Reagan Administration Defense Policy: Departure from Containment," in *Eagle Resurgent? The Reagan Era in American Foreign Policy,* ed. Kenneth A. Oye, Robert J. Lieber, and Donald Rothchild (Boston: Little, Brown, 1987), 75–114. Two works that argue that developing states matter are Desch, *When the Third World Matters,* 6–9; and Steven R. David, *Choosing Sides: Alignment and Realignment in the Third World* (Baltimore: Johns Hopkins University Press, 1991).

87. Gerald R. Ford, *A Time to Heal: The Autobiography of Gerald R. Ford* (New York: Harper and Row/Readers Digest Association, 1979), 302. See also Chris P. Ioannides, *Realpolitik in the Eastern Mediterranean: From Kissinger and the Cyprus Crisis to Carter and the Lifting of the Turkish Arms Embargo* (New York: Pella, 2001), 33, 253–74.

88. Iain Guest, *Behind the Disappearances: Argentina's Dirty War against Human Rights and the United Nations* (Philadelphia: University of Pennsylvania Press, 1990), 181–85; and Joseph S. Tulchin, *Argentina and the United States: A Conflictual Relationship* (Boston: Twayne, 1990), 150.

89. Hansard, *Hansard Parliamentary Debates,* 3rd series, vol. 231 (1876): 214 (hereafter simply "Hansard").

90. U.S. Senate Committee on Foreign Relations, Subcommittee on Multinational Corporations, *Multinational Corporations and United States Foreign Policy,* Part 2, 93rd Cong., 1st Sess., 20, 21, 22, 27, 28, 29 March and 4 April 1973, 542–43, cited in James Petras, and Morris Morley, *The United States and Chile* (New York: Monthly Review Press, 1975), 29–30, 124–25. See also Henry Kissinger, *The White House Years* (Boston: Little, Brown, 1979), 656–57.

91. Quote from George P. Shultz, *Turmoil and Triumph: My Years as Secretary of State* (New York: Scribner's, 1993), 1123. See also Chester A. Crocker, *High Noon in Southern Africa: Making Peace in a Rough Neighborhood* (New York: Norton, 1992), 7–10, 76. For a discussion on the apparent exaggerations about strategic minerals, see Michael Shafer, "Mineral Myths," *Foreign Policy* 47 (Summer 1982): 154–71.

92. Crocker, *High Noon,* 239.

93. Kenneth W. Waltz, *Theory of International Politics;* and Hans J. Morgenthau, *Politics among Nations: The Struggle for Peace and Power,* brief ed. (New York: McGraw-Hill, 1993).

94. Waltz, *Theory of International Politics,* 161–94.

95. Glenn H. Snyder, *Alliance Politics* (Ithaca: Cornell University Press, 1997), 43.

96. Waltz, *Theory of International Politics,* 118–27, 164–75; Morgenthau, *Politics among Nations,* 183–93; and Stephen M. Walt, "Why Alliances Endure and Collapse," *Survival* 39, no. 1 (Spring 1997): 158–59.

97. George Liska, *Nations in Alliance* (Baltimore: Johns Hopkins University Press, 1968), 89.

98. Paul K. Huth, *Extended Deterrence and the Prevention of War* (New Haven: Yale University Press, 1988), 43; Glenn H. Snyder, *Alliance Politics,* 43–47; idem, "The Security Dilemma in Alliance Politics," *World Politics* 36, no. 4 (July 1984): 471–77; and Walt, "Why Alliances Endure," 160–61.

99. Martin, *Democratic Commitments,* 3; James Fearon, "Domestic Political Audiences and the Escalation of International Disputes," *American Political Science Review* 88, no. 3 (September 1994): 577–92; and Peter F. Cowhey, "Domestic Institutions and the Credibility of International Commitments: Japan and the United States," *International Organization* 47, no. 2 (Spring 1993): 299–326.

100. Martin, *Democratic Commitments,* 3–17.

101. Fearon, "Domestic Political Audiences"; Kurt Taylor Gaubatz, "Democratic States and Commitments in International Relations," *International Organization* 50, no. 1

(Winter 1996): 109–39; and Brett Ashley Leeds, "Domestic Political Institutions, Credible Commitments, and International Cooperation," *American Journal of Political Science* 43, no. 4 (October 1999): 979–1002.

102. Martin, *Democratic Commitments,* 64.

103. Robert O. Keohane, "Compliance with International Commitments: Politics within a Framework of Law," *Proceedings of the American Society of International Law* 86 (1992): 176–80; John S. Duffield, "International Regimes and Alliance Behavior: Explaining NATO Conventional Force Levels," *International Organization* 46, no. 4 (Autumn 1992): 819–55; and Abram Chayes and Antonia Handler Chayes, "On Compliance," *International Organization* 47, no. 2 (Spring 1993): 175–205.

104. Martin, *Democratic Commitments,* 21–80. See also Cowhey, "Domestic Institutions"; and Gaubatz, "Democratic States."

105. Fearon, "Domestic Political Audiences"; and Leeds, "Domestic Political Institutions."

106. Leeds discusses this as well as democratic institutionalist dyadic expectations for cooperation. See Leeds, "Domestic Political Institutions."

107. Arthur A. Stein, *Why Nations Cooperate: Circumstances and Choice in International Relations* (Ithaca: Cornell University Press, 1990), 31.; and Vinod K. Aggarwal, *Liberal Protectionism: The International Politics of Organized Textile Trade* (Berkeley: University of California Press, 1985).

108. Robert D. Putnam, "Diplomacy and Domestic Politics: The Logic of Two-Level Games," *International Organization* 42, no. 3 (Summer 1988): 427–60.

109. For trade examples of appeasing domestic constituencies, Vinod K. Aggarwal, "The Unraveling of the Multi-Fiber Arrangement, 1981: An Examination of International Regime Change," *International Organization* 37, no. 4 (Autumn 1983): 617–45; and Gilbert R. Winham, *International Trade and the Tokyo Round of Negotiations* (Princeton: Princeton University Press, 1986).

110. Keohane, *After Hegemony,* 215–16.

111. A lone AI report, for instance, helped bring about the end of U.S. military aid to Uruguay.

112. John Gallagher and Ronald Robinson, "The Imperialism of Free Trade," *Economic History Review* 6, no. 1 (1953): 1–15.

113. Ibid., 6.

114. Ibid., 7, 11. Gallagher and Robinson discuss informal imperial relations with the Ottoman Empire and in the Balkan region, which is of primary interest to this study.

115. Waltz, *Foreign Policy,* 204, 209, 210–21.

116. Ibid., 207. See also William H. Mott, *United States Military Assistance: An Empirical Perspective* (Westport, CT: Greenwood Press, 2002); John D. Montgomery, *The Politics of Foreign Aid* (New York: Praeger, 1962); and Edward S. Mason, *Foreign Aid and Foreign Policy* (New York: Harper and Row, 1964).

117. Mott, *United States Military Assistance,* 32, 87–92. William Mott describes security assistance pledges as "legal commitments," given their "treaty-like" arrangements under Mutual Defense Assistance Agreements (MDAAs). See also Samuel Hale Butterfield, *U.S. Development Aid—An Historic First: Achievement and Failure in the 20th Century* (Westport, CT: Praeger, 2004), 14–29, 44–50, 77–80; Vernon Ruttan, *United States Development Assistance Policy: The Domestic Politics of Foreign Economic Aid* (Baltimore: Johns Hopkins University Press, 1996), 62–63, 74–78, 92–93; William H. Becker and William M. McClenahan Jr., *The Market, the State, and the Export-Import Bank of the United States, 1934–2000* (Cambridge: Cambridge University Press, 2003), 28–34, 66–67, 77–89; and Jordan J. Hillman, *The Export-Import Bank at Work: Promotional Financing in the Public Sector* (Westport, CT: Quorum, 1983), 20–22. These sources dis-

cuss the strategic rationale for many commitments. The United States initiated security and economic development assistance during the Cold War under the same legislation that involved signed agreements with partners, committing Washington to unspecified amounts of funding until both sides mutually agreed to end the arrangement. Trade financing, like Export-Import Bank funding, came under similar terms.
118. For instance, Owen, *Liberal Peace.*
119. On the advantages of case studies for theory-building and the assessment of internal validity, see Gary King, Robert O. Keohane, and Sidney Verba, *Designing Social Inquiry: Scientific Inference in Qualitative Research* (Princeton: Princeton University Press, 1994), 226–28; and Steven Van Evra, *Guide to Methods for Students of Political Science* (Ithaca: Cornell University Press, 1997).
120. This technique was suggested in King, Keohane, and Verba, *Designing Social Inquiry,* ch. 6.
121. For methods on avoiding sampling on the dependent variable, see ibid., 128–37.

Chapter 2. Suffering Christians in British-Ottoman Relations

1. M. E. Yapp, *The Making of the Modern Middle East, 1892–1923* (London: Longman, 1987), 47–57, 69–70; and R. T. Shannon, *Gladstone and the Bulgarian Agitation of 1876,* 2nd ed. (Hamden, CT: Archon Books, 1975), 15–16.
2. Cited in Barbara Jelavich, *The Ottoman Empire, the Great Powers and the Straits Question, 1870–1887* (Bloomington: University of Indiana Press, 1973), 21–22.
3. Shannon, *Gladstone,* 28.
4. Reginald Coupland, *The British Anti-Slavery Movement* (London: Frank Cass, 1933), 86–135; and Suzanne Miers, *Britain and the Ending of the Slave Trade* (New York: Africana, 1975), 3–7.
5. James Walvin, "The Propaganda Campaign," in *Slavery and British Society 1776–1846,* ed. James Walvin (Baton Rouge: Louisiana State University Press, 1982), 51.
6. George Carslake Thompson, *Public Opinion and Lord Beaconsfield, 1875–1880,* vol. 1 (London: Macmillan, 1886), 73–84; and Richard Millman, *Britain and the Eastern Question, 1875–1878* (Oxford: Clarendon, 1979), 1–2.
7. L. Carl Brown, *International Politics and the Middle East: Old Rules, Dangerous Games* (Princeton: Princeton University Press, 1984), 46–56.
8. In order, Sir J. Mackintosh, the Marquess of Londonberry, Viscount Goderich and Lord Holland, cited in Hansard, 2nd series, vol. 7 (1822): 1650, 1652, 1730, 1171.
9. Hansard, 2nd series, vol. 7 (1822): 1651.
10. Brown, *International Politics,* 46–56; and M. S. Anderson, *The Eastern Question, 1774–1923* (New York: St. Martin's Press, 1966), ch. 3.
11. Shannon shows that in drafting the Treaty of Paris, British Prime Minister Lord Palmerston explicitly blocked efforts to make the reform promise of the Porte a quid pro quo for the support of Ottoman integrity and independence. He did not want to give Russia any excuse to invade Turkey. Shannon, *Gladstone,* 15–16.
12. Anderson, *Eastern Question,* 156–59.
13. Hansard, 3rd series, vol. 160 (1860): 604, 614.
14. Ibid., 622.
15. Ibid., 647–48.
16. Anderson, *Eastern Question,* 156–59; and Jelavich, *Ottoman Empire,* 23–24.
17. Charles and Barbara Jelavich, *The Establishment of the Balkan National States, 1804–1820* (Seattle: University of Washington Press, 1977), 53–64.
18. Hansard, 3rd series, vol. 171 (1862): 6–10.

19. Ibid., 12.

20. Richard Cobden in ibid., 129, 139–40.

21. Ibid., 140.

22. Following an 1866 revolt in Crete, the Ottoman government also reformed its government there to allow far-reaching autonomy. Jelavich, *Establishment*, 64–65; and Anderson, *Eastern Question*, 159–62.

23. Richard H. S. Crossman, *The Myths of Cabinet Government* (Cambridge, MA: Harvard University Press, 1972), 31.

24. Ibid., 30–40; and Kenneth W. Waltz, *Foreign Policy and Democratic Politics: The American and British Experience* (Boston: Little, Brown, 1967), 55–62.

25. Crossman, *Myths of Cabinet Government*, 33.

26. Ibid., 33–37.

27. Jelavich, *Ottoman Empire*, 19.

28. Ibid., 29–47, 87.

29. Ibid., 83–84.

30. "Greek Brigands in Turkey," *Times* (London), 19 January 1871; and "Turkey and Tunis," *Times* (London), 31 October 1871.

31. "Turkey," *Times* (London), 28 July 1971; and "Russia and Turkey," *Times* (London), 24 January 1971.

32. Hansard, 3rd series, vol. 205 (1871): 966.

33. Hansard, 3rd series, vol. 208 (1871): 313.

34. Activist groups did not form on the issue of Turkish Christians until 1875.

35. Hansard, 3rd series, vol. 204 (1871): 239–47, 840–64.

36. Ibid., 894–974.

37. Millman, *Britain and the Eastern Question*, 17–19, ch. 3; Alan Palmer, *The Decline and Fall of the Ottoman Empire* (London: J. Murray, 1992), 140–43; and Walter G. Wirthwein, *Britain and the Balkan Crisis, 1875–1878* (New York: Columbia University Press, 1935), 16.

38. "The Herzegovina and Turkestan," *Times* (London), 12 August 1875; "The Herzegovina," *Times* (London), 13 August 1875; "The Herzegovina," *Times* (London), 14 August 1875; "The Herzegovina," *Times* (London), 17 August 1875; and "Herzegovina," *Times* (London), 21 April 1876.

39. Millman, *Britain and the Eastern Question*, ch. 4; R. W. Seton-Watson, *Disraeli, Gladstone, and the Eastern Question: A Study in Diplomacy and Party Politics* (London: Frank Cass, 1962), 27–31.

40. Millman, *Britain and the Eastern Question*, 87–88, 92–93, 100–107.

41. Ibid., 58–59, 119; and Shannon, *Gladstone*, 36–42.

42. For coverage of a meeting that demonstrated this plus the nature of activist appeals, see "A Meeting was Held Yesterday by the 'League in Aid of the Christians in Turkey,'" *Times* (London), 20 July 1876.

43. Seton-Watson, *Disraeli, Gladstone*, 17, 36–37; and Millman, *Britain and the Eastern Question*, 15–18, 112.

44. Hansard, 3rd series, vol. 229 (1876): 1891.

45. Ibid., 1053. See also Seton-Watson, *Disraeli, Gladstone*, 34–35; and David Harris, *Britain and the Bulgarian Horrors* (Chicago: University of Chicago Press, 1939), 66–68.

46. Hansard, 3rd series, vol. 229 (1876): 1606.

47. Hansard, 3rd series, vol. 230 (1876): 267–68.

48. Seton-Watson, *Disraeli, Gladstone*, 37. It should be noted that domestic reform was not viewed by MPs and Cabinet members as a way to make the Ottoman Empire stronger. Rather, it was believed that these reforms would help sustain the Porte's control over its subject populations, removing all excuses for other states, especially

Russia, to interfere in Ottoman affairs. For examples of this policy in action, see Millman, *Britain and the Eastern Question.*

49. Harris, *Britain and the Bulgarian Horrors,* 20–23; Shannon, *Gladstone,* 22–23; and Seton-Watson, *Disraeli, Gladstone,* 51–54.

50. Wirthwein, *Britain and the Balkan Crisis,* 63–70; Thompson, *Public Opinion,* vol. 1, 310–13; and Millman, *Britain and the Eastern Question,* 123–25.

51. "Turkish Outrages in Bulgaria," *Times* (London), 18 July 1876; "The Atrocities in Bulgaria," *Times* (London), 1 August 1876; "The Atrocities in Bulgaria," *Times* (London), 2 August 1876; and "The Bulgarian Atrocities," *Times* (London), 15 August 1876.

52. Thompson, *Public Opinion,* vol. 1, 310.

53. See Hansard, 3rd series, vol. 230 (1876): 874, 879, 881, 1180, 1184–85, and vol. 231 (1876): 130, 139, 154. The unidentified speakers are, in order, Henry Bruce and Sir H. Drummond Wolff.

54. Hansard, 3rd series, vol. 231 (1876): 224, 198, 203, 214.

55. Derby noted the "excitement" in Parliament. Wirthwein, *Britain and the Balkan Crisis,* 70; and Thompson, *Public Opinion,* vol. 1, 345–51.

56. Seton-Watson, *Disraeli, Gladstone,* 80.

57. Shannon, *Gladstone,* 48. See also, Thompson, *Public Opinion,* vol. 1, 423–24.

58. Harris, *Britain and the Bulgarian Horrors,* 147–62; and Wirthwein, *Britain and the Balkan Crisis,* 74.

59. Harris, *Britain and the Bulgarian Horrors,* 147–62; and Wirthwein, *Britain and the Balkan Crisis,* 74.

60. Shannon, *Gladstone,* 54.

61. Hansard, 3rd series, vol. 231 (1876): 729, 745–46, 1088, 1096, 1123–25.

62. Ibid., 1108, 1140 and 1146.

63. Cited in Harris, *Britain and the Bulgarian Horrors,* 268–69.

64. Cited in Millman, *Britain and the Eastern Question,* 158. See also, Seton-Watson, *Disraeli, Gladstone,* 56–57.

65. Millman, *Britain and the Eastern Question,* 112–24, 165–66.

66. Cited in Harris, *Britain and the Bulgarian Horrors,* 269–70.

67. Ibid., 270–71; and Shannon, *Gladstone,* 68.

68. Shannon, *Gladstone,* 59–78, ch. 5.

69. Harris, *Britain and the Bulgarian Horrors,* 252.

70. Shannon, *Gladstone,* 147–48; and Thompson, *Public Opinion,* vol. 1, 387–99.

71. As part of their activities, Farley and Freeman kept up a spirited debate in the British newspapers. J. Lewis Farley, "The Wounded in Servia," letter to the editor, *Times* (London), 22 August 1876; William Wood, G. W. Gibraltar and Edward A. Freeman, "Turkish Atrocities," letter to the editor, *Times* (London), 28 August 1876; and Edward A. Freeman, "The Servian Sick and Wounded," letter to the editor, *Times* (London), 26 September 1876.

72. For example, see James Baker, "Atrocities in Bulgaria," letter to the editor, *Times* (London), 11 July 1876.

73. Seton-Watson, *Disraeli, Gladstone,* 83–85; Shannon, *Gladstone,* 57–89; Harris, *Britain and the Bulgarian Horrors,* 196–97; and Wirthwein, *Britain and the Balkan Crisis,* 78–86.

74. Shannon, *Gladstone,* 90–112.

75. Harris, *Britain and the Bulgarian Horrors,* 224–25; Wirthwein, *Britain and the Balkan Crisis,* 90; and Thompson, *Public Opinion,* vol. 1, 389–94.

76. Cited in Millman, *Britain and the Eastern Question,* 166.

77. Thompson, *Public Opinion,* vol. 1, 389.

78. Millman, *Britain and the Eastern Question,* 171.

79. Cited in ibid., 169–71. Other members of the cabinet spoke to the same effect; see 171–72.

80. Cited in Seton-Watson, *Disraeli, Gladstone*, 88, 308–10.

81. Millman, *Britain and the Eastern Question*, 173–74; and Seton-Watson, *Disraeli, Gladstone*, 91–92, 96.

82. Cited in Millman, *Britain and the Eastern Question*, 197.

83. See Gladstone's comments cited in Agatha Ramm, ed., *The Political Correspondence of Mr. Gladstone and Lord Granville, 1876–1886*, vol. 1 (Oxford: Clarendon, 1962), 1, 18.

84. Millman, *Britain and the Eastern Question*, 197–98, 208–13.

85. Disraeli was angry with Salisbury for the threat posed to British imperial interests. Lord Carnarvon, a cabinet member, observed in December, for instance, that Disraeli did not distinguish between "British interests and support of Turkey" and was intent on a British war against Russia to protect Ottoman integrity. See Seton-Watson, *Disraeli, Gladstone*, 131.

86. Cited in Millman, *Britain and the Eastern Question*, 212 and 209.

87. Ibid., 222.

88. Salisbury pleaded with Disraeli to sign the protocol, noting that if Britain did not sign and Russia declared war, the Cabinet would face Parliament in the politically unstable position of appearing as a friend to Turkey. Seton-Watson, *Disraeli, Gladstone*, 159–80; Millman, *Britain and the Eastern Question*, 254–79; and Wirthwein, *Britain and the Balkan Crisis*, 171–74, 195–205.

89. Hansard, 3rd series, vol. 233 (1877): 582, 601; Mr. Baillie Cochran and Mr. Bourke in 579–80, 589–98.

90. Cited in Millman, *Britain and the Eastern Question*, 270–71. Seton-Watson noted that the Parliamentary debate "undoubtedly influenced the decision to send him to Vienna and replace Layard." Seton-Watson, *Disraeli, Gladstone*, 180.

91. Hansard, 3rd series, vol. 234 (1877): 402–56.

92. Ibid., 457–72.

93. Ibid., 809–10, 932, 698.

94. Ibid., 664–781, 787.

95. Cited by Millman, *Britain and the Eastern Question*, 298.

96. Ibid., 375–461; and Palmer, *Decline and Fall*, 155–62.

97. Seton-Watson, *Disraeli, Gladstone*, 120–21.

98. Ibid., 233–427; and Millman, *Britain and the Eastern Question*, 311–402.

99. Cited in Harris, *Disraeli*, 269–70.

100. Millman, *Britain and the Eastern Question*, 31–36, 99–100, 232; and Seton-Watson, *Disraeli, Gladstone*, 92–93.

101. On Andrassy's deep distrust of Russia, see Seton-Watson, *Disraeli, Gladstone*, 141, 143, 269–70.

102. Ibid., 198–99; and Millman, *Britain and the Eastern Question*, 282–84.

103. Cited by Seton-Watson, *Disraeli, Gladstone*, 200.

104. Cited by Millman, *Britain and the Eastern Question*, 364–65. See also Seton-Watson, *Disraeli, Gladstone*, 107, 293–95.

105. Thompson, *Public Opinion*, vol. 1, 230–32.

106. Yapp, *Making of the Modern Middle East*, 7.

107. Wirthwein, *Britain and the Balkan Crisis*, 266–74.

108. Cited by Millman, *Britain and the Eastern Question*, 172, 167–68.

109. R. J. Hammond, *Portugal and Africa, 1815–1910: A Study in Uneconomic Imperialism* (Stanford: Stanford University Press, 1966), 80–82; Roger Anstey, *Britain and the Congo in the Nineteenth Century* (Clarendon, UK: Clarendon Press, 1962), 37–51; and G. K. Fieldhouse, *The Colonial Empires from the 18th Century* (New York: Dell, 1965), 350.

110. Anstey, *Britain and the Congo*, 52–56, 85–106.
111. Ibid.
112. See Anstey, *Britain and the Congo*, 162; S.E. Crowe, *The Berlin West Africa Conference, 1884–1885* (Westport, CT: Negro University Press, 1970) 24–27.
113. Anstey, *Britain and the Congo*, 36. See also ch. 3
114. Cited in Hammond, *Portugal*, 54–55.
115. Anstey, *Britain*, 40–87; Hammond, *Portugal*, 43–63; and Fieldhouse, *Colonial Empires*, 349–50.
116. Hansard, 3rd series, vol. 356 (1883): 1289–92, 1305; and Anstey, *Britain and the Congo*, 113.
117. Cited in Anstey, *Britain and the Congo*, 115–20.
118. Ibid., 121–32.
119. See Hansard, 3rd series, vol. 356 (1883): 1284–92, 1295–96, 1300, 1314.
120. Sir Charles Wentworth Dilke cited in Anstey, *Britain and the Congo*, 136.
121. Hansard, 3rd series, vol. 356 (1883): 1300–13, 1322–37.
122. Anstey, *Britain and the Congo*, 143, 144–46.
123. Ibid., 151–55, 159.
124. Cited in ibid., 159, 160.
125. Ibid., 160–67; and Crowe, *Berlin West Africa Conference*, ch. 8; and Jean Stengers, "The Congo Free State and the Belgian Congo," in *Colonialism in Africa, 1870–1960*, vol. 1, ed. L. H. Gann and Peter Duignan (Cambridge: Cambridge University Press, 1969), 261–92.

Chapter 3. Torture and Summary Execution in U.S.–Latin American Relations

1. Cited in James Petras and Morris Morley, *The United States and Chile: Imperialism and the Overthrow of Allende* (New York: Monthly Review Press, 1975), 124–25; Frank Robinson Pancake, "Military Assistance as an Element of United States Foreign Policy in Latin America, 1850–1968," Ph.D. dissertation, University of Virginia, 1969, 30–50, 72–73, ch. 5; and Lars Schoultz, *Human Rights and United States Policy toward Latin America* (Princeton: Princeton University Press, 1981), 212–17, 246. See also Paul Y. Hammond, David J. Louscher, Michael D. Salomone, and Norman A. Graham, *The Reluctant Supplier: The U.S. Decision for Arms Sales* (Cambridge, MA: Oelgeshlager, Gunn, and Hain, 1983), 141–42. Throughout the Cold War, the United States financed nearly all security assistance to Latin America by waiving debt, issuing grants, and subsidizing credit provided by U.S. financial institutions.

2. Pancake, "Military Assistance," 30–50, 72–73, ch. 5; Luigi Einaudi, "U.S. Relations with the Peruvian Military," in *U.S. Foreign Policy and Peru*, ed. Daniel A. Sharp (Austin: Institute of Latin American Studies, University of Texas at Austin, 1972), 38; and Lawrence A. Clayton, *Peru and the United States: The Condor and the Eagle* (Athens: University of Georgia Press, 1999), 179–81.

3. William H. Mott, *United States Military Assistance: An Empirical Perspective* (Westport, CT: Greenwood, 2002), 32, 87–92; Richard Grimmett, "The Role of Security Assistance in Historical Perspective," in *U.S. Security Assistance: The Political Process*, ed. Ernest Graves and Steven A. Hildreth (Lexington, MA: Lexington Books, 1985), 6–8.

4. Mott, *United States Military Assistance*, 32, 92.

5. Cynthia McClintock, *Revolutionary Movements in Latin America: El Salvador's FMLN and Peru's Shining Path* (Washington, D.C.: U.S. Institute of Peace, 1998), 210–14; and Pancake, "Military Assistance," 63–64.

6. For examples of how this influenced U.S. policy, see Pancake, "Military Assistance," 65–66, 118–19, 125, 128–33; and Schoultz, *Human Rights*, 177–81.

7. John Salzberg and Donald M. Young, "The Parliamentary Role of Implementing International Human Rights: A U.S. Example," *Texas Journal of International Law* 12, nos. 2–3 (Spring/Summer 1977): 251.

8. Cited in David Weissbrodt, "Human Rights Legislation and U.S. Foreign Policy," *Georgia Journal of International and Comparative Law,* supplement to vol. 7 (Summer 1977): 239–40.

9. Cited by Patricia Weiss Fagen, "U.S. Foreign Policy and Human Rights: The Role of Congress," in *Parliamentary Control over Foreign Policy,* ed. Antonio Cassese (Alphen aan den Rijn, The Netherlands: Sijtohoff and Noordhoff, 1980), 114.

10. Schoultz, *Human Rights,* 197–98.

11. Ibid., 195–98; Weissbrodt, "Human Rights Legislation," 241–50; Tom Harkin, "Human Rights and Foreign Aid: Forming an Unbreakable Link," in *Human Rights and U.S. Foreign Policy: Principles and Applications,* ed. Peter G. Brown and Douglas MacLean (Lexington, MA: Lexington Books, 1979), 15–26.

12. *Congressional Record,* 94th Cong., 1st Sess., 1975, 121, pt. 22: 28306–11.

13. Cynthia Brown, ed., *With Friends like These: The Americas Watch Report on Human Rights and U.S. Policy in Latin America* (New York: Pantheon, 1985), 12, 241–50.

14. John Salzberg, "Monitoring Human Rights Violations: How Good Is Information?" in *Human Rights and U.S. Foreign Policy,* ed. Brown and MacLean, 177–78.

15. Other actions included the punishment of people responsible for torture, the ending of torture, and the lifting of states of emergency or states of siege. Harkin, "Human Rights and Foreign Aid," 24.

16. Philip A. Ray Jr. and Sherrod J. Taylor, "The Role of Nongovernmental Organizations in Implementing Human Rights in Latin America," *Georgia Journal of International and Comparative Law,* supplement to vol. 7 (Summer 1977): 477–506; Arthur Schlesinger Jr., "Human Rights and the American Tradition," *Foreign Affairs* 57, no. 3 (Winter 1978/79): 501–26; and David P. Forsythe, "American Foreign Policy and Human Rights: Rhetoric and Reality," *Universal Human Rights* 2, no. 3 (July–September 1980): 40–41.

17. Ray and Taylor, "Role of Nongovernmental Organizations," 478.

18. Laurie Wiseberg and Harry M. Scoble, "Monitoring Human Rights Violations: The Role of Nongovernmental Organizations" in *Human Rights and American Foreign Policy,* ed. Donald P. Kommers and Gilbert D. Loescher (Notre Dame: University of Notre Dame Press, 1979), 189–92; and idem, "The International League for Human Rights: The Strategy of a Human Rights NGO," *Georgia Journal of International and Comparative Law,* supplement to vol. 7 (Summer 1977): 292–95.

19. Wiseberg and Scoble, "Monitoring Human Rights Violations," 183–85; and Ray and Taylor, "Role of Nongovernmental Organizations," 479–87.

20. Salzberg and Young, "Parliamentary Role," 265.

21. Ray and Taylor, "Role of Nongovernmental Organizations," 498.

22. Schoultz, *Human Rights,* 107, 84.

23. Donald M. Fraser, "Congress's Role in the Making of International Human Rights Policy" in *Human Rights and American Foreign Policy,* 248.

24. Brown, *With Friends like These,* 72–90; and Weissbrodt, "Human Rights Legislation," 261–62.

25. Barry M. Rubin, "Carter, Human Rights, and U.S. Allies," in *Human Rights and U.S. Foreign Policy,* ed. Barry M. Rubin and Elizabeth P. Shapiro (Boulder, CO: Westview Press, 1979), 121; and "Democracy Dawns in Bolivia," *Update Latin America,* vol. 7, no. 6 (November–December 1982), 1, 10–11.

26. Margaret E. Keck and Kathryn Sikkink, *Activists beyond Borders: Advocacy Networks in International Politics* (Ithaca: Cornell University Press, 1998), 110–16.

27. Rubin, "Carter, Human Rights," 122–23; and David Weissbrodt, "The Role of Nongovernmental Organizations in the Implementation of Human Rights," *Texas International Law Journal,* 52, no. 3 (Spring/Summer 1977), 305–14.

28. David P. Forsythe, *Human Rights and United States Foreign Policy* (Gainesville: University of Florida Press, 1988), 90–96.

29. For more on U.S.-Chilean relations, see William F. Sater, *Chile and the United States: Empires in Conflict* (Athens: University of Georgia Press, 1990); Petras and Morley, *United States and Chile;* Luis Roniger and Mario Sznajder, *The Legacy of Human Rights Violations in the Southern Cone: Argentina, Chile, and Uruguay* (Oxford, UK: Oxford University Press, 1999); and Brown, *With Friends like These.*

30. Roniger and Sznajder, *Legacy,* 16; Sater, *Chile and the United States,* chs. 8 and 9; and Harold Molineau, *U.S. Policy toward Latin America: From Regionalism to Globalism* (Boulder, CO: Westview Press, 1986), 171–72.

31. Terri Shaw, "Junta Says Chile Calm; Others Report Fighting," *Washington Post,* 15 September 1973; Marvine Howe, "Chile Hunt Nets a Left-Wing Hero," *New York Times,* 21 September 1973; Ralph A. Dungan, "The Junta's Challenge in Chile," *New York Times,* 13 October 1973; and Jonathan Kandell, "Chile's Junta Tells, in 264 Pages, Why It Started Coup," *New York Times,* 31 October 1973.

32. *Congressional Record,* 93rd Cong., 2nd Sess., 1974, 120, pt. 19: 24732; Molineau, *U.S. Policy,* 171–72; Cecil V. Crabb Jr. and Pat M. Holt, *Invitation to Struggle: Congress, the President, and Foreign Policy* (Washington, D.C.: Congressional Quarterly, 1992), 230–32; and Schoultz, *Human Rights,* 198–99.

33. There was no foreign assistance authorization or appropriations bill before Congress in 1975.

34. Pamela Constable and Arturo Valenzuela, *A Nation of Enemies: Chile under Pinochet* (New York: Norton, 1991), 20.

35. Schoultz, *Human Rights,* 12.

36. Constable and Valenzuela, *Nation of Enemies,* 32–33.

37. These figures are not intended to demonstrate or measure media pressure but merely to illustrate that information about political developments in Chile was flowing into the U.S. policy process. *The New York Times Index 1973: A Book of Record,* vol. 1 (New York: New York Times Co., 1974), 384–95. I chose the *New York Times* index because it offers a synopsis of topics included in each article published. See also *Washington Post Index, 1973* (Wooster, OH: Bell and Howell, 1975), 069B–071A. By way of comparison, only one *New York Times* article in 1973 prior to the coup noted anything approximating a pattern of abuses. The political turmoil under Allende in 1973 plus various liberal steps stand out far more. This follows secondary source accounts. See Brown, *With Friends like These,* 45–46; and Constable and Valenzuela, *A Nation of Enemies,* 15–29.

38. "Chilean Junta Picks Cabinet, Tightens Grip," *Washington Post,* 14 September 1973.

39. "Chile Junta Says Fighting Persists and Warns Foes," *New York Times,* 17 September 1973.

40. Marvine Howe, "2 Britons Freed in Chile Report Brutal Conditions," *New York Times,* 20 September 1973; "Mass Executions Reported," *New York Times,* 24 September 1973; and Terri Shaw, "Two Assert Chilean Junta Is Killing Many Prisoners," *Washington Post,* 25 September 1973.

41. "Chile's Junta Said to Plan Military Trials for 5,200," *New York Times,* 18 September 1973; Jonathan Kandell, "Military Junta in Chile Outlaws Marxist Parties," *New*

York Times, 22 September 1973; and "Chile's Christian Democrats Hit Junta Constitution Plans," *Washington Post,* 23 September 1973.

42. *Congressional Record,* 93rd Cong., 1st Sess., 1973, 119, pt. 24, 30958.

43. Congressmen John Moakley and Dante Fascell, in *Congressional Record,* 93rd Cong., 1st Sess., 119, pts. 23, 24, 25: 29530 and 29402–03. See also comments by Michael Harrington, Robert Drinan, and Fraser, 30785, 31444–45, 31689, 30615.

44. *Congressional Record,* 93rd Cong., 1st Sess., 1973, 119, pt. 25: 32570–72.

45. Ibid., 32570; and Sater, *Chile and the United States,* 190–91.

46. Spencer Rich, "Smallest Aid Bill Is Voted by Senate," *Washington Post,* 3 October 1973.

47. Shaw, "Two Assert," A9.

48. Schoultz, *Human Rights,* 74–75.

49. Subcommittee to Investigate Problems Connected with Refugees and Escapees of the Senate Committee on the Judiciary, *Refugee and Humanitarian Problems in Chile,* 93rd Cong., 1st Sess., 28 September 1973, 43.

50. *Congressional Record,* 93rd Cong., 1st Sess., 1973, 119, pt. 24: 30808–9, 30907, 31776.

51. Schoultz, *Human Rights,* 198–99, 74–75.

52. For the hearing excerpts, see *Congressional Record,* 93rd Cong., 2nd Sess., 1974, 120, pt. 15: 20403–4. For Hill statements, *Congressional Record,* 93rd Cong., 2nd Sess., 1974, 120, pt. 2: 2279–80 and *Congressional Record,* 93rd Cong., 2nd Sess., 1974, 120, pt. 15: 19555–56.

53. Henry Kissinger, *The White House Years* (Boston: Little, Brown, 1979), 656–57.

54. *Congressional Record,* 93rd Cong., 2nd Sess., 1974, 120, pt. 25: 33254; and William F. Nicholson, "U.S. Sells Fighters to Chile," *Washington Post,* 7 October 1974.

55. Brown, *With Friends like These,* 53–54.

56. Constable and Valenzuela, *A Nation of Enemies,* 94, 118; see also *The New York Times Index 1974: A Book of Record,* vol. 1 (New York: New York Times Co., 1975), 357–63; *The New York Times Index 1975: A Book of Record,* vol. 1 (New York: New York Times Co., 1976), 389–93; and *The New York Times Index 1976: A Book of Record* (New York: New York Times Co., 1976 and 1977), 266–68.

57. "Amnesty Group Prepares Charges of Chilean Torture," *New York Times,* 12 December 1973; "IEC Protests Executions in Chile," *Amnesty International Newsletter,* vol. 4, no. 1 (January 1974), 3; "Foreign 'Experts' Helped in Torture of Prisoners, AI Mission Report Says," *Amnesty International Newsletter,* vol. 4, no. 2 (February 1974), 1; and *Congressional Record,* 93rd Cong., 2nd Sess., 1974, 120, pt. 1: 763–65. The report noted a lack of information to determine exact numbers. It was estimated that in Santiago alone 550 were awaiting trial and another 1,000 were in "preventative detention" who might never receive a trial.

58. "New AI Report Documents Repression of Human Rights by Military Junta in Chile," *Amnesty International Newsletter,* vol. 4, no. 10 (October 1974), 2–3; *Congressional Record,* 93rd Cong., 2nd Sess., 1974, 120, pt. 21: 28868–70; and Schoultz, *Human Rights,* 12.

59. "Chile and Uruguay: Contrasts and Comparisons," *The Review,* vol. 12 (June 1974), 5–7 and *Congressional Record,* 93rd Cong., 2nd Sess., 1974, 120, pt. 12: 16234–35. The ICJ estimated four thousand detained without charges, "ill-treatment" of prisoners including "systematic" and "severe torture," and trials that seriously hampered defense attorneys and offered no means of appeal. Jonathan Kandell, "Church Group Reports Torture on Chilean Prisoners," *New York Times,* 17 May 1974.

60. Schoultz, *Human Rights,* 84.

61. None of these members cited public opinion or any other reason for action. Fur-

thermore, none of the opponents of action against Chile and none of the secondary sources note that public opinion factored into the congressional decision process.

62. U.S. Senate Committee on the Judiciary, The Subcommittee to Investigate Problems Connected with Refugees and Escapees, *Refugee and Humanitarian Problems in Chile Part II*, 93rd Cong., 2nd Sess., 23 July 1974, 49–61.

63. *Congressional Record*, 93rd Cong., 2nd Sess., 1974, 120, pt. 20: 26634–35.

64. U.S. House Committee on Foreign Affairs, Subcommittees on Inter-American Affairs and the International Organizations and Movements, *Human Rights in Chile*, 93rd Cong., 2nd Sess., 12 June 1974, 131–35, appendices VII–IX.

65. U.S. House Committee on Foreign Affairs, *Report on the Foreign Assistance Act of 1974*, 93rd Cong., 2nd Sess., 25 October 1974, House Report 93–1471, 40.

66. Numerous members made statements citing NGO information from early to mid-1974. See *Congressional Record*, 93rd Cong., 2nd Sess., 1974, 120, pt. 22: 28864–67, and pts. 20, 28, 30: 26446–47, 37360–61, 39896–97.

67. *Congressional Record*, 93rd Cong., 2nd Sess., 1974, 120, pt. 25: 33251–55, 33257, 33256.

68. Ibid., 33519.

69. James P. Sterna, "Ford Signs Bill but Attacks Cuts in Funds to Help Indochina," *New York Times*, 21 December 1974.

70. David Binder, "Chile Accused of Torture by O.A.S. Investigators," *New York Times*, 10 December 1974; "Chile Frees Some but Repression Continues," *Amnesty International Newsletter*, vol. 5, no. 2 (February 1975), 4; and "New Arrests in Chile," *Amnesty International Newsletter*, vol. 6, no. 7 (July 1976), 1. See also *Congressional Record*, 94th Cong., 1st Sess., 1975, 121, pt. 13: 16659.

71. For congressional complaints, see *Congressional Record*, 94th Cong., 1st Sess., 1975, 121, pt. 4: 4568–70; *Congressional Record*, 94th Cong., 1st Sess., 1975, 121, pt. 9: 11415; *Congressional Record*, 94th Cong., 1st Sess., 1975, 121, pt. 13: 16658–62; and *Congressional Record*, 94th Cong., 1st Sess., 1975, 121, pt. 27: 35673–76. Congressional committees also remained active, calling numerous NGOs to testify. U.S. House Committee on Foreign Affairs, Subcommittee on International Organizations, *Chile: The Statute of Human Rights and Its Relationship to U.S. Economic Assistance Programs*, 94th Cong., 2nd Sess., 29 April and 5 May 1976; and U.S. House Committee on International Relations, *International Security Assistance and Arms Export Control Act of 1976*, 94th Congress, 2nd Sess., 31 March 1976.

72. House Subcommittee on International Organizations of the Committee on Foreign Affairs, *Chile: The Statute of Human Rights and Its Relationship to U.S. Economic Assistance Programs*, 94th Cong., 2nd Sess., 29 April and 5 May 1976; House Committee on International Relations, *International Security Assistance and Arms Export Control Act of 1976*, 94th Cong., 2nd Sess., 31 March 1976; Senate Committee on Foreign Relations, *Report of the Committee on Foreign Relations of the United States Senate on S. 2662, to Amend the Foreign Assistance Act of 1961 and the Foreign Military Sales Act, and For Other Purposes*, 94th Cong., 2nd Sess., 30 January 1976, S. Report 94–605, 5; and House Committee on Foreign Affairs, *Report of the Committee on International Relations on HR 11963 to Amend the Foreign Assistance Act of 1961 and the Foreign Military Sales Act, to Authorize International Security Assistance for Fiscal Year 1976, to Provide for the Termination of Grant Military Assistance Programs at the End of the Fiscal Year 1977, and For Other Purposes*, 94th Cong., 2nd Sess., 24 February 1976, House Report 94–848, 42–43.

73. *Congressional Record*, 94th Cong., 2nd Sess., 1976, 122, pt. 3: 3601. See also House Committee, *Report of the Committee on International Relations on HR 11963*, 43; and Senate Committee, *Report of the Committee on Foreign Relations of the United States Senate on S. 2662*, 58.

74. *Congressional Record,* 94th Cong., 2nd Sess., 1976, 122, pt. 3: 3598–3601.

75. Joseph S. Tulchin, *Argentina and the United States: A Conflictual Relationship* (Boston: Twayne, 1990), 132–41.

76. Ibid., 141.

77. Quotation from Joanne Oman, "30 Bodies Discovered on Road in Argentina," *Washington Post,* 21 August 1976. See also Juan de Ones, "Argentina Steps up War against Leftists," *New York Times,* 14 November 1976; and idem, "Harsh Steps Check Argentine Guerillas," *New York Times,* 28 July 1976.

78. Brown, *With Friends like These,* 98–99; Roniger and Sznajder, *Legacy,* 21–25; and Ian Guest, *Behind the Disappearances: Argentina's Dirty War against Human Rights and the United Nations* (Philadelphia: University of Pennsylvania Press, 1990), 20–22.

79. The totals break down as follows: 39 articles in the second half of 1974, 53 in 1975, and 26 in the first five months of 1976. *New York Times Index 1974,* 101–5; *New York Times Index 1975,* 107–11; and *New York Times Index 1976,* 84–88.

80. "The Plight of Defense Lawyers in Argentina," *The Review,* vol. 14 (June 1975), 1–3.

81. "Lawyers Confirm Torture in Argentina," *Amnesty International Newsletter,* vol. 5, no. 7 (July 1975), 4; "AI Sends Argentine President List of 461 Political Murders," *Amnesty International Newsletter,* vol. 5, no. 11 (September 1975), 2; and *The Amnesty International Report, 1 June 1975—31 May 1976* (London: Amnesty International Publications, 1976), 85–87.

82. *Congressional Record,* 94th Cong., 1st Sess., 1975, 121, pt. 4, 4568–70; pt. 9, 11415.

83. See *Congressional Record,* 94th Cong., 1st Sess., 1975, 121, pt. 27: 35673–76.

84. The article breakdown: 1974: 24 left-wing, 10 right-wing; 1975: 32 left-wing, 16 right-wing; and 1976: 12 left-wing, 8 right-wing.

85. "Mrs. Peron Said to Confer on Leftists," *New York Times,* 8 September 1974; "Argentine Rightists Admit Killings," *New York Times,* 22 September 1974; "Terrorism in Argentina," *New York Times,* 10 November 1974; Jonathan Kandell, "Beleaguered Mrs. Peron Clings to Power, but Argentines Ask, How Long?" *New York Times,* 20 March 1975; and idem, "New Kidnapping Stirs Argentina," *New York Times,* 18 June 1974.

86. Guest, *Behind the Disappearances,* 17–22; and Tulchin, *Argentina and the United States,* 141.

87. Joanne Omang, "Lopez Rega's Departure Focuses Argentina's Ills," *Washington Post,* 21 July 1975; idem, "Mrs. Peron's Aide Accused," *Washington Post,* 15 July 1975; and Juan de Onis, "Mrs. Peron, under Pressure, Moves against Ex-Strongman," *New York Times,* 3 December 1975.

88. Jonathan Kandell, "Rumors of Argentine Coup Rebutted by Military Chief," *New York Times,* 26 August 1975; De Onis, "Mrs. Peron, under Pressure"; idem, "Mrs. Peron Calls Talks on Terror," *New York Times,* 5 December 1975; idem, "Top Commanders Warn Mrs. Peron to Yield Powers," *New York Times,* 20 December 1975.

89. "Junta Members Have Long Worked Closely Together," *New York Times,* 25 March 1976; Juan de Onis, "Argentine Military, Firmly in Control, Eases Curbs," *New York Times,* 26 March 1976; "Argentine Junta Names a Cabinet," *New York Times,* 29 March 1976; and Joanne Omang, "Argentine Leader Reported Trying to Curb Death Squads," *Washington Post,* 11 September 1976.

90. Rubin, "Carter, Human Rights," 124.

91. Members of Congress made very few public statements about Argentina in 1975 and 1976. See the indexes in *Congressional Record,* 93rd Cong., 2nd. Sess., 1974, 120, pt. 1: 66; and *Congressional Record,* 94th Cong., 1st Sess., 1975, 121, pt. 1: 64; *Congressional Record,* 94th Cong., 1st Sess., 1975, 121, pt. 15: 19243; *Congressional Record,* 94th Cong., 2nd Sess., 1976, 122, pt. 6: 7575.

92. See, for instance, *Congressional Record,* 94th Cong., 2nd Sess., 1976, 122, pt. 15: 18406–8; *Congressional Record,* 94th Cong., 2nd Sess., 1976, 122, pt. 12: 15144–45; *Congressional Record,* 94th Cong., 2nd Sess., 1976, 122, pt. 18: 22417; and *Congressional Record,* 94th Cong., 2nd Sess., 1976, 122, pt. 6: 7388–89.

93. *Congressional Record,* 94th Cong., 2nd Sess., 1976, 122, pt. 19: 24513.

94. U.S. House Committee on International Relations, Subcommittee on International Organizations, *Human Rights in Argentina,* 94th Cong., 2nd Sess., 28 September 1976, 1–2.

95. *Congressional Record,* 94th Cong., 2nd Sess., 1976, 122, pt. 15: 18198; and 94th Cong., 2nd Sess., 1976, 122, pt. 16: 20365; *Congressional Record,* 94th Cong., 2nd Sess., 1976, 122, pt. 18: 22417.

96. Brown, *With Friends like These,* 98–99; Roniger and Sznajder, *Legacy,* 21–25; and Guest, *Behind the Disappearances,* 20–22.

97. *The New York Times Index 1976,* 84–88 and *The New York Times Index 1977: A Book of Record* (New York: New York Times Co., 1978), 65–67.

98. "Repression in Argentina," *New York Times,* 26 May 1976; "U.S. Help Sought for Latin American Exiles," *New York Times,* 20 June 1976; "3 Nuns, 5 Clergymen Murdered in Argentina," *Washington Post,* 5 July 1976; Marvine Howe, "Union's Protest Policies," *New York Times,* 6 July 1976; Juan de Onis, "Harsh Steps Check Argentine Guerillas," *New York Times,* 28 July 1976; idem, "Argentina Beset by Arrest Queries," *New York Times,* 13 August 1976; idem, "Argentine Extremists Kill 46 in Two Mass Murders," *New York Times,* 21 August 1976; idem, "Argentina Steps up War against Leftists," *New York Times,* 14 November 1976; and Joanne Omang, "30 Bodies Discovered on Road in Argentina," *Washington Post,* 21 August 1976.

99. *Congressional Record,* 94th Cong., 2nd Sess., 1976, 122, pt. 15: 18406–08, 18198.

100. House Subcommittee, *Human Rights in Argentina,* 1.

101. Ibid., 27–30.

102. Guest, *Behind the Disappearances,* 85.

103. "AI Mission Investigates Human Rights Violations in Argentina," *Amnesty International Newsletter,* vol. 6, no. 13 (December 1976), 3; "AI Publishes Report of Mission to Argentina" *Amnesty International Newsletter,* vol. 7, no. 4 (April 1977), 1; *Amnesty International Report 1977* (London: Amnesty International Publications, 1977), 118–23; Guest, *Behind the Disappearances,* ch. 6.

104. Guest, *Behind the Disappearances,* 85. See also Schoultz, *Human Rights,* 84.

105. Guest, *Behind the Disappearances,* 165; Judith F. Buncher, ed., *Human Rights and American Diplomacy: 1975–77* (New York: Facts on File, 1977), 175; and Lester D. Langley, *America and the Americas: The United States in the Western Hemisphere* (Athens, GA: University of Georgia Press, 1989), 233–34.

106. See, for instance, the comments of several who opposed assistance termination in *Congressional Record,* 95th Cong., 1st Sess., 1977, 123, pt. 7: 15897–15904 and *Congressional Record,* 95th Cong., 1st Sess., 1977, 123, pt. 16: 20279–81.

107. Schoultz, *Human Rights,* 107.

108. U.S. House Committee on Appropriations, *Foreign Assistance and Related Programs Bill,* Report no. 95–417, 95th Cong., 1st Sess., 15 June 1977, 8–9, 58–60.

109. *Congressional Record,* 95th Cong., 1st Sess., 1977, 123, pt. 16: 19268–72.

110. *Congressional Record,* 95th Cong., 1st Sess., 1977, 123, pt. 13: 15897–04.

111. Ibid., 15900.

112. *Congressional Record,* 95th Cong., 1st Sess., 1977, 123, pt. 16: 20278–89; and Schoultz, *Human Rights,* 107.

113. *Congressional Record,* 95th Cong., 1st Sess., 1977, 123, pt. 16: 20278–89; and "Carter Signs Aid Bill; Some Nations Barred," *New York Times,* 2 November 1977.

114. Guest, *Behind the Disappearances*, 181–85. See also, Tulchin, *Argentina and the United States*, 150.

115. Anthony Lake, *Somoza Falling* (Boston: Houghton Mifflin, 1989), 18–22.

116. Ibid., 20–22; and Bernhard Diederich, *Somoza and the Legacy of U.S. Involvement in Latin America* (New York: E. P. Dutton, 1981), 123–30, 141.

117. *The New York Times Index, 1975: A Book of Record*, vol. 2 (New York: New York Times Co., 1976); and *The New York Times Index 1976*.

118. U.S. House Subcommittee on Foreign Assistance of the Committee on Appropriations, *Foreign Assistance and Related Agencies Appropriations for 1978, Part 3: Special Hearings Testimony of Public Witnesses*, 94th Cong., 1st Sess., April 1977, 12–15; and Diederich, *Somoza*, 141.

119. Morris H. Morley, *Washington, Somoza, and the Sandinistas: State and Regime in U.S. Policy toward Nicaragua, 1969–1981* (Cambridge: Cambridge University Press, 1994), 98–99; Robert Kagan, *A Twilight Struggle: American Power and Nicaragua, 1977–1980* (New York: Free Press, 1996), 30; and Lake, *Somoza Falling*, 22.

120. Shirley Christiansen, *Nicaragua: Revolution in the Family* (New York: Random House, 1985), 40.

121. Alan Riding, "Rights Organization Accuses Nicaragua Regime of Widespread Abuses," *New York Times*, 16 August 1977, 6.

122. Diederich, *Somoza*, 141.

123. U.S. House Subcommittee, *Foreign Assistance and Related Agencies Appropriations for 1978, Part 3*, 2, 508–30.

124. Ibid., 593.

125. Ibid.

126. *Congressional Record*, 95th Cong., 1st Sess., 1977, 123, pt. 17: 20579, 20581–82, 20586; see Congressman Rudd's comment at 20585.

127. Ibid., 20590–93.

128. Ibid., 20582, 20591–93; see Representative Mario Biaggi's comments at 20595.

129. Ibid., 20595.

130. Morley, *Washington, Somoza*, 98–100.

131. Ibid., 104; and Lake, *Somoza Falling*, 22–24.

132. The amount for training included more than $500,000 for the National Guard in 1978. *Congressional Record*, 95th Cong., 2nd Sess., 1978, 124, pt. 23: 30825.

133. Morley, *Washington, Somoza*, 101–4.

134. Kagan, *Twilight Struggle*, 60–61; and Morley, *Washington, Somoza*, 115–16.

135. Christiansen, *Nicaragua*, 51; Diederich, *Somoza*, 162–63; and Morley, *Washington, Somoza*, 115–16.

136. Diederich, *Somoza*, 190–203; and Christiansen, *Nicaragua*, 61.

137. *The New York Times Index, 1978: A Book of Record* (New York: New York Times Co., 1979), 764.

138. Lake, *Somoza Falling*, 195.

139. *Congressional Record*, 95th Cong., 2nd Sess., 1978, 124, pt. 23: 30825.

140. "Political Killings, Arrests Continue in Nicaragua," *Amnesty International Newsletter*, vol. 9, no. 1 (January 1979), 1; *Amnesty International Report 1977* (London: Amnesty International Publications, 1977), 150–52; *Amnesty International Report 1979* (London: Amnesty International Press, 1979), 69; Karen DeYoung, "All of Nicaragua Put under Rule of Armed Forces," *Washington Post*, 14 September 1978; John M. Goshko, "U.S. Urges Somoza to Discipline Troops, Investigate Slayings," *Washington Post*, 21 September 1978; James E. Goff, "Latin American Churches Want Somoza to Resign," *Washington Post*, 13 October 1978; and Karen DeYoung, "Christians Call for U.S. to Help Remove Somoza," *Washington Post*, 9 November 1978.

141. Karen DeYoung, "Rights Unit Finds 'Grave' Abuse by Somoza's Troops," *Washington Post*, 8 November 1978; and Morley, *Washington*, 124–25.

142. *Congressional Record*, 95th Cong., 2nd Sess., 1978, 124, pt. 23: 30823–26, 30873–74, 30876, 30879; and Morley, *Washington, Somoza*, 134–35.

143. Morley, *Washington, Somoza*, 134.

144. *Congressional Record*, 95th Cong., 2nd Sess., 1978, 124, pt. 23: 30879.

145. Lake, *Somoza Falling*, 194, 209–10.

146. McClintock, *Revolutionary Movements*, 217–19; and Schoultz, *Human Rights*, 63–64.

147. Frederick B. Pike, *United States and the Andean Republics: Peru, Bolivia, and Ecuador* (Cambridge, MA: Harvard University Press, 1977), 318–19; and McClintock, *Revolutionary Movements*, 99–102.

148. McClintock, *Revolutionary Movements*, 96–101; Pike, *United States and the Andean Republics*, 329–47, 352–54, 366; Petras and Morley, *United States and Chile*, 69; and Molineau, *U.S. Policy*, 99.

149. U.S. Senate Committee on Foreign Relations, Subcommittee on Foreign Assistance, *Foreign Assistance Authorization, Arms Sales Issues*, 93rd Cong., 2nd Sess., 18 June 1975, 142.

150. U.S. House Committee on International Relations, *International Security Assistance Act of 1976*, 94th Cong., 1st Sess., 3 February 1976, 696.

151. "Peru," *The Review*, vol. 13 (December 1974), 19–25; "Latin America—Expulsion, the Right to Return, and Passports," *The Review*, vol. 14 (June 1975), 3–8; "Postcards from Prisoners: Julio Armancanqui Flores, Peru," *Amnesty International Newsletter*, vol. 4, no. 5 (May 1974), 3–4; "AI News in Brief," *Amnesty International Newsletter*, vol. 4, no. 7 (July 1974), 4; "AI Officials Arrested in Peru and Nepal; Police Detain S. Korean Committee Member," *Amnesty International Newsletter*, vol. 4, no. 2 (November 1974), 1, 4; "Peru Detains Lawyers," *Amnesty International Newsletter*, vol. 6, no. 2 (February 1976), 1; and *The Amnesty International Report, 1 June 1975 – 31 May 1976*, 108–10.

152. McClintock, *Revolutionary Movements*, 102–3 and *Peru: Paths to Poverty* (London: Latin American Bureau, 1985), 66–74.

153. *The Amnesty International Report 1977*, 154–57; *The Amnesty International Report, 1978* (London: Amnesty International Publications, 1978), 136–38; *The Amnesty International Report, 1979*, 72–74; and Brown, *With Friends like These*, 215–17.

154. McClintock, *Revolutionary Movements*, 96–102.

155. Pike, *United States and the Andean Republics*, 351, 368.

156. McClintock, *Revolutionary Movements*, 102.

157. "Military Regimes In Latin America," *The Review*, vol. 17 (December 1976), 13–26.

158. "Tortures Charged in Peru," *Amnesty International Campaign for the Abolition of Torture Monthly Bulletin*, vol. 2, no. 8 (August 1975), 2; and "Peruvian Torturers Go on Trial," *Amnesty International Campaign for the Abolition of Torture Monthly Bulletin*, vol. 3, no. 5 (May 1976), 2.

159. See, for instance, U.S. House Committee on International Relations, *H.R. 11963, International Security Assistance Act of 1976*, 94th Cong., 2nd Sess., 4 February 1976, 704–5.

160. U.S. House Committee on International Relations, *International Security Assistance and Arms Export Control Act of 1976*, 94th Cong., 2nd Sess., 31 March 1976, 183, 195–96; and U.S. House Committee on Foreign Affairs, *H.R. 11963*, 704–5.

161. Brown, *With Friends like These*, 211–12.

162. U.S. House Committee on International Relations, *Human Rights and U.S. Policy:*

Argentina, Haiti, Indonesia, Iran, Peru, and the Philippines, 94th Cong., 2nd Sess., 31 December 1976, 23–27.

163. U.S. Senate Report, *Study Mission to Latin America,* 95th Cong., 1st Sess., Doc. 95–67, September 1977, 11–12.

164. U.S. Senate Committee on Foreign Relations, *Perspectives on Latin America: Report of a Study Mission to Costa Rica, Panama, Peru, and Venezuela,* 95th Cong., 2nd Sess., December 1978, 25–33. These assessments were echoed in U.S. Senate Foreign Relations Committee and U.S. House Committee on Foreign Affairs, *Report on Human Rights Practices in Countries Receiving U.S. Aid by the U.S. Department of State,* 96th Cong., 1st Sess., 8 February 1979, 324–31.

165. *Congressional Record,* 96th Cong., 2nd Sess., 1980, 126, pt. 12: 25548.

166. McClintock, *Revolutionary Movements,* 236–42.

167. Theodore H. White, *Breach of Faith: The Fall of Richard Nixon* (New York: Atheneum, 1975); Staff of *The New York Times, The End of a Presidency* (New York: Holt, Rinehart, and Winston, 1974); and Raymond L. Garthoff, *Détente and Confrontation: American-Soviet Relations from Nixon to Reagan* (Washington., D.C.: Brookings Institution, 1985), 330, 355–56, 368–85.

168. See notes 172–76.

169. Mott, *United States Military Assistance,* 19–25, 93–95; and Lewis Sorley, *Arms Transfers Under Nixon: A Policy Analysis* (Lexington, KY: University of Kentucky Press, 1983), 153.

170. David Ronfeldt and Caesar Sereseres, *U.S. Arms Transfers, Diplomacy, and Security in Latin America and Beyond* (Santa Monica, CA: Rand Corporation, 1977), 9–10; and Sorley, *Arms Transfers,* 158.

171. Sorley, *Arms Transfers,* 153–60; and Hammond et al., *The Reluctant Supplier,* 72–74. Between 1970 and 1977, the share of trade to the Soviet Union coming from Latin America (excluding Cuba) rose from 0 to 12 percent.

172. Robert S. Litwak, *Détente and the Nixon Doctrine: American Foreign Policy and the Pursuit of Stability, 1969–1976* (Cambridge: Cambridge University Press, 1984), 50–78, 81–116, 120–47; and Dana H. Allin, *Cold War Illusions: America, Europe and Soviet Power, 1969–1989* (New York: St. Martin's Press, 1994), 27–29, 51.

173. Robert Pastor, *Congress and the Politics of U.S. Foreign Economic Policy, 1929–1976* (Berkeley: University of California Press, 1980), ch. 9; Joan Hoff, *Nixon Reconsidered* (New York: Basic Books, 1994), 158–59; and Vernon Ruttan, *United States Development Assistance Policy: The Domestic Politics of Foreign Economic Aid* (Baltimore: Johns Hopkins University Press, 1996), ch. 6.

174. Hammond et al., *Reluctant Supplier,* 193–94; and Sorley, *Arms Transfers,* 24–25.

175. Richard Nixon, *U.S. Foreign Policy for the 1970s: Building for Peace* (Washington, D.C.: U.S. Government Printing Office, 1971), cited in Sorley, *Arms Transfers,* 30.

176. Sorley, *Arms Transfers,* ch. 2; and Hammond et al., *Reluctant Supplier,* 66–77, 193–94.

177. Hammond et al., *Reluctant Supplier,* 75–77, 128–30; Richard Grimmett, "Role of Security Assistance," 14–36; Mott, *United States Military Assistance,* 26–42; and Sorley, *Arms Transfers,* chs. 1, 2. The security assistance program consisted of three components: the Military Assistance Program (MAP), Foreign Military Sales (FMS), and International Military Education and Training (IMET). The United States granted packages to MDAA signatories that included portions of each. Responding to economic pressure and seeking to end programs that presumably pulled the U.S. into Vietnam, Congress eradicated MAP, the training portion of the assistance program, in 1973. FMS funding for grants, loans and cash sales during the decade more than made up for the end to the relatively small MAP.

178. Hammond et al., *Reluctant Supplier*, 129, 141–42. The United States financed nearly all transfers to Latin American through debt waivers, grants, or supply of credit provided by U.S. financial institutions.

179. Mott, *United States Military Assistance*, 98. Assistance to Chile doubled. The Ford administration transferred $49 million in weapons to the new Argentine government in less than a year. By comparison, from 1966 to 1975, the United States provided a total of $105.6 million in FMS to Buenos Aires.

180. Crabb and Holt, *Invitation to Struggle*, 209–10; and Garthoff, *Détente and Confrontation*, 326–27. For factors aside from détente, see Kathryn Sikkink, "The Power of Principled Ideas: Human Rights Policies in the United States and Western Europe," in *Ideas and Foreign Policy: Beliefs, Institutions, and Political Change*, ed. Judith Goldstein and Robert O. Keohane (Ithaca: Cornell University Press, 1993), 140; Pastor, *Congress and the Politics*, 313; and Rubin, "Carter, Human Rights," 111.

181. Pastor, *Congress and the Politics*, 313.

182. Thomas G. Paterson, *Contesting Castro: The United States and the Triumph of the Cuban Revolution* (New York: Oxford University Press, 1994), 125–38; and Brown, *With Friends like These*, 107–8. The Cuban termination probably facilitated Castro's successful revolution. Meanwhile, The U.S. resumed Chilean and Argentine assistance only after both returned to democracy.

183. For the history of the aid program, see John D. Montgomery, *The Politics of Foreign Aid: American Experience in Southeast Asia* (New York: Frederick A. Praeger, 1962), 212; Edward S. Mason, *Foreign Aid and Foreign Policy* (New York: Harper and Row, 1964), 33–36; Hammond et al., *Reluctant Supplier*, 43–75, 61–75, 125–47; and Grimmett, "Role of Security Assistance," 1–8.

184. For cases from international economics, see Vinod K. Aggarwal, *Liberal Protectionism: The International Politics of Organized Textile Trade* (Berkley: University of California Press, 1985).

185. In Latin America alone, Brazil, El Salvador, Guatemala, Paraguay, Nicaragua, and Uruguay faced unilateral desertion as well, despite their loyalty as U.S. allies.

186. Argentine government files cited in Guest, *Behind the Disappearances*, 164.

187. Augusto Varas, "Hemispheric Relations and Security Regimes in Latin America," in *Hemispheric Security and U.S. Policy in Latin America*, ed. Augusto Varas (Boulder, CO: Westview Press, 1989), 33–66; and John Child, *Unequal Alliance: The Inter-American Military System, 1938–1978* (Boulder, CO: Westview Press, 1980). For Chilean actions along these lines, see Petras and Morley, *United States and Chile*, 39.

188. McClintock, *Revolutionary Movements*, 95–96; and Clayton, *Peru*, 254–55.

189. *Congressional Record*, 94th Cong., 1st Sess., 1975, 121, pt. 16: 27196; and *Congressional Record*, 94th Cong., 2nd Sess., 1976, 122, pt. 27: 35600; *Congressional Record*, 94th Cong., 2nd Sess., 1976, 122, pt. 9: 11286; and U.S. Senate Subcommittee on Foreign Assistance, *Foreign Assistance Authorizations*, 18 June 1975, 141–42.

CHAPTER 4. APARTHEID IN U.S.–SOUTH AFRICAN RELATIONS

1. Richard W. Hull, *American Enterprise in South Africa: Historical Dimensions of Engagement and Disengagement* (New York: New York University Press, 1990), 296–359, 315, 381; Christopher Coker, *The United States and South Africa, 1968–1985: Constructive Engagement and Its Critics* (Durham, NC: Duke University Press, 1986), ch. 1; Robert K. Massie, *Loosing the Bonds: The United States and South Africa in the Apartheid Years* (New York: Doubleday, 1997), 128; and Thomas Borstelmann, *Apartheid's Reluctant*

Uncle: The United States and Southern Africa in the Early Cold War (New York: Oxford University Press, 1993).

2. "U.S.-Mozambique: The State Department Perspective," *Africa Report* 28, no. 1 (January–February 1983): 46–48; Allen Isaacman, "In Machel's Footsteps," *Africa Report* 32, no. 1 (January–February 1987): 25–27; David Hoile, *Mozambique: A Nation in Crisis* (London: Claridge Press, 1989), ch. 7; Chester A. Crocker, "U.S. Policy toward Mozambique," *State Department Bulletin*, Bureau of Public Affairs, U.S. Department of State, 1987, 1–2; Alex Vines, *Renamo: Terrorism in Mozambique* (Bloomington: Indiana University Press, 1991), 42–43; Gilliam Gunn, "Learning from Adversity: The Mozambican Experience," in *Regional Conflict and U.S. Policy: Angola and Mozambique*, ed. Richard J. Bloomfield (Algonac, MI: Reference Publications, 1988), 160–66; idem, "Post-Nkomati Mozambique," *CSIS Africa Notes*, vol. 38 (8 January 1985), 6–7; Pauline H. Baker, *The United States and South Africa: The Reagan Years* (New York: Ford Foundation/Foreign Policy Association, 1989), 2; and J. Stephen Morrison, "The Battle for Mozambique," *Africa Report* 32, no. 5 (September–October 1987): 44–45.

3. ExIm funding began in the early 1950s with the initiative to secure strategic minerals. See Hull, *American Enterprise*, 204–5, 220, 264–65; and Borstelmann, *Apartheid's Reluctant Uncle*, chs. 7, 8. South Africa joined the GATT in 1948. South Africa received a commitment to deliver approximately thirty-nine thousand tons of sugar annually starting in 1962. This was renewed and re-approved by Congress with its regular review of the Sugar Act of 1937. E. W. Kenworthy, "U.S. Sugar Quota—How It Works," *New York Times*, 21 February 1960; "Bill by Kennedy Would End South African Sugar Quota," *New York Times*, 19 April 1969; and Massie, *Loosing the Bonds*, 265–66.

4. Hull, *American Enterprise*, 220.

5. John Felton and Nancy Green, "Senate, after 4 Years, Votes a Foreign Aid Bill," *CQ Weekly*, vol. 43, no. 20 (18 May 1985), 926. Aid would flow if Mozambique continued to "reduce dependence on Moscow, reassert its independence and nonalignment, and reach out the West," said Crocker. Crocker, "U.S. Policy," 4.

6. Hull, *American Enterprise*, 341–42; and Baker, *United States and South Africa*, 138–44.

7. Winrich Kuhne, "What Does the Case of Mozambique Tell Us about Soviet Ambivalence toward Africa?" *CSIS Africa Notes*, vol. 46 (30 August 1985), 3.

8. Baker, *United States and South Africa*, 58; and Gunn, "Learning," 166.

9. Massie, *Loosing the Bonds*, 255–56; and Coker, *United States and South Africa*, 82.

10. Massie, *Loosing the Bonds*, chs. 9–11; and Coker, *United States and South Africa*, ch. 7.

11. Hull, *American Enterprise*, 301–11.

12. Ibid.; and Massie, *Loosing the Bonds*, 407–14.

13. Hull, *American Enterprise*, 305, 315.

14. *Congressional Record*, 95th Cong., 1st Sess., 1977, 123, pt. 28: 35966, 35969.

15. Coker, *United States and South Africa*, 149.

16. Hull, *American Enterprise*, 308–9.

17. *Congressional Record*, 95th Cong., 2nd Sess., 1978, 124, pt. 21: 29026, 29027, 29029. A bipartisan coalition in the House and Senate also monitored U.S. policy toward South Africa. David Hauck, Meg Voorhes, and Glenn Goldberg, *Two Decades of Debate: The Controversy over U.S. Companies in South Africa* (Washington, D.C.: Investor Responsibility Research Center, 1983), 43.

18. Chester Crocker, *High Noon in Southern Africa: Making Peace in a Rough Neighborhood* (New York: Norton, 1992), 78. Emphasis in original.

19. Cited in Coker, *United States and South Africa*, 160. See also Chester A. Crocker, "South Africa: Strategy for Change," *Foreign Affairs* 59, no. 2 (Winter 1980/81): 323–51.

20. Hull, *American Enterprise*, 319.

21. *Congressional Record*, 98th Cong., 1st Sess., 1983, 129, pt. 12: 16432.

22. *Congressional Record*, 98th Cong., 1st Sess., 1983, 129, pt. 21: 29636

23. *The Washington Star*, 10 June 1981, reprinted in *Congressional Record*, 97th Cong., 1st Sess., 1981, 127, pt. 12: 15765.

24. Senator Richard G. Lugar, *Letters to the Next President* (New York: Simon and Schuster, 1988), 211.

25. *Congressional Record*, 97th Cong., 2nd Sess., 1982, 128, pt. 4: 5269–73.

26. John F. Burns, "South Africa Clashes Subside," *New York Times*, 20 June 1980; idem, "At Least 8 Killed in South Africa as Police and Demonstrators Clash," *New York Times*, 18 June 1980; idem, "South Africa, in Bid to Avoid Unrest, Extends Ban on Political Meetings," *New York Times*, 1 July 1980; "Three Killed in South Africa as Rioting Follows Funeral," *New York Times*, 28 July 1980; "South Africa Government Silences Two Black Papers," *New York Times*, 21 January 1981; Joseph Lelyveld, "Crackdown Under Way in South Africa," *New York Times*, 23 June 1981; idem, "14 Unionists Seized by South Africans," *New York Times*, 28 November 1981; idem, "South Africa Recasting Its Security Laws," *New York Times*, 15 May 1982; and "Cape Town Authorities Seize Hundreds of Black Squatters," *New York Times*, 27 February 1983.

27. *Amnesty International Report, 1977* (London: Amnesty International Publications, 1977), 102; and *Amnesty International Report, 1978* (London: Amnesty International Publications, 1978).

28. Hauck, Voorhes, and Goldberg, *Two Decades*, 7–29, 41; See also, Massie, *Loosing the Bonds*, ch. 5, 558, 526–41; and "Interview with Randall Robinson, Executive Director of TransAfrica," *Africa Report* 25, no. 1 (January–February 1980): 13–14.

29. Hauck, Voorhes, and Goldberg, *Two Decades*, 44–45; and Massie, *Loosing the Bonds*, 498.

30. Massie, *Loosing the Bonds*, 473–522; and Coker, *United States and South Africa*, 161–65.

31. There were many critics as well. See Massie, *Loosing the Bonds*, 509–22; and Coker, *United States and South Africa*, 164–73.

32. Lugar, *Letters*, 21l and *Congressional Record*, 97th Cong. 2nd Sess., 1982, 128, pt. 4: 5269.

33. Massie, *Loosing the Bonds*, 496–98.

34. While I do not condone these categories, they are the official, racially based descriptions of different groups of people used in South Africa at the time. Hence, I report them as used. So-called whites, Indians, and Coloreds were each given a separate house in the new tricameral legislature. How the government determined racial categories was complex and changed at numerous points throughout the apartheid years. For examples and a discussion, see Massie, *Loosing the Bonds*, 21 and 221–23.

35. Hull, *American Enterprise*, 323–27.

36. For example, see Alan Cowell, "Pretoria Will Use Army to End Riots," *New York Times*, 8 October 1984; "South African Army Enters Black Towns; Hundreds are Held," *New York Times*, 24 October 1984; and "South Africa Accused of Detaining 1,000," *New York Times*, 8 November 1984.

37. *Congressional Record*, 98th Cong., 2nd Sess., 1984, 130, pt. 18: 24780, and pt. 21: 28850, 28851.

38. *Congressional Record*, 98th Cong., 2nd Sess., 1984, 130, pt. 18: 25883. For the full debate, see 25877–95.

39. Lugar, *Letters*, 212.

40. Cited by Baker, *United States and South Africa,* 125–27. See also Robert S. Walker, "A Conservative Viewpoint against Apartheid," *Africa Report* 30, no. 3 (May–June 1985): 55.

41. Crocker, *High Noon,* 217.

42. For example, see Nancy Green, "Export Controls Act Thwarted by a Standoff on Capitol Hill," *CQ Weekly Report,* vol. 42, no. 41 (13 October 1984), 2672, 2717.

43. Massie, *Loosing the Bonds,* 479–81, 523–41; Hauck, Voorhes, and Goldberg, *Two Decades,* 16–29; and Hull, *American Enterprise,* 329–30.

44. Hauck, Voorhes, and Goldberg, *Two Decades,* 50, 25–26, 45.

45. Massie, *Loosing the Bonds,* 558–60.

46. For examples, see Barbara Gamarekian, "Apartheid Protest Takes Page from 60's History," *New York Times,* 30 November 1984; and Leslie Maitland Warner, "Protests Spreading in U.S. against South Africa Policy," *New York Times,* 5 December 1984.

47. Massie, *Loosing the Bonds,* 560–68, 584.

48. Stephen Engelberg, "House Panel Favors Pretoria Sanctions," *New York Times,* 3 May 1985; Larry Rohter, "Activism at Schools Seems to Be Stirring as Protests Continue," *New York Times,* 25 April 1985; and Massie, *Loosing the Bonds,* 575–79.

49. Hull, *American Enterprise,* 332. See also Crocker, *High Noon,* 257–58.

50. Massie, *Loosing the Bonds,* 567–85; and Robert A. Manning, "Toward Constructive Disengagement?" *Africa Report* 30, no. 5 (September–October 1985): 82.

51. Crocker, *High Noon,* 259.

52. Lugar, *Letters,* 212; and idem, "Making Foreign Policy: The Congress and Apartheid," *Africa Report* 31, no. 5 (September–October 1986): 34.

53. Massie, *Loosing the Bonds,* 583–84.

54. Lugar, *Letters,* 217.

55. For the debates, see *Congressional Record,* 99th Cong., 1st Sess., 1985, 131, pt. 10: 12741–91, 13997–14311; pt. 13: 18324–39; and pt. 14: 18754–18843.

56. *Congressional Record,* 99th Cong., 1st Sess., 1985, 131, pt. 14: 18768, 18772, 18788.

57. In order, Representatives Stephen Solarz, Representative Chalmers Wylie, Representative Stewart McKinney, and Representative Howard Berman. *Congressional Record,* 99th Cong., 1st Sess., 1985, 131, pt. 10: 12747, 12759, 12760, 12769.

58. Ibid., 12750, 12773.

59. In order, Senators Steven Symms and Malcolm Wallop in *Congressional Record,* 99th Cong., 1st Sess., 1985, 131, pt. 14: 18787, 18804–7. For a similar statement by Congressman Robert Walker in the House, see *Congressional Record,* 99th Cong., 1st Sess., 1985, 131, pt. 10: 12791.

60. For examples, see *Congressional Record,* 99th Cong., 1st Sess., 1985, 131, pt. 16: 22540–60.

61. Lugar, *Letters,* 218; and Massie, *Loosing the Bonds,* 585.

62. Crocker, *High Noon,* 273–77.

63. Lugar, *Letters,* 221.

64. "Transcript of Reagan's Remarks on South Africa," *Washington Post,* 10 September 1985.

65. Lena Williams, "Pressure Rises on Colleges to Withdraw South Africa Interests," *New York Times,* 2 February 1986; and Matthew L. Wald, "College Officials Fear Divestment May Cut Corporate Giving," *New York Times,* 6 May 1986.

66. Crystal Nix, "Many in U.S. Protests on South Africa," *New York Times,* 12 October 1985; "Ongoing Protests at Embassy Yield No Arrests for 1st Time," *Washing-*

ton Post, 22 November 1985; and Karlyn Barker, "Antiapartheid Movement to Mark Anniversary," *Washington Post,* 27 November 1985.

67. Karlyn Barker and Keith Harriston, "Shell Boycott Plan Boosts Tutu's 'People Effort,' " *Washington Post,* 10 January 1986; Robin Toner, "Shell Oil Boycott Urged; Pretoria Policy at Issue," *New York Times,* 10 January 1986; "NAACP Director Urges Boycott of Shell Oil," *New York Times,* 17 February 1986; and Hull, *American Enterprise,* 339.

68. Massie, *Loosing the Bonds,* 595–609.

69. Juan Williams, "Antiapartheid Actions Await Turn of Events," *Washington Post,* 28 September 1985.

70. "U.S. Welcomes Speech," *New York Times,* 1 February 1986.

71. Alan Cowell, "Botha Woos South Africa's Blacks With Advertisement," *New York Times,* 3 February 1986; Alan Cowell, "Pretoria Ends Emergency Decree and Releases 327 From Prisons," *New York Times,* 8 March 1986; and Edward A. Gargan, "Pretoria Rescinds Pas-Law Control on Blacks' Moves," *New York Times,* 19 April 1986.

72. Bernard Gwertzman, "U.S. Hails South Africa for Easing of Apartheid," *New York Times,* 25 April 1986.

73. Crocker, *High Noon,* 305–6. See also, Lugar, *Letters,* 224–27; and Massie, *Loosing the Bonds,* 604–7.

74. *Congressional Record,* 99th Cong., 2nd Sess., 1986, 132, 8: 11751, 11755–56. See also Alan Cowell, "South African President Warns of Further Raids," *New York Times,* 2 May 1986.

75. Cited in Crocker, *High Noon,* 304–5.

76. Lugar, *Letters,* 227–30; Massie, *Loosing the Bonds,* 605, 614–17; and Crocker, *High Noon,* 316–24.

77. Massie, *Loosing the Bonds,* 607–19.

78. *Congressional Record,* 99th Cong., 2nd Sess., 1986, 132, pt. 10: 14225–91, pt. 15: 21470–21510, pt. 15: 21785–21869.

79. *Congressional Record,* 99th Cong., 2nd Sess., 1986, 132, 19: 27832, 27834, 27843, 27853. See also, 27842–43, 27644, 27646–48, 27663–64, 27668.

80. Steven V. Robert, "House Passes Pretoria Sanctions; President Is Expected to Veto Bill," *New York Times,* 13 September 1986.

81. Steven V. Roberts, "Senate, 78 to 21, Overrides Reagan's Veto and Imposes Sanctions on South Africa," *New York Times,* 3 October 1986.

82. Cited in Barry Sussman, "Activists Stimulate S. African Sanctions," *Washington Post,* 24 July 1985.

83. Edward Walsh, "Grass-Root Pleas Stir Lawmakers," *Washington Post,* 16 September 1985, A1; and Lugar, *Letters,* 237–38.

84. Kenneth E. Sharpe, "U.S. Policy toward Central America: The Post-Vietnam Formula under Siege," in *Crisis in Central America: Regional Dynamics and U.S. Policy in the 1980s,* ed. Nora Hamilton, Jeffry Frieden, Linda Fuller, and Manuel Pastor Jr. (Boulder, CO: Westview Press, 1988), 24–28; and John Felton, "House Votes Amendment-Laden Foreign Aid Bill," *CQ Weekly Report,* vol. 42, no. 28 (13 July 1985), 1359–61.

85. Cynthia Arnson, "The Reagan Administration, Congress, and Central America: The Search for Consensus," in *Crisis in Central America,* ed. Hamilton, Frieden, Fuller, and Pastor, 38.

86. Sharpe, "U.S. Policy," 26.

87. Felton, "House Votes," 1360; and Felton and Green, "Senate, after 4 Years," 923–36.

88. Crocker, *High Noon,* 290–99.

89. Baker, *United States and South Africa,* 53–56.

90. *Congressional Record*, 99th Cong., 1st Sess., 1985, 131, pt. 13: 18489, 18490, 18492, 18496.

91. Gunn, "Learning," 166–67.

92. Baker, *United States and South Africa*, 53. See also Vines, *Renamo*, notes 43 and 52.

93. Vines, *Renamo*, 42–46; and Karl Maier, "Between Washington and Pretoria," *Africa Report* 33, no. 6 (November–December 1988): 44.

94. Vines, *Renamo*, 43; Baker, *United States and South Africa*, 57; and Charles A. Moser, "Support for Mozambique Freedom Fighters during Official Visit of Mozambique Dictator Samora Machel," *Freedom Fighter* 1, no. 4 (September 1985): 1.

95. Cited in Moser, "Support for Mozambique Freedom Fighters," 4–5.

96. "The Resistance Can Win in Mozambique," *National Security Record* 92 (June 1986): 1–6. On Capitol Hill, members of Congress cited information from this and other Heritage reports. *Congressional Record*, 99th Cong., 1st Sess., 1985, 131, pt. 18: 24362; and *Congressional Record*, 99th Cong., 2nd Sess., 1986, 132, pt. 13: 18017.

97. *The Amnesty International Report, 1 June 1975–31 May 1976* (London: Amnesty International Publications, 1976), 67; *The Amnesty International Report, 1977* (London: Amnesty International Publications, 1977), 84; *The Amnesty International Report, 1978* (London: Amnesty International Publications, 1978), 61–62; *The Amnesty International Report, 1980* (London: Amnesty International Publications, 1980), 63–64; *The Amnesty International Report, 1982* (London: Amnesty International Publications, 1982), 61–62; *The Amnesty International Report, 1981* (London: Amnesty International Publications, 1981), 67–68; *The Amnesty International Report, 1984* (London: Amnesty International Publications, 1984), 72–76; *The Amnesty International Report, 1986* (London: Amnesty International Publications, 1986), 67–70.

98. "The Resistance Can Win in Mozambique," 6.

99. Moser, "Support for Mozambique Freedom Fighters," 1–5; and "The Resistance Can Win in Mozambique," 6.

100. "The Resistance Can Win in Mozambique," 6.

101. Vines, Renamo, 48; and Morrison, "Battle for Mozambique," 44–47.

102. *Congressional Record*, 100th Cong., 1st Sess., 1987, 133, pt. 8: 10874.

103. *Congressional Record*, 100th Cong., 1st Sess., 1987, 133, pt. 15: 21104.

104. *Congressional Record*, 100th Cong., 1st Sess., 1987, 133, pt. 14: 21107.

105. Neil A. Lewis, "Shultz Assures Mozambique Aide U.S. Won't Withdraw Its Support," *New York Times*, 23 May 1987; and "Shultz Meets Helms and Dole on Mozambique Policy Rift," *New York Times*, 15 July 1987.

106. Neil A. Lewis, "U.S. Meets a Mozambique Rebel Figure," *New York Times*, 13 July 1987.

107. "Mozambique: The Policy Quagmire," editorial, *Washington Post*, 6 October 1987.

108. *The Amnesty International Report, 1985* (London: Amnesty International Publications, 1985), 69; *The Amnesty International Report, 1986*, 67; and *The Amnesty International Report, 1987* (London: Amnesty International Publications, 1987), 76.

109. Crocker, "U.S. Policy"; Karl Maier, "Chissano's Challenge," *Africa Report* 32, no. 4 (July–August 1987): 67–69; and Mota Lopes, "The MNR: Opponents or Bandits," *Africa Report* 31, no. 1 (January–February 1986): 67–73.

110. Morrison, "Battle for Mozambique," 70; "Mozambique Says Rebels Massacre 380," *Washington Post*, 22 July 1987; "Mozambique Says Rightist Guerillas Massacred 380 Civilians," *New York Times*, 22 July 1987; William Claiborne, "South Africa Reassures Mozambique," *Washington Post*, 25 July 1987; and "72 Said Dead in Mozambique Raid," *Washington Post*, 13 August 1987.

111. Allen Isaacman, "Chissano's Friends and Enemies," *Africa Report* 32, no. 5 (September–October 1987): 49.

112. *Congressional Record,* 100th Cong., 1st Sess., 1987, 133, pt. 15: 21103, 21106–7.

113. Senator Helms, *Congressional Record,* 100th Cong., 1st Sess., 1987, 133, pt. 17: 23529, 23534, 23535, 23527, 23547, 23537.

114. Sibyl W. Cline, *Renamo: Anti-Communist Insurgents in Mozambique: The Fight Goes On* (Washington, D.C.: United States Global Strategy Council, 1989), 24–25; and Hilary Anderson, *Mozambique: A War against the People* (New York: St. Martin's Press, 1992), 46–75.

115. Sibyl W. Cline, "Forgotten Freedom Fighters: Mozambique's RENAMO Lost in a Maelstrom of Misinformation," *Soldiers of Fortune* (January 1990), 38.

116. Vines, *Renamo,* 44.

117. Audie Klotz, *Norms in International Relations: The Struggle against Apartheid* (Ithaca: Cornell University Press, 1995).

118. For a similar point, see Jeffrey T. Checkel, "The Constructivist Turn in International Relations Theory," *World Politics* 50, no. 2 (January 1998): 342–44.

119. George P. Shultz, *Turmoil and Triumph: My Years as Secretary of State* (New York: Scribner's, 1993), 1123.

120. Crocker, *High Noon,* 76.

121. Coker, *United States and South Africa,* chs. 7–10.

122. Crocker, *High Noon,* 237–39.

123. Massie, *Loosing the Bonds,* 382–83; and Crocker, *High Noon,* 305–6.

124. Robert M. Price, "Creating New Political Realities," in *African Crisis Areas and U.S. Foreign Policy,* ed. Gerald R. Bender, James S. Coleman, and Richard L. Sklar (Berkeley: University of California Press, 1985), 64–88.

125. Ibid.; Gerald R. Bender, "American Policy toward Angola: A History of Linkage," and Allen F. Isaacman, "Mozambique: Tugging at the Chains of Dependency," in *African Crisis Areas,* 110–28, 129–57.

126. *Congressional Record,* 99th Cong., 1st Sess., 1985, 131, pt. 14: 18830.

127. *Congressional Record,* 99th Cong., 1st Sess., 1985, 131, pt. 13: 18327.

128. "Transcript of Talk By Reagan on South Africa and Apartheid," *New York Times,* 23 July 1986.

129. Gregory F. Treverton, "Introduction: Framing the Issues," and The Right Honorable Lord Pym, "Strains among Friends: Coordinating Western Policy toward South Africa," both in *Europe, America, and South Africa,* ed. Gregory F. Treverton (New York: Council on Foreign Relations, 1988), 8–9, 34–35.

130. Treverton, "Introduction," 8.

131. Walker, "A Conservative Viewpoint."

132. Allen Isaacman, "After the Nkomati Accord," *Africa Report* 30, no. 1 (January–February 1985): 12.

133. Isaacman, "In Machel's Footsteps," 25–27.

134. "The Resistance Can Win in Mozambique," 2.

135. Hoile, *Mozambique,* 104, 106–7.

136. "The Resistance Can Win in Mozambique," 2.

137. Sam Levy, "Broken Promises," *Africa Report* 3, no. 1 (January–February 1986): 77.

CHAPTER 5. HUMAN RIGHTS AND VITAL SECURITY

1. Jerome Alan Cohen, "Arms Sales and Human Rights: The Case of South Korea," in *Human Rights and U.S. Foreign Policy: Principles and Applications,* ed. Peter G. Brown and Douglas MacLean (Lexington, MA: Lexington Books, 1979), 255.

2. A. James Gregor, *Crisis in the Philippines: A Threat to U.S. Interests* (Washington, D.C.: Ethics and Public Policy Center, 1984), 16–21.

3. Ibid., 10–11, 28–29.

4. Fred Poole and Max Vanzi, *Revolution in the Philippines: The United States in the Hall of Cracked Mirrors* (New York: McGraw-Hill, 1984), 2.

5. Cohen, "Arms Sales," 255–56; and William G. Gleysteen Jr., *Massive Entanglement, Marginal Influence: Carter and Korea in Crisis* (Washington, D.C.: Brookings Institution Press, 1999), 10–13.

6. Cohen, "Arms Sales," 261; and Gleysteen, *Massive Entanglement*, 13.

7. Manwoo Lee, "Anti-Americanism and South Korea's Changing Perception of America," in *Alliance under Tension: The Evolution of South Korean–U.S. Relations*, ed. Manwoo Lee, Ronald D. McLaurin, and Chung-in Moon (Boulder, CO: Westview Press, 1988), 10–20.

8. Richard P. Claude, "Human Rights in the Philippines and U.S. Responsibility," in *Human Rights and U.S. Foreign Policy*, 232; and Gregor, *Crisis in the Philippines*, 28–29, 33, 67.

9. Poole and Vanzi, *Revolution*, 90–103.

10. Manwoo Lee, "Double Patronage toward South Korea: Security Versus Democracy and Human Rights," in *Alliance under Tension*, ed. Lee, McLaurin, and Moon, 45; David Weissbrodt, "The Role of Nongovernmental Organizations in the Implementation of Human Rights," *Texas International Law Journal* 52, no. 3 (Spring/Summer 1977): 303; John Salzberg and Donald Young, "The Parliamentary Role in Implementing International Human Rights: A U.S. Example," *Texas Journal of International Law* 12, nos. 2–3 (Spring/Summer 1977): 266; and John Salzberg, "Monitoring Human Rights Violations: How Good is Information?" in *Human Rights and U.S. Foreign Policy: Principles and Applications*, ed. Peter G. Brown and Douglas MacLean (Lexington, MA: Lexington Books, 1979), 175.

11. Salzberg and Young, "Parliamentary Role," 267; Norman D. Levin and Richard L. Sneider, "Korea in Postwar U.S. Security Policy," in *The U.S.–South Korean Alliance: Evolving Patters in Security Relations*, ed. Gerald L. Curtis and Sung-joo Han (Lexington, MA: D. C. Heath, 1984), 48–49.

12. Salzberg and Young, "Parliamentary Role," 268.

13. David P. Forsythe, *Human Rights and United States Foreign Policy* (Gainesville: University of Florida Press, 1988), 116; and Lee, "Double Patronage," 35.

14. Claude, "Human Rights," 238–39.

15. Cited in Claude, "Human Rights," 239.

16. Ronald D. McLaurin and Chung-in Moon, "Problems of U.S.–South Korean Relations: Autonomy vs. Dependence, Authoritarianism vs. Democracy," in *Alliance under Tension*, ed. Lee, McLaurin, and Moon, 223.

17. Claude, "Human Rights," 238. From 1969 to 1972, the U.S. offered the Philippines $80 million in military assistance. Under the early period of martial law from 1972 to 1976, Washington granted $166.4 million. That represented an increase of 108 percent.

18. Jon V. Kofas, *Under the Eagle's Claw: Exceptionalism in Postwar U.S.-Greek Relations* (Westport, CT: Praeger Publishers, 2003), 13–14, 21, 24, 63–64, 102, 107; Chris P. Ioaniddes, *Realpolitik in the Eastern Mediterranean: From Kissinger and the Cyprus Crisis to Carter and the Lifting of the Turkish Arms Embargo* (New York: Pella, 2001), 33, 253–54, 255–70; and Laurence Halley, *Ancient Affections: Ethnic Groups and Foreign Policy* (New York: Praeger Publishers, 1985), 1.

19. Kofas, *Under the Eagle's Claw*, 30; and Clifford P. Hackett, "The Role of Congress and Greek-American Relations," in *Greek America Relations: A Critical Review*, ed. Theodore A. Couloumbis and John O. Iatrides (New York: Pella, 1980), 56.

20. Kofas, *Under the Eagle's Claw*, 59–88; and Robert McDonald, "The Colonels' Dicta-

torship: 1967–1974," in *Background to Contemporary Greece,* ed. Marion Sarafias and Martin Eve (London: Merlin Press, 1990), 264–70.

21. Kofas, *Under the Eagle's Claw,* 84–96; McDonald, "Colonels' Dictatorship," 264–65; and Laurence Stern, *The Wrong Horse: The Politics of Intervention and the Failure of American Diplomacy* (New York: Times Books, 1977), 53.

22. For a discussion of both reports, see *Torture in Greece: The First Tortures' Trial in 1975* (London: Amnesty International Publications, 1977), 11.

23. Kofas, *Under the Eagle's Claw,* 95.

24. *Torture in Greece,* 12, 15, 83. AI noted that the report "created a climate of public opinion which the [Council of Europe] Ministers could not ignore. The Council of Europe had never received so much attention."

25. Theodore A. Coulombis, *The United States, Greece, and Turkey: A Troubled Triangle* (New York: Praeger Publishers, 1983), 51; Stern, *The Wrong Horse,* 49–51, 58–59; and Kofas, *Under the Eagle's Claw,* 89–90, 98–99.

26. Stern, *The Wrong Horse,* 61–62, 66–67.

27. Kofas, *Under the Eagle's Claw,* 98, 101–2, 106.

28. Cited in Stern, *The Wrong Horse,* 67.

29. Kofas, *Under the Eagle's Claw,* 103, 105.

30. Ibid., 106–8, 115.

31. *Congressional Record,* 92nd Cong., 2nd Sess., 1971, 116, pt. 29: 32156, and 117, pt. 29: 38231, 38232, 38235.

32. Ioannides, *Realpolitik,* 47–50; Van Coufoudakis, "The Reverse Influence Phenomenon: The Impact of the Greek-American Lobby on the Foreign Policy of Greece," in *Diasporas in World Politics: The Greeks in Comparative Perspective,* ed. Dimitris C. Constas and Athanassios G. Platias (London: Macmillan, 1993), 53–54; and Paul Y. Watanabe, *Ethnic Groups, Congress, and American Foreign Policy: The Politics of the Turkish Arms Embargo* (Westport, CT: Greenwood Press, 1984), 148–49.

33. Hackett, "Role of Congress," 143.

34. Watanabe, *Ethnic Groups,* 78–84; and Hackett, "Role of Congress," 135–40.

35. Watanabe, *Ethnic Groups,* 83–84.

36. Ibid., 84–86.

37. Ioannides, *Realpolitik,* 13.

38. Halley, *Ancient Affections,* 37–39.

39. Watanabe, *Ethnic Groups,* 135–46. For additional information on the grassroots initiative, see Hackett, "Role of Congress," 142; and Halley, *Ancient Affections,* 32–33.

40. Watanabe, *Ethnic Groups,* 153. The scale and force of the movement was so surprising to many in Congress that it created the impression of a very broad public movement. "What is also clear is that the virulence and the energy of their representations startled legislators into a belief that the Greek-American community could be dangerous to electoral aspirations of many." Halley, *Ancient Affections,* 36.

41. Watanabe, *Ethnic Groups,* 112, 122, 141.

42. Cited in ibid., 153.

43. Halley, *Ancient Affections,* 44.

44. Watanabe, *Ethnic Groups,* 109; and Ioannides, *Realpolitik,* 33, 253–74. Those warnings were justified in the context of U.S. perceived security interests: Turkish military effectiveness declined substantially during the embargo years. Turkey also promptly closed six U.S. military bases, harming among other things U.S. intelligence gathering inside the USSR. The Turks also increased Soviet naval passage through the Turkish Straits and began to receive substantial amounts of Soviet assistance.

45. Halley, *Ancient Affections,* 56.

46. Cited in Watanabe, *Ethnic Groups*, 56.
47. Halley, *Ancient Affections*, ch. 9.
48. Coufoudakis, "Reverse Influence," 57.
49. Michael C. Desch, *When the Third World Matters: Latin America and United States Grand Strategy* (Baltimore: Johns Hopkins University Press, 1993), 116–28. Desch argues that for these reasons and access to important sea lanes, Central America and the Caribbean were particularly vital to the U.S. and Europe in the 1980s.
50. Formal congressional aid termination followed El Salvador's renunciation of assistance following the Carter administration's criticism. Michael McClintock, *The American Connection: State Terror and Popular Resistance in El Salvador*, vol. 1 (London: Zed Books, 1985), 171–94.
51. Tom Buckley, *Violent Neighbors: El Salvador, Central America, and the United States* (New York: Times Books, 1984), 241–53; and Lars Schoultz, "Guatemala: Social Change and Political Conflict," in *Trouble in Our Backyard and the United States in the Eighties*, ed. Martin Diskin (New York: Pantheon Books, 1983), 175–83.
52. McClintock, *American Connection*, 193–94, 262–65.
53. Terry Karl, "Exporting Democracy: The Unanticipated Effects of U.S. Electoral Policy in El Salvador," in *Crisis in Central America: Regional Dynamics and U.S. Policy in the 1980s*, ed. Nora Hamilton, Jeffry A. Frieden, Linda Fuller, and Manuel Pastor Jr. (Boulder, CO: Westview Press, 1988), 175.
54. McClintock, *American Connection*, 262–64, 276.
55. Ibid., 302; Cynthia J. Arnson, *Crossroads: Congress, the President, and Central America: 1976–1993*, 2nd ed. (University Park: Pennsylvania State University, 1993), 60–62, 84–85; and Martin Diskin and Kenneth Sharpe, *The Impact of U.S. Policy in El Salvador, 1979–1985* (Berkeley, CA: Institute of International Studies, University of California, Berkeley, 1986), 26–27.
56. McClintock, *American Connection*, 246, 249–51.
57. Ibid., 249–79; and Arnson, *Crossroads*, 40–51.
58. Cited in Arnson, *Crossroads*, 42, 73.
59. Ibid., 54–72, quotation 73; and McClintock, *American Connection*, 246–88.
60. On the first certification and the fallout from it, see Arnson, *Crossroads*, 84–91.
61. McClintock, *American Connection*, 291.
62. In fact, Secretary of State Alexander Haig threatened the right in El Salvador that the United States would terminate all military assistance if there was not a moderate civilian president. Edward Best, *U.S. Policy and Regional Security in Central America* (New York: St. Martin's Press, 1987), 41–43. See also Arnson, *Crossroads*, 91–101.
63. Arnson, *Crossroads*, 96–100.
64. Guerrillas made major strategic gains by seizing several major towns. In addition, the number of recruits swelled in the latter half of 1982 and the beginning of 1983. Karl, "Exporting Democracy," 179; Arnson, *Crossroads*, 116; and Buckley, *Violent Neighbors*, 300–303.
65. Best, *U.S. Policy*, 43–48.
66. Arnson, *Crossroads*, 123.
67. Ibid., 137–39.
68. Cited in ibid., 143.
69. Best, *U.S. Policy*, 49.
70. Ibid., 50, 100.
71. Ibid., 50.
72. Arnson, *Crossroads*, 160–62. For other assessments, see Best, *U.S. Policy*, 50; Karl, "Exporting Democracy," 180; and Diskin and Sharpe, *Impact of U.S. Policy*, 31.

73. Schoultz, "Guatemala," 197–98; Shelton H. Davis, "State Violence and Agrarian Crisis in Guatemala," in *Trouble in Our Backyard and the United States in the Eighties,* ed. Diskin 164–67; and Gabriel Aguilera Peralta, "The Hidden War: Guatemala's Counterinsurgency Campaign," in *Crisis in Central America,* ed. Hamilton, Frieden, Fuller, and Pastor, 153–55.

74. Cited by Schoultz, "Guatemala," 197–98.

75. Buckley, *Violent Neighbors,* 252.

76. Peralta, "Hidden War," 157; Schoultz, "Guatemala," 185, 195; and Davis, "State Violence," 164–65.

77. Schoultz, "Social Change," 184–85; Buckley, *Violent Neighbors,* 303–24; and Peralta, "Hidden War," 157.

78. Davis, "State Violence," 158; and Schoultz, "Guatemala," 185–86.

79. Best, *U.S. Policy,* 36.

CHAPTER 6. THE IMPLICATIONS OF ENFORCED HUMANITARIAN NORMS

1. President George W. Bush himself said, "We must move beyond the 1972 Anti-Ballistic Missile Treaty, a treaty that was written in a different era, for a different enemy." Cited in Bradley Graham and Mike Allen, "Bush to Tell Russia U.S. Will Withdraw from '72 ABM Pact," *Washington Post,* 12 December 2001. See also Mike Allen, "Bush Cites Need to Overhaul Military," *Washington Post,* 12 December 2001; and Steven Mufson and Dana Milbank, "U.S. Sets Missile Treaty Pullout," *Washington Post,* 14 December 2001.

2. Glenn H. Snyder, *Alliance Politics* (Ithaca: Cornell University Press, 1997), 223.

3. Barbara Jelavich, *A Century of Russian Foreign Policy* (Philadelphia: J.B. Lippincott, 1964), 177–81; Karel Durman, *The Time of the Thunderer: Mikhail Katkov, Russian Nationalist Extremism, and the Failure of the Bismarckian System, 1871–1887* (Boulder, CO: East European Monographs, 1988), 198–208; and Benedict H. Summer, *Russia and the Balkans, 1970–1880* (Hamden, CT: Archon Books, 1962), 275–82.

4. Donald S. Zagoria, *The Sino-Soviet Conflict, 1956–1961* (Princeton: Princeton University Press, 1962), 152–331; and Adam B. Ulam, *Expansion and Co-Existence: Soviet Foreign Policy, 1917–73,* 2nd ed. (New York: Holt, Rinehart, and Winston, 1974), 606–36. On Somalia, see Melvin Goodman, "The Soviet Union and the Third World: The Military Dimensions," in *The Soviet Union and the Third World: The Last Three Decades,* ed. Andrzej Korbanski and Francis Fukuyama (Ithaca: Cornell University Press, 1987), 56; Colin Legum, "U.S.S.R. Policy in Sub-Saharan Africa," in *The Soviet Union and the Third World,* 230–42; and Colin Legum and Bill Lee, *Conflict in the Horn of Africa* (London: Rex Collings, 1977).

5. Gary Clyde Hufbauer, Jeffrey J. Schott, and Kimberly Ann Elliott, *Economic Sanctions Reconsidered: Supplemental Case Studies,* 2nd ed. (Washington, D.C.: Institute for International Economics, 1990), 498–504.

6. Of these cases, only Peru escaped congressional action. In all other cases, the government resumed repressive measures that sparked de-commitment actions. Peru, on the other hand, completed a transition to democracy on schedule.

7. Margaret Thatcher, *The Downing Street Years* (New York: Harper Collins, 1993), 520–23.

8. Martin Holland, *The European Community and South Africa: European Political Cooperation under Strain* (London: Pinter, 1988); and Gregory F. Treverton, ed., *Europe, America, and South Africa* (New York: New York University Press, 1988).

9. Jon V. Kofas, *Under the Eagle's Claw: Exceptionalism in Postwar U.S.-Greek Relations* (Westport, CT: Praeger, 2003), 83–124.

10. For recent work, see Martha Finnemore, *The Purpose of Intervention: Changing Beliefs about the Use of Force* (Ithaca: Cornell University Press, 2003); and Neta Crawford, *Argument and Change in World Politics: Ethics, Decolonization, and Humanitarian Intervention* (Cambridge: Cambridge University Press, 2002).

11. David Dessler and John Owen, "Constructivism and the Problem of Explanation," *Perspectives on Politics* 3, no. 3 (September 2005), 597–610.

12. These suggestions build upon and add to those made by others. See Margaret E. Keck and Kathryn Sikkink, *Activists beyond Borders: Advocacy Networks in International Politics* (Ithaca: Cornell University Press, 1998); Ethan Nadelman, "Global Prohibition Regimes: The Evolution of Norms in International Society," *International Organization* 44, no. 4 (Autumn 1990): 479–526; and Richard Price, "Reversing the Gun Sights: Transnational Civil Society Targets Land Mines," *International Organization* 52, no. 3 (Summer 1998): 613–44.

13. For an example of work that does posit some type of opportunity space before alternative policy ideas are considered, see Jeffrey W. Legro, *Rethinking the World: Great Power Strategies and International Order* (Ithaca: Cornell University Press).

14. Lisa Martin, *Democratic Commitments: Legislatures and International Commitments* (Princeton: Princeton University Press, 2000); and James D. Fearon, "Domestic Political Audiences and the Escalation of International Disputes," *American Political Science Review* 88, no. 3 (September 1994): 577–92.

15. The terms *single-play* and *iterated* here do not necessarily imply interaction between actors, but are meant instead to convey the picture of single versus multiple considerations of a commitment by legislatures across the life of a pledge.

16. It should be noted that domestic institutionalists do not necessarily claim this outright. Yet their silence on the issue, very strong expectations of socio-legislative consistency across time, and lack of attention to how and when socio-legislative interests might change makes the assumption natural and logical.

17. There is nothing in my argument that indicates that these partners are or must be nondemocratic states. While generally less likely, it is possible that a liberal state could terminate pledges to another liberal state when different understandings about what is humane and inhumane exists between them. Britain, for instance, took several punitive steps against other liberal states in Europe on the basis of its antislavery norms.

18. Robert O. Keohane, *After Hegemony: Cooperation and Discord in the World Political Economy* (Princeton: Princeton University Press, 1984), 94, 100, emphasis added. For similar points about the reduction rather than negation of uncertainty, see Kenneth A. Oye, "Explaining Cooperation Under Anarchy: Hypotheses and Strategies," in *Cooperation Under Anarchy*, ed. Kenneth A. Oye (Princeton: Princeton University Press, 1986), 14.

19. Jim Nichol, *Central Asia: Regional Developments and Implications for U.S. Interests* (Washington, D.C.: Congressional Research Service, 24 January 2006), 8–10.

20. Jeffrey S. Smith, "Senators Fault Pentagon as New Photos Emerge," *Washington Post*, 10 May 2004; "Bush Rejects Detainee Abuse Commission," *Washington Post*, 21 June 2005; and Charles Babington and Shailagh Murray, "Senate Supports Interrogation Limits," *Washington Post*, 6 October 2005.

21. "Elections, Democracy and Stability in Pakistan," *Asia Report of the International Crisis Group*, no. 137 (31 July 2007), 21; K. Alan Kronstadt, *Pakistan's Political Crisis* (Washington, D.C.: Congressional Research Service, 3 January 2008), 22–24.

22. Robin Wright, "Rice, on Way to Central Asia, Reprimands Uzbekistan," *Washington Post*, 11 October 2005; and idem, "Uzbeks Stop Working with U.S. against Terrorism," *Washington Post*, 30 September 2005.

23. For a discussion and detailed cases, see Gary Clyde Hufbauer, Jeffrey J. Schott, and Kimberly Ann Elliott, *Economic Sanctions Reconsidered: History and Current Policy*, 2nd ed. (Washington, D.C.: Institute for International Economics, 1990), 1–15; and idem, *Economic Sanctions Reconsidered: Supplemental Case Studies*.

24. Anthony Lake, *Somoza Falling* (Boston: Houghton Mifflin, 1989), chs. 2 and 3; and Robert Kagan, *A Twilight Struggle* (New York: Free Press, 1996), chs. 5, 6, 8.

Index

Gallagher, John, 38
Gamson, William, 24
Gann, L. H., 197n125
García, Fernando Romeo Lucas, 161–62
Garthoff, Raymond L., 206n167
Geisel, Ernesto, 81
General Agreement on Tariffs and Trade
  (GATT), 35, 113, 140
Germany, 49, 64
  Belgium and, 68, 71
  Black Sea Conference and, 47
  Greece and, 173
  rise of, 32, 63, 166, 167
Gersony Report, 135
Gladstone, William, 47, 49, 52, 56, 59–62,
  65–66, 70
Glenn, John, 120
Gleysteen, William, 214n5
Goldberg, Glenn, 208n17
Goldstein, Judith, 207n180
Goldwater, Barry, 88, 124
Gorbachev, Mikhail, 141
Goschen, George, 61
Gradison, Willis, 124
Granville, Lord, 71
Graves, Ernest, 197n3
Gray, William, 123, 126
Greece, 48
  Council of Europe and, 148–49, 152, 173,
    215n24
  Cyprus and, 23–25, 151–55
  NATO and, 147, 150–51, 173
  U.S. relations with, 147–51, 162–63
  war of independence of, 44, 45
Greek Orthodox Church, 23, 151, 153
Gregor, A. James, 213n2
Gregory, William, 45
Guantanamo Bay, Cuba, 1, 179
Guatemala, 79t, 81, 155–56, 160–63,
  207n185
Guest, Ian, 91, 94, 191n88, 202n78
Guevara, Angel Aníbal, 161
Guyana, 79t

Haas, Mark L., 188n51
Hackett, Clifford, 151
Haiti, 79t, 81–82
Halley, Laurence, 154, 214n18
Hamilton, Alexander, 188n39
Hamilton, Nora, 211n84
Hammond, Paul Y., 197n1
Hammond, R. J., 196n109
Hardy, Gathorne, 57
Harkin, Tom, 77
Harrington, Michael, 104
Harris, David, 194n45

Hartington, Marquess of, 50, 52, 61
Hartke, Vance, 150
Hatfield, Mark, 101
Hauck, David, 208n17
Helms, Jesse, 124, 133–35
Heritage Foundation, 130–33
Herzegovina, 49, 50, 55, 58
Hildreth, Steven A., 197n3
Hillman, Jordan J., 192n117
Hinckley, Barbara, 188n50
Hoff, Joan, 206n173
Hoile, David, 208n2
Holland, Martin, 217n8
Hollings, Ernest, 105
Honduras, 80t, 81
Hufbauer, Gary Clyde, 217n5
Hughes, Harold, 88
Hull, Richard, 113, 115, 122, 207n1
humanitarian norms, 3–18, 164–83, 165t, 170t
  British-Ottoman relations and, 15, 43–62,
    71–73, 72t
  "freedom fighters" and, 129–31
  hypothesis of, 25–29, 25t
  nonstate actors and, 19–25, 21t
  U.S. Latin American policies and, 77–82,
    79t–80t, 108, 110–11
  U.S. southern African policies and, 40t,
    138–139, 142t
Human Rights Watch, 22, 146
Human Rights Working Group, 78
Humphrey, Hubert, 84
Huth, Paul, 32, 191n98
Hutton, James, 69–71

IACHR. *See* Inter-American Commission
  on Human Rights
Iakovos, Archbishop, 153, 154
Ignatieff, Michael, 14, 186n10, 186n15
Ignatiev, Nicholas, 58, 59
ILHR. *See* International League for Human
  Rights
IMF. *See* International Monetary Fund
India, 42–43
Indochina War, 32
Inter-American Commission on Human
  Rights (IACHR), 88, 90, 100, 155, 162
International Commission of Jurists (ICJ),
  78, 79t–80t
  Argentina and, 90
  Chile and, 86, 87
  El Salvador and, 155, 163
  Guatemala and, 162, 163
  Peru and, 104
  Philippines and, 146
International League for Human Rights
  (ILHR), 79t–80t, 94

Index

United Democratic Front (UDF), 119,
121, 122
United Kingdom, 15
Austria and, 32, 42, 63–65, 167
Congo and, 67–72
India and, 42–43
Ottoman Empire and, 2, 18, 40t, 42–67,
71–73, 72t, 165t, 170t, 180
Portugal and, 2, 38, 67–72, 137, 165t, 169
Russia and, 32, 42–43, 63–65, 166–68
South Africa and, 126, 127
United Mine Workers, 126
United States Catholic Conference (USCC),
78, 79t, 175
Argentina and, 94
Chile and, 86, 87
United States Committee for Democracy in
Greece, 148
Uruguay, 80t, 81, 92, 207n185
Uzbekistan, 4, 178, 179

Valenzuela, Arturo, 188n45, 199n34
Vance, Cyrus, 147
Van Evra, Steven, 193n119
Vanzi, Max, 145, 214n4
Velasco Alvarado, Juan, 102–5
Venezuela, 29, 80t, 81
Videla, Jorge Rafael, 89–93
Vietnam
China and, 168
United States and, 12, 27, 32, 106–8, 172
Vines, Alex, 208n2
Vorrhes, Meg, 208n17

Walker, Jack L., Jr., 189n55
Walker, Robert, 210n59
Wallop, Malcolm, 132, 210n59

Waltz, Kenneth, 17, 188n49, 191n86
Walvin, James, 44
war on terror, 1–7, 13–14, 176–82, 185n6
Washington Office on Africa (WOA),
117–18
Washington Office on Latin America
(WOLA), 78
Argentina and, 94, 95
El Salvador and, 156
Nicaragua and, 97, 98
Watanabe, Paul, 215n32
Watergate scandal, 105–6, 172
Weicker, Lowell, 123
Wells, Melissa, 133–35
White, Theodore H., 206n167
Whitley, Edward, 70
Wilberforce, William, 11, 44
Wilson, Charles, 98, 99
Wilson, Richard Ashby, 186n10
Winham, Gilbert, 192n109
Wirthwein, Walter G., 194n37
WOLA. *See* Washington Office on Latin
America
Wolff, H. Drummond, 54, 60, 195n53
Wolpe, Howard, 127
World War I, 62, 63, 166
World War II, 74, 108, 147, 148
Wright, Jim, 160
Wylie, Chalmers, 210n57

Yapp, M. E., 193n1

Zablocki, Clement, 159
Zagoria, Donald, 217n4
Zambia, 127, 138
Zimbabwe, 127, 137, 138, 140, 141, 167
See also Rhodesia